£1.50

THE DICKENS HERO

THE DICKENS HERO

Selfhood and Alienation
in the Dickens World

❧

BETH F. HERST

WEIDENFELD AND NICOLSON
LONDON

This book is dedicated to my parents,
Murray and Roslyn Herst

Contents

ॐ

Acknowledgments

This book began life as a doctoral thesis for the University of London. I am grateful to the Association of Commonwealth Universities (UK) for the financial support of a Commonwealth Scholarship which made my three years of study in England possible. Dr Michael Slater offered advice, encouragement and enthusiasm at every stage of the original writing – as both supervisor and exemplary Dickensian. This book owes its existence to his continued support. I am grateful too to Dr Robin Gilmour for his kind criticism and suggestions at a later stage in its development. Finally, many thanks are due to Carol Percy and Judith Wilkinson, for their friendship, encouragement and patient willingness to listen and discuss 'outside their field'.

A portion of Chapter 1 first appeared, in somewhat different form, in *The Dickens Quarterly*. I am grateful to the editor for permission to reprint it here.

Quotations from Stephen Wall's Introduction to *Our Mutual Friend* (Harmondsworth, 1971) are reproduced by permission of Penguin Books Ltd; George Lukács, *The Theory of the Novel* (London, 1971) by permission of Merlin Press Ltd; John Gross and Gabriel Pearson (eds.), *Dickens and the Twentieth Century* (London, 1962) by permission of Routledge Ltd; Julian Moynahan, 'The Hero's Guilt: The Case of *Great Expectations*' (*Essays in Criticism* 10 (1960)) by permission of the editors; H. M. Daleski, *Dickens and the Art of Analogy* (London, 1970) by permission of Faber and Faber Ltd; F. R. and Q. D. Leavis, *Dickens the Novelist* and Steven Marcus, *Dickens: From Pickwick to Dombey* (London, 1970, 1965) by permission of Chatto and Windus; Philip Collins, *Dickens and Education* (London, 1963) by permission of Macmillan Ltd; Robert Garis, *The Dickens Theatre* (Oxford, 1965) by permission of Oxford University Press; Franco Moretti, *The Way of the World: The Bildungsroman in European Culture* (London, 1987) by permission of Verso; Erich Kahler, *The Inward Turn of Narrative* and Winifred Hughes, *The Maniac in the Cellar: Sensation Novels of the 1860s* (Princeton, 1973,

Note on Texts and Sources

Primary Texts

Where possible I have used the Clarendon edition of Dickens's novels: *The Pickwick Papers*, ed. James Kinsley (1986); *Oliver Twist*, ed. Kathleen Tillotson (1966); *Martin Chuzzlewit*, ed. Margaret Cardwell (1982); *Dombey and Son*, ed. Alan Horsman (1974); *David Copperfield*, ed. Nina Burgis (1981); *Little Dorrit*, ed. H. P. Sucksmith (1979); and *The Mystery of Edwin Drood*, ed. Margaret Cardwell (1972). For the remaining novels, I have used the Oxford Illustrated Dickens. I am grateful to Oxford University Press for permission to quote from these two editions. All references are to page number and are given in parentheses.

References to John Forster's *Life of Charles Dickens* are to J. W. T. Ley's edition (London: Cecil Palmer, 1928).

Secondary Criticism

I have attempted to keep references to the monumental – and ever-increasing – body of Dickens scholarship to a minimum in the hope of allowing my own argument free play. The Bibliographic Essay at the end of the volume, divided by chapters, seeks to outline briefly a critical context and indicate possible directions for further reading. Full details of the works discussed in the Essay can be found in the Bibliography which follows it.

THE DICKENS HERO

cℐℰ

Introduction

In the opinion of Angus Wilson, recorded in his well-known essay 'The Heroes and Heroines of Dickens', to examine Dickens's heroes is, simply, 'to dwell on his weaknesses and failures'.[1] Wilson's verdict has been shared by generations of critics and readers alike. Dickens's male protagonists have long been considered the least interesting thing about the novels they inhabit: drably virtuous stick-figures overshadowed by the imaginative exuberance that surrounds them. Fashions in Dickens criticism have changed and changed again in the twenty-five years and more since the appearance of Wilson's essay. The once neglected early novels now command equal attention with the later, allowing the comic genius to re-emerge from the shadow of his 'dark' alter ego. The 'Inimitable' has been both re-read and deconstructed. Yet, while exceptions are increasingly being made, most consistently for David Copperfield, Arthur Clennam and Pip, the received wisdom as to Dickens's young male protagonists remains for the most part unquestioned. Nor was Wilson himself, by any means, the initiator of the trend. The tradition of dismissal for which he speaks extends back as far as the novelist Margaret Oliphant, writing in *Blackwood's Magazine* in April 1855. There she compares, as many subsequent critics would do, the limited scope of Dickens's 'respectable' young man, that 'thoroughly refined and gentle-hearted boy', with the much wider sphere of Thackeray's Pendennis, frequenter of 'dens of vice and unknown mysteries . . . David Copperfield could not enter without pollution'.[2] And the comparison is scarcely in David's favour. It is the aim of this study to challenge this tradition, to place noted 'exceptions' like David Copperfield, Clennam and Pip within a sustained progression, and to demonstrate that, *pace* Angus Wilson, an examination of the heroes of Dickens brings one, not to weakness and failure, but rather closer still to the heart of his imaginative world.

But do Dickens's novels possess heroes at all? There are no Carlylean 'Great Men' among the young male protagonists who people their pages, nothing to suggest the transcendent qualities of the 'Hero-soul' to be worshipped. His young men are not 'heroes' but 'heroes of novels', a different species of the genus, subject to imaginative norms that do not easily assimilate the epic, 'heroic' mode. The fact is not simply a function of characteristic Dickensian 'weaknesses'. The apparent limitation is inseparable from the evolution of the novel form itself. The domestication of the heroic in English fiction is frequently identified as a peculiarly nineteenth-century development, the literary expression of the triumph of a middle-class ethic valuing above all the 'ordinary' and the 'real', and secure in the possession of their meaning. Yet, from at least the first apologetic introduction of Fielding's foundling upon the stage of *Tom Jones*, 'who bad as he is, must serve as the heroe of this history,' the 'hero' in his larger-than-life incarnation has been – to borrow the title of the classic study of the phenomenon – in eclipse. The tradition rises with the rise of the novel itself. One might, indeed, trace its origins to sixteenth-century Spain and the anti-heroic, picaresque literature of the delinquent developed there, a literature no less engaged with the common details of ordinary life than the most 'realistic' Victorian novel. Richardson's Sir Charles Grandison, it is true, conceived as a fictional response to the unheroic 'lowness' of Tom Jones, might be seen as the embodiment of an alternative idealizing tendency: the *picaro* replaced by the paragon. But if Grandison is a paragon, he is a paragon of private life, and it is as much the diminished sphere of activity as the idealization that he bequeaths to his heirs. The tradition of limitation has a history identical with the novel genre itself: the hero's eclipse is a long-standing one. The work of the great Victorian practitioners of the form, Dickens, Thackeray, Trollope, Eliot, Gaskell and the Brontës, simply continues the process begun by their great predecessors, making the eclipse almost total. The fictions of all might with justice borrow the subtitle of *Vanity Fair* and call themselves 'A Novel Without a Hero'.

In defining its literary heroes, abandoning past models and creating new, each age also defines itself. The figure of the hero serves as a literal embodiment of the values, assumptions and beliefs – both acknowledged and unconscious – that shape it. The major Victorian novelists' shared preoccupation with the steady contraction of the possibilities of 'heroic' action, their redefinition of the 'hero' out of existence in their fiction, is itself a profound expression of the spirit of their age. For them the discrepancy between the moral and technical meanings of the term 'hero' – the hero as great soul; the hero as central protagonist in a literary work – has become a fact of life, the very gap between the two the special province of their art. From Charlotte Brontë's rebellious governess to George Eliot's failed Saint Theresa, the problem of the literary hero – the 'hero' as literary problem – is inescapable. Dickens himself, most unusually for him, gives explicit voice to his particular form of the common concern in a letter to his friend John Forster, written during a lengthy stay in France:

Similarly I have always a fine feeling of the honest state into which we have got, when some smooth gentleman says to me or to someone else when I am by, how odd it is that the hero of an English book is always uninteresting – too good – not natural, etc. I am continually hearing this of Scott from English people here, who pass their lives with Balzac and Sand. But O my smooth friend, what a shining impostor you must think yourself and what an ass you must think me, when you suppose that by putting a brazen face upon it you can blot out of my knowledge the fact that this same unnatural young gentleman (if to be decent is to be necessarily unnatural), whom you meet in those other books and in mine, *must* be presented to you in that unnatural manner, and is not to have, I will not say any of the indecencies you like, but not even any of the experience, trials, perplexities, and confusions inseparable from the making or unmaking of all men![3]

The fictional protagonist as 'Hero-soul' is not the issue here. Dickens's concern is rather the already manifestly domesticated 'hero of an English book', an ordinary young man who has emerged, in the novels of Scott at least if not of his less talented contemporaries, as a soul of very ordinary dimensions. Still more, Dickens's anger is directed at the public hypocrisy that dismisses this characteristically limited English hero as uninteresting for lacking the very weaknesses it will not allow him to possess. The 'smooth gentleman' and 'brazen face' of this 1856 letter anticipate *Our Mutual Friend*'s Podsnap nine years later, jealously guarding the blushing cheek of his Young Person. And Dickens clearly links this particular species of cant to the general condition of England, that 'honest state into which we have got' about which he had written despondently to Forster the previous year. Convinced that 'mere form and conventionalities usurp, in English art, as in English government and social relations, the place of living force and truth',[4] Dickens here directly relates the problem of the hero to the ethos of the age. The fictional hero is 'unnatural', and in eclipse in this important sense too, because the form and convention that are stifling English social life forbid his being anything else.

Six years earlier, in 1850, Thackeray's preface to his novel *Pendennis* had similarly protested the enforced emasculation of the 'hero of an English book', in terms which find an echo here:

Even the gentleman of our age – this is an attempt to describe one of them, no better nor worse than most educated men – even these we cannot show as they are, with the notorious foibles and selfishness of their lives and their education. Since the author of 'Tom Jones' was buried, no writer of fiction among us has been permitted to depict to his utmost power a MAN. We must drape him and give him a certain conventional simper. Society will not tolerate the Natural in our Art.[5]

Yet, however similar the terms of engagement, the two authors are not fighting an identical battle. Both kick against the convention of reticence which forbids reference to a young man's sexual experience – 'indecencies' in Dickens's phraseology, 'notorious foibles' in Thackeray's – except by such oblique means. But Dickens's concerns do not rest here. For him 'the Natural' suggests a hero possessed not merely of a sexual life but of a range of 'experiences, trials, perplexities, and confusions' extending beyond the scandal of Pendennis's amorous escapades with porters' daughters. Indeed, the conventional decency of the fictional 'gentlemen of our age' is not to him the necessarily unnatural thing it appears to be to Thackeray. Immunity to the consequences of involvement in the society in which such gentlemen necessarily move represents a much more serious falsification.

In 1853, three years after the *Pendennis* preface, Thackeray returns to Tom Jones in *The English Humourists of the Eighteenth Century* with a critical ambivalence not shown before. Concerned now with 'Art and Ethics' rather than 'the Natural in our Art', he finds Fielding's creation a much more problematic model:

If it is right to have a hero whom we may admire, let us at least take care that he is admirable: if, as is the plan of some authors (a plan decidedly against their interests be it said), it is pronounced that there exists in life no such being, and therefore that in novels, the picture of life, there should appear no such character; then Mr. Thomas Jones becomes an admissable person, and we examine his defects and good qualities, as we do those of Parson Thwackum, or Miss Seagrim. But a hero with a flawed reputation; a hero sponging for a guinea; a hero who can't pay his landlady, and is obliged to let his honour out to hire, is absurd and his claim to heroic rank untenable.[6]

Thackeray, perhaps, never does resolve the confusion he here exhibits over the two meanings of the term 'hero' and the proper relation between them. And Dickens too, in his early experiments with the idea of a natural hero, will demonstrate a similar ambivalence, subverting convention and yet never entirely abandoning it. But by 1856 – the year of his letter to Forster – he has gone well beyond questioning 'if it is right to have a hero whom we may admire'. Indeed, from *David Copperfield* onward, the idea of the literary hero as either public great man or private paragon is entirely abandoned. What Dickens creates instead is his own unique protagonist, a 'hero of an English book' who embodies the experience of the individual in society as Dickens perceives it, a figure of and for his time. This distinctive Dickens 'hero' – there is a qualification implicit in the term – as he evolves in the novels between 1848 and 1870 is preeminently the 'fictional special case' described by Erich Kahler in *The Inward Turn of Narrative*, a case 'so selected and so shaped, so intensified that it becomes the essence of humanity, presenting a fundamental aspect of human life as conditioned by a certain era, or the human condition of an era'.[7] He is, indeed, inseparable from the deepest meaning of Dickens's novels themselves.

The evolution of this distinctive, and distinctively qualified, hero falls roughly into four successive phases. The novels to *Dombey and Son* see a series of experiments with the idea of a natural 'hero' which sets the process in motion. Nicholas Nickleby, Dick Swiveller, Martin Chuzzlewit and Walter Gay all represent attempts to combine the familiar figure and function – the young man of spirit in pursuit of love, fortune and a happy ending – with a realism of presentation that allows for weakness and imperfection, not quite 'indecencies' perhaps (they are more central to Thackeray's fictional concerns), but natural failings at least. The experiment is not, on the whole, successful. Only Dick Swiveller, by means of inspired comic invention, transcends the static 'heroism' dogging his counterparts to become a genuinely original creation. Yet the repeated attempts, however unsuccessful, are themselves significant, testifying to Dickens's early dissatisfaction with the doubly conventional 'hero of an English book', and to his growing commitment to redefining, or rather recreating, the figure.

Such recreation truly begins with David Copperfield. For, in David, Dickens brings together two ideas that had separately pervaded the earlier novels, fusing the natural hero, a figure imperfect and dynamic, and the abandoned child, a waif alternately beseiged and forlorn, to give birth to a new fictional protagonist. It is in David that the characteristic plight of the Dickens hero takes shape. Homeless in a hostile world, divided in and from himself, it is David who establishes the search for selfhood – an integrated sense of identity, role and place – as the essence of that hero's experience. And the two novels that follow extend the process still further. In *Bleak House* and *Hard Times* the homeless hero acquires a social context. The psychic divisions which are the result of David Copperfield's personal history become in Richard Carstone, Esther Summerson and Tom Gradgrind the inevitable consequence of involvement in a society they cannot escape. There is for the Dickens hero as he here emerges no retreating to the paradisal refuge granted to predecessors like Nicholas Nickleby. He is, literally from birth, enmeshed in a world which proves increasingly inimical to emotional and moral wholeness. The characteristic psychic estrangement of the Dickens hero becomes, paradoxically, the symbol of his inescapable social engagement.

It is a paradox which fuses the 'psychological' and the 'social' aspects of Dickens's art, making the two essentially coextensive in their terms of analysis no less than their thematic significance. The self, for the Dickens hero, is preeminently a social entity, seeking definition in relation to the world which surrounds it. He is haunted less by the previous century's anxieties concerning selfhood, perception and epistemology, and more by a new fear that integrity of self is impossible in the industrialized, urbanized society to which that century had given birth. For Dickens, the first great English novelist of the city, it is a society symbolized above all by the 'great wilderness' of London, as Nicholas Nickleby calls it. For him the city increasingly becomes an emblem of an inescapable predicament, a condition of existence no less than a physical place. And it is precisely in the city that the Dickens hero must, in a double sense, find himself. In the later novels the hero's plight as he literally and figuratively seeks to find a home becomes the focus for Dickens's vision of the human condition of an era which was spreading the urban wilderness farther and faster than ever before. Indeed, the hero's plight *is* that vision in its most personal form, reaching beyond the boundaries of its era to the condition of modern social existence generally. From *Hard Times* onward, Dickens explores the implications of the link he there effects between his hero's personal history and its social (and urban) contexts. And, as he does so, the hero himself becomes steadily more implicated in the alienation that is his hallmark, steadily more compromised by his exposure to the corrupting world he inhabits. It is an infection that will lead, in the final novels, to the ultimate 'indecency' of murder.

While the hero's experience thus develops from novel to novel, moving towards its grim conclusion, there is an identifiable pattern informing it throughout: a movement from an increasingly symbolic psychic estrangement, through self-discovery, to a social alienation which emerges as the price of selfhood. The idea of self-discovery as a cycle of separation and reunion, and of the presence of this cycle as a structuring principle in a wide range of Victorian novels, has received considerable critical attention of late. Yet, however wide the initial separation and extensive the significance attributed to it, some form of reintegration is generally seen to follow. *Violation and Repair in the English Novel: The Paradigm of Experience from Richardson to Woolf* is the title of a recent, and representative, study. The Dickens hero, however, experiences a rather different paradigm. For him, selfhood increasingly proves an achievement incompatible with social integration. There is violation in abundance, but less and less repair. Given the nature of the world he moves in, the homeless hero cannot wish to be more at home. It is not that he can never attain emotional wholeness – though it will become steadily more elusive – but that he must accept a further, and permanent, estrangement with it. Alienation, in the specific sense of being forever an alien in a society inimical to him, is his fate, and separation his only choice.

Focusing, as Dickens increasingly does, on the social formation of his young male protagonists, he might be said to be working within the familiar tradition of the *Bildungsroman*, or novel of development, exemplified and essentially initiated by Goethe's *Wilhelm Meister's Apprenticeship* (translated into English by Carlyle in 1824). Certainly, he shares the *Bildung* novelist's concern with the relation between social pressures and psychic needs, charting the interaction between world and self. A recent historian of the genre, however, has asserted that 'A *Bildung* is truly such only if, at a certain point, it can be seen as *concluded*: only if youth passes into maturity, and comes to a stop there. And with it, time stops – narrative time at least.'[8] Judged in these terms, what Dickens creates through the experience of his hero's search for selfhood is, effectively, an anti-*Bildungsroman*. For, as the prospect of social integration grows steadily more elusive for the Dickens hero, so too does the prospect of closure. Narrative time may stop with a vengeance for an early 'hero' like Nicholas Nickleby, who is even allowed to return to his childhood home and fill it with children of his own. David Copperfield, the transitional figure in the evolution we are tracing, is able to secure only a much more compromised 'happy ending' won amid betrayal, death and continuing loss. And his successors achieve still less, their histories left suspended in a narrative irresolution that is the formal expression of their social fate. The only Dickens heroes to achieve an unequivocal 'ending' are those who, like Sydney Carton, find in death a resolution unavailable to them in life. Structurally no less than thematically, Dickens's hero stands at the heart of his fictional world, the experience of that hero defining both the form and the content of the narratives he inhabits, his continued estrangement their own deepest meaning.

I am very much indebted in the chapters that follow to a whole range of critical studies, both of the novel generally and of Dickens and Victorian fiction in particular, studies embracing an equally wide range of theoretical approaches. In the Bibliographic Essay at the end of the volume, I have attempted to acknowledge the indebtedness and indicate those works I have found most helpful to my argument, most challenging, or both. As for my own critical first principles, I trust they will both reveal and justify themselves adequately in the course of this book. Dickens wrote out of a conviction that the complex realities he perceived at work in the world around him could find expression in the constructed, fictive world of his art. It is the aim of this study to trace the ways in which his changing perception of those realities seeks, and finds, a focus in the changing figure of the Dickens hero, the human heart of Dickens's decentred narrative world.

৺1৻

Young Men Out of Nature:
The Early Heroes

There is only one other point on which I would desire to offer a remark. If Nicholas be not always found to be blameless or agreeable, he is not always intended to appear so. He is a young man of an impetuous temper and of little or no experience; and I saw no reason why such a hero should be lifted out of nature.

(*Nicholas Nickleby* – Preface to the First Cheap Edition)

Following on the heels of the venerable Pickwick and the very young Oliver Twist, Nicholas Nickleby represents Dickens's first full-scale version of the familiar literary 'hero', a figure effectively defined by G. K. Chesterton as 'young, poor, brave, unimpeachable, and ultimately triumphant',[1] and one typically engaged in a quest for the twin goals of love and fortune. But if Nicholas is Dickens's first full-length portrait in this style, the type has not gone completely unrepresented in his earliest work. Though *The Pickwick Papers* and *Oliver Twist* substitute, respectively, a bachelor who was never young and a child who never grows old for the sort of *jeune premier* Chesterton describes, Dickens does not dispense with him entirely. Mr Pickwick's young friends Winkle and Snodgrass offer comic versions of the 'hero'/lover's usual experience of adventure and romance: Winkle with his agonized attempts to sidestep an unwanted duel; Snodgrass ending a clandestine meeting with his beloved locked in her father's bedroom, dodging distractedly among the furniture. And they supply too the traditional denouement with wedding bells Pickwick, by reason of age and character, cannot provide. Harry Maylie plays a similarly supplementary role, though in more serious fashion, in *Oliver Twist*, assuming the courtship and marriage functions – standard preoccupations of the young male literary protagonist – from which little Oliver, like the elderly Pickwick, has been deliberately disqualified. With no real part to play in its plot – he assists at the capture of Sikes but is hardly instrumental even there – Harry is introduced into the novel with a descriptive vagueness which

9

suggests generic status: 'He seemed about five-and-twenty years of age, and was of the middle height; his countenance was frank and handsome; and his demeanour singularly easy and prepossessing' (222). The adjectives reveal nothing that is specific to him and, indeed, his presence in *Oliver Twist* contributes little more than a pretext for two unnecessary love scenes: the first when the angelic Rose renounces him for his own sake, the second when Harry takes his turn 'heroically' renouncing all the world for her.

Yet, however perfunctory such a conventional sketch might seem, the simple fact of its inclusion is itself revealing. Dickens's first two novels may displace the traditional figure of the 'hero', but they do not reject it outright. If Winkle and Snodgrass parody the typical 'heroic' experience – and even they are paired off very conventionally at novel's end – Harry Maylie plays it straight. Though all three are deliberately moved to the periphery of the main plot, while Pickwick and Oliver take the 'hero' 's place, all are equally deliberately retained there, to enact their familiar rituals. In *Nicholas Nickleby* the 'hero' simply returns, quite literally, to centre stage after an initial period of waiting in the wings. It is, perhaps, a deliberate concession to the expectations of a reading public accustomed to encounter in novelists as diverse as Scott, Marryat and Bulwer-Lytton protagonists who are young (but not *too* young), active and possessed of romantic potential. Or perhaps, more fundamentally, it is a testament to a less conscious assumption in Dickens himself that this third book, the book which in Forster's estimation truly established his credentials as a novelist,[2] required a 'hero' in the established mode to do so, however much he may subsequently have claimed to be challenging that very requirement.

Nicholas Nickleby is, undoubtedly, impetuous and inexperienced as Dickens claims. But he is also young, handsome, romantic and high-spirited, and being so owes more than Dickens chooses to acknowledge in his 1848 preface to a long line of similarly equipped novel heroes. Nicholas is not in the same imaginative league as his two predecessors as title-figures. He lacks the symbolic force which renders the benevolent Mr Pickwick truly 'immortal' and has made Oliver Twist's plea far more familiar to many who have never read the novel in which it features. What Nicholas indisputably does have, however, is a recognizable pedigree. His roots lie deep in a fictional world at least as old as Dick Whittington. It is a world familiar from the pages of Fielding and Smollett, where penniless youths journey to the city to make their fortunes – and do – and gallant young men generally succeed to beautiful wives, large estates and happy endings. Much like Harry Maylie, Nicholas suggests a certain standard-issue brand of literary 'heroism' consisting of good looks, courage, charm perhaps, luck certainly, some measure of intelligence, and nothing much that could be called distinctive character.

And yet, by Dickens's own account, Nicholas represents a deliberate rejection of just such a formulaic 'hero' figure. Designed to be neither unfailingly blameless nor even, necessarily, agreeable, never artificially lifted to a perfection he could not naturally own, Nicholas emerges from Dickens's somewhat cryptic consideration, added to the novel's preface for the 1848 edition, as both 'hero' and 'natural young man', and the conjunction is clearly significant. Indeed, the proffered 'remark' plainly constitutes a defence of what Dickens at least – and presumably some of *Nickleby*'s first readers as well, hence the need for its addition – perceived to be a distinctive feature of the novel: the casting of an ordinary young man of the middle class, complete with the ordinary faults natural to him, in the role of literary hero.[3] Ten years after the fact, Dickens reemphasizes his protagonist's distance from such *un*natural figures as Bulwer-Lytton's Pelham (eponymous hero of the 1828 novel), a consummate dandy in the Beau Brummel mode, or Disraeli's Duke of St James (of *The Young Duke*, 1830), a fabulously wealthy aristocrat who manages to lose a hundred thousand pounds in a gambling den before reforming into an exemplary husband and peer. Nor is Nicholas intended to be a sentimental exquisite like Befillaire, 'the young, the slim, the low-voiced' (359), hero of Mrs Wititterly's fashionable 'novel in three volumes' (358) which Dickens parodies so enthusiastically in *Nickleby* itself. Certain aspects of Nicholas's character, his peripatetic tendencies, physical attractiveness and pronounced naivete, suggest rather that Dickens may have been glancing back to his favourite eighteenth-century authors, to Le Sage, Fielding and Smollett, for his inspiration, substituting an older tradition for that of the sentimental/fashionable 'novel in three volumes'. If nothing else, these writers' choice of a picaresque rather than a heroic mode offers an obvious precedent for Dickens's own declared determination not to lift his young male protagonist 'out of nature'. And the outline of Nicholas's life and adventures does seem to recall the pattern of experience typical of earlier, English picaros in particular: the constant wanderings, the unexpected triumphs and equally unexpected reverses, the shifting roles. His journeyings too, like Peregrine Pickle's or Tom Jones's, provide the only real structure possessed by the novel which bears his name.

But if the 'naturalness' Dickens later claims for Nicholas owes something to the example of these earlier models, the debt proves, like the 'naturalness', to be partial at best, and to lie largely in the first half of the novel. For it is there that the 'natural' faults – distinguishing traits, really, rather than moral defects – Nicholas might be said to inherit from his picaresque predecessors feature most prominently. In these early chapters Dickens repeatedly underlines his protagonist's impetuosity, quick temper and occasional naive obtuseness. Nicholas is not always blameless or agreeable here, and his inexperience and touchy pride actually serve as the source of a comedy which lifts him, at least for the time, out of the ranks of the generic literary 'hero'. Nicholas desperately, and tactlessly, fending off the amorous Fanny Squeers to the accompaniment of her extraordinary mating-call – ' "I never saw such legs in the whole course of my life!" ' (103) – has something of the flavour of Fielding's Joseph Andrews, similarly besieged by an ardent Mrs Slipslop, though a flavour refined for family consumption. With memories of this previous 'hero' 's beleaguered virtue hovering in the background, it is an encounter which shows Nicholas at his least 'heroic', most comic and, consequently, most credible.

Yet Dickens remains fundamentally uncertain how far he wishes to undercut the conventional dignity and propriety of the 'hero'. Young Nicholas's flirtatiousness and reiterated physical charms, both most unusual in a Dickens protagonist, may recall the amorous naturalness of Tom Jones. But it is very much the 'child's Tom Jones, a harmless creature' of David Copperfield's early reading (*DC* 48), a figure free of the sexual fallibility which occasionally besets Fielding's 'heroe'. While a penniless Tom may, characteristically, allow himself to be kept by the infatuated Lady Bellaston (the very sin which so offended Thackeray), Nicholas is incapable of similarly exploiting Fanny Squeer's romantic 'extravagance':

She [Fanny] had not failed to recollect, either, how much more agreeable she could render his situation if she were his friend, and how much more disagreeable if she were his enemy; and doubtless, many less scrupulous young gentlemen than Nicholas would have encouraged her extravagance had it been only for this very obvious and intelligible reason. However, he had thought proper to do otherwise, and Miss Squeers was outrageous.   (142)

However 'natural', even comic, in design, Nicholas is never allowed to be anything less than 'scrupulous' in conduct. With his highly developed sense of rectitude and acute consciousness of family responsibility, he never approaches the moral waywardness of a Peregrine Pickle, or even of the much more benign Tom Jones. Dickens's commitment to 'naturalness', in other words, proves much less consistent, or at least much more limited, in practice than his subsequent theory would suggest. And while one might attribute this failure of commitment to the convention of reticence he would later attack in his 1856 letter to Forster, there would seem to be other significant, and perhaps more characteristic, impulses underlying it.

It is, in fact, the fundamental weakness of the 'young gentleman' that he fluctuates between the 'natural' and the 'scrupulous' in this way. Opportunities for laughter at Nicholas's expense diminish noticeably after his second return to London (Chapter 32), although they never disappear entirely, decreasing as the narrative emphasis shifts away from the occasionally ridiculous young man of impetuous temper and little experience of the novel's earlier chapters to a much more serious, and more conventional, figure. And this change in Nicholas's dominant mode is significant. Increasingly forced by the demands of Dickens's preposterous plot (or rather plots) to play a traditional 'heroic' part – championing outraged maidenhood, confounding dastardly enemies, winning beautiful heroines – Nicholas reverts to traditional 'heroic' type, shedding claims to naturalness, and comedy, in the process. Most readers of the novel find its title-figure least interesting on these later occasions. And the impossibly rhetorical style he falls into, stiff with echoes of stage melodrama and fictional cliché, suggests that Dickens himself is not much more fully engaged. The letter Nicholas is allowed to pen, to take just one example, after discovering his uncle's treachery to Kate, sounds suspiciously like something borrowed from the pages of Fanny Burney or Ann Radcliffe, fit reading-matter for that typically Gothic 'stately terrace' in Italy to which Dickens himself will later refer (605):

'Your brother's widow and his orphan child spurn the shelter of your roof, and shun you with disgust and loathing. Your kindred renounce you, for they know no shame but the ties of blood which bind them in name with you.

'You are an old man, and I leave you to the grave. May every recollection of your life cling to your false heart, and cast their darkness on your death-bed.' (425)

The distinctive sense of high spirits, of sheer imaginative exuberance, which characterizes *Nicholas Nickleby*'s most memorable episodes – the Yorkshire school, Mantalini at home, Crummles's troupe – not to mention nature itself, tend to evaporate in the face of this sort of 'heroic' posturing. Only Nicholas's rescue of Smike, enacted amid the grotesque tragicomedy of Dotheboys Hall, achieves a genuine rather than mechanical energy. The hungry young man who makes 'fearful ravages on the bread and butter' at Fanny Squeers's tea-party (108), while standing fiercely on his dignity as a gentleman, would seem to be the product of one sort of creative impulse; the humourless paragon who hurls defiance at his wicked uncle – ' "Remember that you come near me at your peril" ' (718) – before bearing off his beloved in his arms, the fruit of quite another. Both are at work, and in tension, throughout the novel. Nicholas encounters a Cecilia Bobster as well as a Madeline Bray. But ultimately it is the conventional impulse which dominates. In spite of Dickens's later claims, the natural and the heroic, though they meet in Nicholas, do not mingle. The ostensibly ordinary young man still ends his adventures with that amalgam of marital bliss, domestic joy and financial security which generally falls to the lot of 'heroes' in books, and to them alone.

In effect, for all Dickens's subsequent protests and claims, Nicholas still owes too much to the conventional literary type of the young paragon 'hero' ever really to break free. If he is naturally impetuous and inexperienced, occasionally disagreeable and not consistently blameless, he is also handsome and gallant, romantic, high-spirited and high-principled. And as the novel progresses it is, increasingly, these latter qualities which are emphasized and called into play. There is the potential for something more than the standard happy ending in Nicholas's Yorkshire predicament, in the combination of degradation, misery and self-reproach he suffers there as the 'aidor and abettor of a system which filled him with honest disgust and indignation' (95–96). And there is thematic promise of a similar sort in the desolation he later experiences in London, where he wanders lonely and oppressed by the anonymity of that urban 'wilderness' (450). At such points Dickens actually seems poised to deepen the meaning of his 'hero''s life and adventures, to show youth, hope and spirit truly embattled in their struggle with a world that rolls on 'from year to year, alike careless and indifferent, and no man seeking to remedy or redress it' (693).

But it is Smike and not Nicholas who plays out the alternative fate suggested by episodes such as these. It is Smike who suffers at the hands of the enemies Nicholas heroically defies; Smike who despairs and is defeated while Nicholas triumphs; and Smike who carries a broken heart to the grave as Nicholas goes on to win both wife and fortune. It is as if the impulse towards the 'natural' and the realistic which, in the early chapters of the novel, finds expression in the comedy Nicholas provides is transposed by novel's end to the near-tragedy of Smike. In this sense, the born victim serves as surrogate for his more fortunate cousin, allowing Dickens to dramatize 'natural' (that is, non-literary, unconventional) possibilities of deprivation, suffering and death without 'making people angry', as he would later put it in the case of *Dombey and Son*'s Walter Gay, by depriving them of the happy ending they would naturally expect.[4] Such sufferings as Nicholas, in contrast to Smike, does endure are, like those of any fairy-tale prince down on his luck, reassuringly short-lived. Benevolent spirits in the shape of the Cheeryble brothers soon intervene on his behalf and he is whisked off, not to a castle, but to the still more solid comfort of a rent-free cottage in the country. Once again, it is the 'natural' that loses ground as the conventional, and Nicholas, win out.

It is the competition of these two strains which defines, and ultimately defeats, Nicholas Nickleby as an attempt at a convincing 'natural' hero. And this same fundamental tension persists, shadowing Nicholas's 'natural' successors in *Martin Chuzzlewit* and *Dombey and Son*, and to similar effect. (Only Dick Swiveller in *The Old Curiosity Shop* fully transcends its influence.) Like Nicholas Nickleby, young Martin Chuzzlewit and Walter Gay are, finally, chiefly remarkable for what they fail to achieve. The novels in which they appear may attest a desire to move beyond the common ground of conventional literary 'heroism', with its stock catalogue of 'chiselled noses, undeniable chins [and] forms that might have served the sculptor for a model' (*MC* 5). Both may indeed propose alternative models in the shape of Tom Pinch, Florence Dombey or Harriet Carker, modest figures 'who are not only not heroic to their valets and waiting-women, but have neither valets nor waiting-women to be heroic to withal!' (*DS* 457). Both may reject, in an increasingly familiar fashion, 'the received idea of heroism and greatness' (*DS* 456), and defy, almost as a matter of course, the authority of 'all the books which treat of such matters' (*MC* 5). In the end, Martin and Walter still emerge as little more than slight variations on the formulaic 'hero' discounted by the *Nickleby* preface. Neither the besetting sin of the one, nor the vestiges of a rejected fate hanging over the other, fully rescues either from the ranks where Nicholas Nickleby too will finally be found. Both hold the promise of something more, as indeed Nicholas had done. But it is a promise unrealized in one case, deliberately abandoned in the other.

The failure is epitomized by Dickens's well-known decision to revise his original proposals for Walter Gay, who was to have reversed Martin Chuzzlewit's career of moral regeneration and declined from early promise into 'negligence, idleness, dissipation, dishonesty, and ruin'.[5] With both young men Dickens projects a new type of 'hero' (loosely anticipated in Nicholas), a culpable hero implicated in his own serious imperfection and developing, for good or ill, as a result. It is a figure whose progress forms part of a larger thematic design, a conception in which the idea of change is integral (it is not in Nicholas), both to the character of the hero himself and to the novel in which he appears. Yet with neither is this first idea carried through. As with Nicholas Nickleby, Dickens retains an ambivalent commitment to the figure he proposes to displace. As he informed Forster in the letter of July 1846 in which he outlined his plans for the character, he undoubtedly considered it 'a good thing' to disappoint the conventional expectations Walter's first appearance in the novel would have aroused: expectations of his further 'happy connection with the story and the heroine', as becomes a novel 'hero'. And yet this was not to be done at the expense of 'making people angry'.[6] So young Martin's selfishness never goes beyond a detachable appendage to an otherwise standard fictional *jeune premier* – handsome, high-spirited, romantic and clearly destined by novel's end for marriage and material success – and Walter Gay is reprieved from ruin to fulfil the same role. Yet the discarded plans remain in prospect, symptoms of a growing incompatibility between the unchanging figure of the 'hero' on the one hand and the maturing concerns of Dickens's fiction on the other. In these earliest novels it is primarily criminal figures like Fagin, Sikes and Jonas Chuzzlewit who possess anything remotely resembling an inner life. Young Martin Chuzzlewit's ostensible conversion bears no comparison with the nightmare intensity of Fagin's breakdown in the condemned cell. Walter Gay never becomes the moral ruin he was initially designed to be, though Jonas Chuzzlewit does descend convincingly to murder and suicide. Yet there is significance to these abortive experiments too. If nothing else they signal Dickens's growing inclination to liberate his 'heroes' from the strait-jacket of their 'heroism', to accord them the sort of psychological vitality his 'villains' early enjoy. As Dickens himself acknowledged in reference to Walter Gay, 'This question of the boy is very important',[7] and it will grow still more so in the novels to come.

It is *The Old Curiosity Shop*, however, and not *Nickleby*, *Chuzzlewit* or *Dombey*, which sees a genuine recreation of the 'hero', effected from the unlikeliest of materials. Dick Swiveller arrives in the novel furnished

with few of the conventional credentials which ultimately guarantee
Nicholas, Martin and Walter their happy 'hero''s fate. His pedigree
extends no further than the young clerks and would-be swells of *Sketches by
Boz*, comic species of London undergrowth Dickens had by now made
peculiarly his own. Dick would indeed seem to owe something to
Dickens's own early days in the law office of Ellis and Blackmore, when he
was himself a particularly youthful, and ambitious, clerk. On first
appearance in the novel, Dick's intended status is doubtful in a way that
even Walter Gay's never is. His involvement with Fred Trent seems to
presage villainies to come. An occasional Wellerish confusion of
consonants – 'conwiviality' (17), 'mutual wiolence' (19) – in the early
chapters equally suggests a comic career. Plainly he cannot be a candidate
for the vacant role of *jeune premier*, for that young gentleman, as George
Orwell noted long ago, always talks the equivalent of 'BBC' in Dickens.[8]

According to Forster, *The Old Curiosity Shop* took form with 'less direct
consciousness of design' on Dickens's part than any of his other major
works, beginning with a plan for 'but a short half-dozen chapters'.[9]
And it is precisely as Dickens's grasp on this the most improvised of his
novels grows visibly surer, as possibilities begin to reveal themselves
and patterns to take shape, that Dick Swiveller receives a promotion.
Fred Trent and his improbable schemes vanish from sight. The errant
'w''s cease to wander. And the good-natured wastrel who saunters into
The Old Curiosity Shop 'a figure conspicuous for its dirty smartness' (16)
gradually emerges as one of its thematic pivots. 'I *mean* to make much of
him,' Dickens informed Forster early in the novel's composition,[10] and
by its close Dick has grown from lightweight cockney villain to serio-
comic hero, possessed of a moral significance Nicholas Nickleby at his
most solemnly conventional, or Martin Chuzzlewit at his most
insistently selfish, never attain. The underlying tensions and competing impulses which dog Dickens's other early 'heroes' find a unique
resolution here. Laughter, far from being avoided as inimical to the
serious 'hero''s serious function, becomes his essence, while the
function itself assumes new and larger dimensions. Unlike Nicholas,
whose experience of life's 'huge aggregate of distress and sorrow' (*NN*
693) still leads only to a country refuge secure from both, or Martin and
Walter who ultimately share a similar happy immunity, Dick is fully
implicated in the sombre possibilities his experience suggests. Armed
with his invincible comic spirit, he both acknowledges and confronts a
world where plain cooks of three feet high are starved in cellars, and
makes his own modest accommodation.

The embodiment of the life force in a novel celebrating the grave (food and drink are his frequent accompaniments), Dick the 'Liverer''s regeneration serves as thematic counterbalance to the death of Nell, holding out hope that goodness need not necessarily retreat with her to the churchyard at the narrative's close. Dick personifies an assurance that kindness, generosity, affection and 'conwiviality' can still live – on an annuity of a hundred and fifty pounds a year – though innocence has died. Neither he nor anyone else can save the fated Nell, for her angelic purity demands death for its preservation. But his marriage with the grown-up Marchioness, the child Dick does succeed in rescuing, proves that there is an alternative to her fate. The union of these two possesses a symbolic fitness which goes well beyond the conventional pairing of Nicholas Nickleby and his shadowy Madeline, or Martin Chuzzlewit and his still more nebulous Mary. Dickens never again creates a 'happy ending' so truly satisfying, or so convincingly earned, as this. The marriage of Florence Dombey and Walter Gay, though clearly intended to carry a comparable thematic weight, lacks a similar emotional appeal. Nor does he create another hero like Dick. The early interest in a 'natural' hero figure, an ordinary, faulty young man, will grow steadily more central to Dickens's concerns, as David Copperfield clearly attests. But it will also increasingly move him away from the comic impulse which finds its apotheosis in Dick, and from the prospect of happy accommodation that impulse holds out for the heroes it creates.

Dickens actually begins his first full-length reconsideration of the 'hero' figure by calling into question the conventional credentials he will himself ultimately affirm. Having described the young Ralph Nickleby's talent for usury, he concludes with a warning which draws once again on the idea of the 'natural' in fiction:

From what we have said of this young gentleman, and the natural admiration the reader will immediately conceive of his character, it may perhaps be inferred that he is to be the hero of the work which we shall presently begin. To set this point at rest for once and for ever, we hasten to undeceive them, and stride to its commencement. (4)

The irony, done somewhat in the Fielding style, may be obvious, but it is also suggestive. For there is a fundamental ambivalence in the novel towards accepted ideas of 'the hero of the work' to which this seemingly incidental bit of narrative byplay gives early voice, an uncertainty that remains significantly unresolved. It is this ambivalence which is responsible for Nicholas's failure to come fully alive as a character. Or rather, it is responsible for his failure to remain so, the ingenuous youth of the novel's early chapters being, on the whole, convincingly rendered. And it is from this underlying ambivalence that the competing impulses stem – the comic and the deadly serious, the 'natural' and the impossibly 'heroic' – which mark Dickens's handling of Nicholas, depriving him, and in the end the novel, of a firm centre. Deliberately experimenting in *Nicholas Nickleby* with the familiar figure of the 'hero', Dickens proves, in the final analysis, unwilling to break free of the conventional limitations this sort of literary heroism imposes, limitations to which Nicholas himself ultimately succumbs.

And yet, with the ironic lines just quoted, a vein of satire is introduced into *Nicholas Nickleby* which will also run throughout, satire directed precisely at conventional notions of heroism and manliness, both in and out of novels. It finds targets in Miss Petowker searching her memory for the word 'aristocratic': '"What do you call it when Lords break off door-knockers and beat policemen, and play at coaches with other people's money, and all that sort of thing?"' (184); and in Miss Knag's brother, an amateur Byron who modelled himself on the heroes of novels, '"took to scorning everything, and became a genius"' (223). Befillaire the exquisite, hero of that exciting epic *The Lady Flabella* which so enthrals Mrs Wititterly, provides yet another butt. And these are only passing shots. More sustained fire is aimed at the distinctive figures of the dandy and the rake, represented in *Nicholas Nickleby* by the characters of Mantalini and Sir Mulberry Hawk. The cynical heartlessness of the fop who 'married on his whiskers' (124), the brutality of the licentious man-about-town, Regency ghosts both, are attacked with an energy which reminds the reader just how *early* - Victorian the moral atmosphere of *Nicholas Nickleby* is. (In later novels Dickens will view the heirs of the dandy figure with increasing interest and, ultimately, sympathy.) And it is specifically in terms of such specious hero figures as these, and of the literary falsities they represent, that Nicholas is defined. Indeed, his 'naturalness' increasingly appears to become less a question of positive than negative identification, residing in his *not* being what other literary young men conventionally are:

And here it may be observed, that Nicholas himself was not, in the ordinary sense of the word a young man of high spirit. He would resent an affront to himself, or interpose to redress a wrong offered to another, as boldly and as freely as any knight that ever set lance at rest; but he lacked that peculiar excess of coolness and great-minded selfishness, which invariably distinguish gentlemen of high-spirit.   (202)

   Nicholas's perfectly ordinary, even endearing faults, his 'headlong rashness and precipitation' (447) and the like, distinguish him, then, from the array of literary types who come within Dickens's satiric sights. Those 'qualities not altogether unnatural at his time of life' (447), by virtue of their naturalness, separate him equally from the polished paragons of the silver fork, *Lady Flabella* school and their more dissolute, but still fascinating, fictional brothers. These latter are, perhaps, a glance at figures like Bulwer-Lytton's Eugene Aram, 'high-spirited' criminal hero of the 1832 novel of that name, and other such heirs of the doomed, 'Byronic' tradition. The 'Byronic' mode as interpreted, and debased, by the fashionable Regency novelists is, indeed, a shaping influence throughout Dickens's early fiction, providing the negative standard of conventional unnaturalness against which he explicitly reacts. Dotheboys Hall, in Dickens's hands, is anything but a prosaic reality. Yet it is precisely the *un*romantic, *un*literary nature of Nicholas's experience there which he stresses. Nicholas himself anticipates a career at 'the Hall' that is straight out of the world of romantic fiction: '"Or suppose some young nobleman who is being educated at the Hall, were to take a fancy to me and get his father to appoint me his travelling tutor when he left, and when we come back from the continent, procured me some handsome appointment. Eh! uncle?"' (27). And there is something both genuine and genuinely appealing about his naive conviction that life will resemble such patent unreality. (In the event, his fate will prove scarcely less improbable.) Nicholas's ingenuous tendency to cast himself as the 'hero' of his adventures, and to wake to disillusionment in consequence, as he does at Dotheboys Hall – 'But the pupils – the young noblemen!' (88) – credibly establishes him as the impetuous, inexperienced youth of Dickens's preface. It invests him with a reality he retains until he is made to play the 'hero' in earnest.
   In fact, on more than one occasion, Dickens uses Nicholas as a means of deflating a variety of traditional, and traditionally literary, 'heroic' postures, making satiric capital out of the obvious disparity which exists between the conventions of fiction and the workings of a rather more commonplace reality. Following Squeers's kidnapping of the unfortunate Smike, Nicholas is bent, as any 'hero' worth the name naturally would be, on revenge. And he meditates accordingly 'a great

variety of schemes for the punishment of the Yorkshire schoolmaster, all of which had their foundation in the strict principles of retributive justice' (513). This is pretty much standard form. There is only one drawback: the schemes are, without exception, 'wholly impracticable' (513). Burning to play the 'hero' in approved fashion and exact a just revenge, Nicholas yet finds himself stopped short, as avenging 'heroes' in novels so seldom seem to be, by that negligible consideration feasibility.

And it is not only in the capacity of avenger that Nicholas fails to make the grade. In the time-honoured role of languishing lover Dickens allows him to be what literary lovers almost never are, at least intentionally, namely funny. His abortive assignation among the beer barrels of the Bobster kitchen provides a ludicrous parody of the standard fictional scene: '"Leave the house, for Heaven's sake! . . ." cried the young lady. "Leave the house or I am ruined and undone for ever"' (526). And Nicholas himself proves conscious of his anomalous position: '"What the devil!"' he demands indignantly, before engaging in the rendezvous, '"Are we to sneak into the kitchen as though we came after the forks?"' (524). Reflecting on the uncomfortable implications of that favourite stock-in-trade of the romantic novelist, love at first sight, he makes a still more indisputable satiric point: 'Still Nicholas was dissatisfied; and there was more in the dissatisfaction than mere revulsion of feeling. He was angry with the young lady for being so easily won, "because", reasoned Nicholas, "it is not as if she knew it was I, but it might have been anybody," which was certainly not pleasant' (523). When it turns out to be the wrong lady who has been won after all, Nicholas goes back happily to loving and languishing 'after the most orthodox models' (519), and Dickens to laughing at both them and him.

In a more serious vein, when Nicholas does discover the identity of his fair unknown, Dickens makes a particular point of contrasting this lovers' meeting with the conventional fictional scene, calling attention to the absence of all the usual appurtenances of the novel or stage: 'And yet Nicholas was in the rules of the King's Bench Prison! If he had been in Italy indeed, and the time had been sunset, and the scene a stately terrace . . .' (605). Do not, the reader is apparently being warned, expect the exaggerated ecstasies of Gothic romance here, nor yet the picturesque rhapsodies of a hundred stage melodramas. The 'natural' world Nicholas inhabits is not that of terraces, and sunsets, and other such familiar dramatic props, but of London, with all its accompanying realities of prison, debt and shabbiness. It is a contrast Dickens will later make explicit in his letter to Forster regarding Walter Gay, a contrast between the common and everyday experience of 'ordinary life' and the unnatural expectations of fiction.

Dickens has, indeed, already grounded much of his satire of 'the most orthodox models' of literary heroism in specific reference to established practice on the stage even more than the page. Though entirely peripheral to *Nicholas Nickleby*'s official plot, Crummles and his troupe of second-rate actors occupy some hundred pages of its action, providing the novel's most extensive parody of both conventional 'heroism' and its usual practitioners. Nicholas, as we have already seen, has a certain 'natural' bent for playing the 'hero'. His aptitude for the part is enthusiastically affirmed by no less an authority than Vincent Crummles, who plainly knows a thing or two about it. '"There's genteel comedy in your walk and manner,"' he tells a startled Nicholas at their first meeting, '"juvenile tragedy in your eye, and touch and go farce in your laugh"' (283). Nicholas's modest disclaimers, '"I don't know anything about it . . . I never acted a part in my life, except at school"' (283), Crummles very rightly ignores. And indeed Nicholas proves a most successful romantic lead in the theatre, whatever difficulties he encounters when attempting the role outside. During his stay with the company, moreover, between the melodramas enacted on-stage and the histrionics indulged in off, the reader is treated to a feast of theatrical convention, cliché and stereotype, all wrought to the point of absurdity, and well beyond. Here, for example, is the grand finale of Nicholas's acting career:

But when Nicholas came on for his crack scene with Mrs. Crummles, what a clapping of hands there was! When Mrs. Cummles (who was his unworthy mother) sneered and called him 'presumptuous boy', and he defied her, what a tumult of applause came on! When he quarrelled with the other gentleman about the young lady, and producing a case of pistols, said, that if he *was* a gentleman, he would fight him in that drawing-room, till the funiture was sprinkled with the blood of one, if not of two – how boxes, pit and gallery joined in one most vigorous cheer! . . . When he was hid behind the curtain in the dark, and the wicked relation poked a sword in every direction, save where his legs were plainly visible, what a thrill of anxious fear ran through the house! (315–316)

It is at this point, however, that one begins to wonder what precisely is being parodied. For Mr Crummles's great melodrama, adapted for him by Nicholas of all people, with its malevolent relation, unworthy

mother, disputed young lady and suggested duel, reads like a deliberate
burlesque of the novel's main action, just as that action is being set in
motion. And Nicholas plays precisely the same role, the 'hero', in both.
His introductory declaration to Sir Mulberry – ' "I am the son of a country
gentleman . . . your equal in birth and education, and your superior, I
trust, in everything besides" ' (417) – clearly indicates his place in the
dramatis personae. If Sir Mulberry is the wicked aristocrat, Nicholas is the
poor but noble gentleman who vanquishes him, familiar figures from
contemporary melodrama. What is more, as Nicholas moves from the
comic parallel plot to the novel's equally unlikely 'serious' action, he
effectively leaves all ironic comment behind. The traditional heroics are
no longer played for laughs. Nicholas confronting his wicked relation *off-*
stage behaves with a thundering theatricality rivalling Crummles's best.
And even Ralph, who had previously shown himself immune to his
nephew's histrionics – ' "I speak plainly, young man, bluster as you will" '
(251) – providing a mocking commentary from the wings, succumbs to
the general infection of unreality:

'My curse, my bitter deadly curse, upon you, boy!'
'Whence will curses come at your command? or what avails a curse or
blessing from a man like you? I warn you, that misfortune and discovery are
thickening about your head; that the structures you have raised through all
your ill-spent life are crumbling into dust; that your path is beset with spies;
that this very day ten thousand pounds of your hoarded wealth have gone in
one great crash!'
' 'Tis false!' cried Ralph, shrinking back.
' 'Tis true . . .' (720)

It is not only misfortunes that are thickening here, but Nicholas's
speech patterns too, with their stagy inverted syntax quite different
from the sort he uses elsewhere. (Compare his 'whence will curses
come' to the much more natural expressions of the Bobster kitchen.) In
a moment he will exit carrying the swooning Madeline in his arms. He
has already discovered, by a quite incredible coincidence, his sister's
persecutor and called the would-be seducer to account in properly
'heroic', and utterly unnatural, terms: ' "I denounce this person as a
liar, and impeach him as a coward . . . You are a base and spiritless
scoundrel! . . . and shall be proclaimed so to the world" ' (414–415).
Heartily as Dickens has been satirizing just this sort of thing, he proves
curiously reluctant to dispense with it himself. The very love scenes
with Madeline quickly descend to the stilted unreality of the Gothic
format they originally defied, with Nicholas perpetrating speeches of a

particularly glaring artificiality. '"You are betrayed, and sold for money – for gold, whose every coin is rusted with tears, if not red with the blood of ruined men, who have fallen desperately by their own mad hands,"' (698) he mildly informs his beloved on one such occasion. Nicholas's entire love affair is, in fact, so completely unconvincing, so lacking in imaginative energy, as to seem little more than an automatic gesture. If Nicholas is to be a 'hero', as by this point it is plain he is, he must have a heroine. And Madeline Bray duly materializes – fainting – in Chapter 40, in distress and ripe for rescuing. All this plainly belongs on a terrace in Italy, or the set of one of Crummles's productions perhaps. Nicholas has, in fact, already engaged in a ludicrous mock duel with Crummles's first tragedian, a duel which effectively parodied the conventions Dickens now calls, seriously, into play (Chapter 29). And in the end there seems very little to choose between Mr Lenville's heroic defiance of his rival – '"Object of my scorn and hatred! . . . I hold ye in contempt"' (379) – and Nicholas's subsequent conduct. In both cases it is the 'hero' with a vengeance.

Nicholas Nickleby is a novel teeming with an abundance of fancy, a monument of comic inventiveness. Yet it has at its centre, in its title-figure, what must ultimately rank as a failure of intention, if not of imagination. For all Dickens's protests, voiced in the preface of 1848 (a preface written, one might note, during the gestation of *David Copperfield*), he fails in this first attempt to conceive a serious 'hero' who is not 'lifted out of nature'. For as soon as Nicholas begins to act like a 'hero', he ceases to resemble, even remotely, anything else. Nor does Dickens succeed in envisioning a function for the hero figure, beyond the provision of the standard happy ending. In the end he remains, in *Nickleby*, committed to, or at least dependent on, the very conventions he claims to reject, conventions Nicholas himself has served to satirize. And this leaves the novel, no less than its hero, to move uneasily between the conflicting impulses that shape it, without ever coming fully to rest. It is, moreover, a conflict that equally undermines both Martin Chuzzlewit and Walter Gay, and this in spite of the very different roles Dickens originally projected for them. Clearly intended to build upon the 'naturalness' of Nicholas, Martin and Walter are, if anything, even less successful. Lacking the humour which could, on occasion, bring their predecessor to life, they remain at best inanimate witnesses to Dickens's as yet unrealized desire: the desire to create a new sort of hero.

Unlike Nicholas Nickleby, the character of young Martin

Chuzzlewit is not accorded a special defence in the preface to the novel which bears his name. Yet he is, in fact, even more in need of the assistance. The problem is not, as Dickens suggested was the case with Nicholas, that the reader cannot like or admire Martin as a person. It is, rather, that he simply never comes alive in any capacity, even the strictly limited one of 'hero'. Certainly, as an imperfect (or culpable) figure, a new definition of hero whose reclamation is to form the essence of his fictional experience, Martin must be accounted a failure. For his imperfection is made to rest solely on the fact of his selfishness and it fails entirely to sustain the weight.

This 'commonest of all the vices', as Dickens calls it in the novel's preface, is plainly intended to show as a crippling moral blight in Martin, 'the one absorbing principle' (245) of his character being equally the great 'failing of his life' (525). Yet it is, for the most part, so trivially substantiated as to appear more like the rudeness of a badly brought-up child than anything truly threatening, Martin asking Tom Pinch to ring a bell whose handle is over his own head. Martin carelessly encumbering Tom with luggage, or laughing at his peculiarities, lacks the imaginative stature of the genuine emotional or psychic cripple. Nothing he does suggests a gravity, or carries a conviction, that would warrant banishment to the swamps of Eden and near-death for its reformation. What is more, Martin's *un*selfishness after his momentous conversion has taken place fails to assume any more convincing or serious form. Where the old Martin unthinkingly keeps Tom Pinch from his share of the fire, the new insists on taking turn and turn about with Mark Tapley. It is a change falling somewhat short of the absolute moral regeneration Dickens would have it be. And, in any event, nothing Martin can do could possibly compare with the career of his hopeful cousin Jonas. His sins, which include attempted parricide, wife-beating and murder, truly show selfishness run wild, while his subsequent descent into paralysing guilt and fear has all the imaginative particularity Martin's counterpointed ascent to selflessness in Eden lacks.

There is, moreover, still another problem with Martin as 'natural' hero which Nicholas Nickleby at least was free from: an over-insistence in the handling of the character which ultimately undermines the credibility it seeks to establish. It is a sort of narrative officiousness which pervades Dickens's presentation, a tacit acknowledgment of Martin's inability to convince on his own, perhaps. Certainly, it is the narrator and not the character who makes the required point in

Martin's parting with Mary, and does so in a typically intrusive series of rhetorical questions:

Was he thinking solely of her care for him, when he took so little heed of her share in the separation; of her quiet monotonous endurance, and her slow anxiety from day to day? Was there nothing jarring and discordant even in his tone of courage, with this one note self for ever audible, however high the strain?   (243)

The same uncertainty, and attendant heavy-handedness, is apparent in the too-explicit use made of characters like Tom Pinch, John Westlock and Mark Tapley. In terms of future technique, the proliferation of these figures, variations on young Martin himself, is an important development of Nicholas's doubling by Smike. It is a method Dickens will employ with increasing sophistication to enhance the depiction of his hero's experience. In later novels such figures will emerge as thematic counterparts, subtle refractions of a central image and situation, yet with an undeniable life and logic of their own. Here, however, they feature primarily as spiritual litmus tests for the imperfect hero. Unwilling to let the obvious significance of these juxtapositions develop itself – egotism personified on the one hand, self-denial on the other – Dickens repeatedly intervenes to point the moral himself: 'No slight circumstance, perhaps, could have better illustrated the difference between John Westlock and Martin Chuzzlewit, than the manner in which each of the young men contemplated Tom Pinch' (203), and so on. The reformed Martin too is no less subject to a similarly blatant moral gauging. Mark Tapley, clearly acting for the author here, deliberately deploys first Tom Pinch and then Mary Graham as a means of sounding the 'singular alteration in Martin' (528), and there is something undignified, even trivializing, in the way Martin is made to jump through these moral hoops: '"I don't know what to make of him," [Mark] thought one night, "he ain't what I supposed. He don't think of himself half as much. I'll try him again"' (528). And try him Mark, and Dickens, do, over and over again.

Plainly, this sort of sign-posting should be unnecessary in a successful depiction of moral and psychological development. If it is not, its introduction will be of little help, as the handling of Martin's actual conversion reveals. Described explicitly as an internal spiritual progress of many months' duration – 'It was long before he fixed the knowledge of himself so firmly in his mind that he could thoroughly discern the truth' (525) – Martin's change emerges from its two pages of compressed narration more like an externally effected miracle cure, in which he himself plays no active part. The whole reform/conversion episode, with its emphasis on Martin's retrospective and prospective nights of the soul while tending the suffering Mark Tapley, invite comparison with Ebenezer Scrooge's miraculous regeneration by similar compressed means. The very illness which is the agent of Martin's cure drops upon him in the course of a single night. (Dickens wrote *A Christmas Carol* while working on the eleventh instalment of *Chuzzlewit*. Martin's 'conversion' comes in the thirteenth.) The more insistent the claims made on Martin's behalf – 'So low had Eden brought him down. So high had Eden raised him up' (525) – the less conviction they carry, for the greater the gap between commentary and action. And it is not only the unconverted or reforming Martin who is not allowed to speak for himself. Dickens demonstrates the same anxiety to insist on the significance of the new Martin's smallest actions, and some of them are very small indeed, as he does with the old:

Their luggage, which was waiting for them at a coach-office, [Martin] conveyed to this new place of refuge; and it was with a glow of satisfaction, which as a selfish man he never could have known and never had, that: thinking how much pains and trouble he had saved Mark, and how pleased and astonished Mark would be: he afterwards walked up and down, in the Temple, eating a meat-pie for his dinner.   (742)

In spite of the increasingly grim character of the Jonas/Tigg subplot, with its catalogue of attempted poisoning, murder and suicide, it is still an essentially comic mode which governs the world of *Martin Chuzzlewit* by its close. Certainly the denouement, complete with ritual unmasking, reconciliation, restoration of inheritance and reunion of lovers, operates recognizably within the traditional comic pattern. And perhaps this goes some way to explaining the ease with which Martin is 'cured' of the great 'failing of his life'. Yet, as Dick Swiveller proves, a predominantly comic form need not preclude either more genuine faults or a more gradual transformation. Ultimately, Dickens simply seems less imaginatively engaged by the prospect of reforming the lightly shadowed 'hero' Martin than the unequivocally disreputable, and un-'heroic', Swiveller. The one remains, in spite of all, little more than a stock figure stretched beyond its capabilities, while the other emerges as a truly original revision.

Still, Martin's interest as an attempt at a revised, 'natural' hero does not rest solely in the fact of his failure, for the failure is not unqualified. Reenacting something of Dickens's own experiences visiting 'God A'mighty's free U-nited States' (345), his disillusion, disgust and indignation – '"Is smartness American for forgery?" asked Martin' (265) – have a genuine ring. More significantly, during his brief sojourn in London, Martin comes rather unexpectedly to life in the archetypal Dickens role of outcast. Like Nicholas Nickleby before him, he is, for a short time, a wanderer in the urban wilderness, bereft of friends, prospects and hope. And, like Nicholas too in this, his predicament, convincingly rendered, lends a new depth and potential to his character, an anticipation of the plight of 'heroes' to come: 'Martin stood in the dark street, with a pretty strong sense of being shut out, alone, upon the dreary world, without the key of it' (218). Prevented by age and social status from finding work – 'He was years and years too old for a cabin-boy, and years upon years too inexperienced to be accepted as a common seaman. His dress and manner, too, militated fatally against any such proposal' (226) – Martin actually succumbs much more fully to the influence of the city than Nicholas ever does, making acquaintance with the pawnshops which will feature so largely in young David Copperfield's London experience. That is to say, he does so until the intervention of his own particular fairy godfather arrests the downward course:

In his first wanderings up and down the weary streets, he counterfeited the walk of one who had an object in his view; but soon there came upon him the sauntering, slip-shod gait of listless idleness, and the lounging at street corners, and plucking and biting of stray bits of straw, and strolling up and down the same place, and looking into the same shop windows, with a miserable indifference, fifty times a day.   (225)

It is, in its limited way, a far more convincingly substantiated transformation than the later experiences in Eden, a reflection, perhaps, of the changing nature of Dickens's imaginative concerns. Certainly, the city will increasingly come to play a key symbolic role in the lives of later Dickens heroes, an emblem of the pressures that divide them. But though both Martin and Nicholas acquire a new reality in their relations with the great wilderness of London, neither is allowed to remain vulnerable to it for long. Having moved momentarily beyond the confines of the 'hero''s conventional experience, each quickly reverts to type. It is no accident that Nicholas and Martin both end their adventures in the country, secure from the threats the city poses. And this too reflects a fundamental imaginative concern: a simultaneous rejection of and adherence to the traditional 'heroic' format already familiar from the pages of *Nickleby*.

Equally interesting in this context is the anti-romanticism with which Dickens at first invests young Martin in his capacity of lover. For this too seems to recall *Nickleby* and its initial willingness to laugh at Nicholas's conduct in the same conventional role. Martin's own views on self-sacrificing, storybook love, of the kind that never tells itself, are designedly unliterary and essentially anti-, or rather counter-, heroic: '"If I didn't tell her I loved her,"' he reasons on one occasion, '"where would be the use of my being in love? . . . unless to keep myself in a perpetual state of worry and vexation?"' (96). And he is no more 'heroic' when anticipating a farewell meeting with his beloved: '"Fine weather indeed," Martin bitterly soliloquized, "to be wandering up and down here in, like a thief! Fine weather indeed, for a meeting of lovers in the open air, and in a public walk!"' (234). Fictional conventions of love and lovers, who generally show themselves immune to considerations of weather, are, in fact, satirized very explicitly in the novel, and not merely through Martin. Dickens combines the maudlin self-pity of the sentimental Man of Feeling with the perpetual gloom of the doomed Byronic hero in the character of Alfred Moddle, exposing all three in Moddle's despairing parting cry: '"I love another. She is Another's. Everything appears to be someone else's. Nothing in the world is mine—"' (828). It is a combination 'Phiz' underlines in his illustration to the chapter ('Mr. Moddle is Both Particular and Peculiar in His Attentions'), in which the smitten Alfred is framed by copies of *Childe Harold* and *The Sorrows of Werther*.

And yet Martin's refusal to conform to the models thus exposed is presented by Dickens solely as a function of his egotism and selfishness: '". . . Of course I shall not think of marrying until I am well able to do so. It would never do, you know, for me to be plunging myself into poverty and shabbiness and love in one room up three pairs of stairs, and all that sort of thing"' (98). This attitude is clearly unacceptable and it is very explicitly reformed out of Martin in Eden, as Mark Tapley goes on to prove only too often. Passionate, self-sacrificing, self-forgetting love and 'all that sort of thing' may be entirely untrue to life as it exists outside of literature, but Martin, apparently, is not to act upon the recognition of any such disparity. Once again the reader is confronted with a by now familiar imaginative tension: a satiric

29

impulse on the one hand, a continued commitment to (or at least exploitation of) the conventions satirized on the other. Martin may not be intended to be a 'hero', his selfishness designed as the badge of his alternative, 'natural' role. Dickens as yet cannot envision anything else for him at novel's end but the enjoyment of the traditional 'hero''s reward: a beautiful wife, a fortune and a future of uninterrupted leisure.

But though Martin does indeed marry the heroine and live happily ever after, his appearances in the role of (reformed) true lover/'hero' are perfunctory and limited at best, Dickens seeming entirely to lose interest once the conversion from selfish 'natural' young man has been effected. It is Tom Pinch who really fulfils the role, with his utterly selfless, and entirely doomed, love for Martin's Mary. And it is Tom Pinch too who provides the novel's positive model of true heroism. Dickens makes the identification very clear: Tom's selflessness in the matter of Mary Graham demands a more genuine courage than 'many and many a deed to which the doubtful trumpet blown by Fame has lustily resounded' (194), a courage infinitely superior to the sham military heroics of Tigg. It is Tom who takes the 'hero''s place in the closing paragraphs of the novel and in its frontispiece. With 'certain ideas of his own upon the subject of glory' (110), moreover, he explicitly frames his own conduct in contrast to the extravagant, and selfish, behaviour of comparable characters in novels:

'. . . people who read about heroes in books, and choose to make heroes of themselves out of books, consider it to be a very fine thing to be discontented and gloomy, and misanthropical, and perhaps a little blasphemous, because they cannot have everything ordered for their individual accommodation. Would you like me to become one of that sort of people?' (763)

In himself Tom Pinch is a distinctly peculiar creation: bald, stooping and of indeterminate age, 'one of those strange creatures who never decline into an ancient appearance but look their oldest when they are very young, and get it over at once' (16), a Dickensian 'grotesque' seemingly, though a patently benignant one. The locus of pathos in a novel which lacks the more obvious source of appeal of an Oliver or a Nell, Tom's ungainliness, simplicity and doomed passion recall Smike, another strange, quasi-tragic figure inhabiting an ostensibly comic world. By deliberately choosing to make this unlikely figure the moral touchstone of the novel, Dickens anticipates his later efforts in *David Copperfield* to redefine heroism in moral terms. Through Tom he calls into question, as David will more famously do, the usual qualifications of 'heroes in books', offering a more 'natural', domesticated redefinition in opposition to the glamour of the 'gloomy, misanthropical and blasphemous' Byronic type. The literary falsities Moddle implicitly parodied, Tom explicitly dismisses. He represents a decisive rejection of the conventional 'hero', substituting devotion, endurance, selflessness and other essentially passive virtues for the more romantic, and more active, attributes which usually attend him. But it is a rejection accompanied as yet by an unwillingness to dispense entirely with some version of the accustomed figure, witness his multiplication in young Martin, John Westlock and Mark Tapley.

It is this same unwillingness, exemplified in the altered proposals for Walter Gay, which speaks through Dickens's own explanation of the change. 'I don't think it would be reasonable to carry it out now,' he wrote to Forster some months after first outlining his plan for the boy. 'I am far from sure it could be wholesomely done, after the interest he has acquired.'[11] The concern appears divided about equally between estimates of popular response (recalling the initial desire to avoid 'making people angry') and artistic considerations (what would be 'reasonable' and could be effected 'wholesomely'). However good the idea in itself, and Dickens originally thought it might be made both 'very powerful and very useful',[12] it is still considered unacceptable to reverse a course apparently set so fair, or to follow it in its downward track. The moral of Walter's ruin is not to be pointed at the expense either of disappointed expectations or charges of deliberate morbidity and he is accordingly reserved, in Forster's words, 'for a happier future' in spite of his 'excellent capabilities' for something more.[13]

And yet Walter's interest, like Martin's and Nicholas's before him, does not rest only in the fact of his failure, a failure epitomized by his abandoned fate. The original proposals, Dickens's first inclinations for the character, also deserve attention. In his final form Walter Gay may be indistinguishable from Tom Pinch's 'heroes in books'. Absent from the novel's action for hundreds of pages, he may scarcely be missed, returning for no more compelling reason than to wed the now marriageable heroine and enact a traditional ritual of reunion and integration. If as nothing else, he is, in fact, significant as the last in a line of attempted variations upon this timeless pattern. But, as originally conceived, he is also something more: an important counterpart to *Martin Chuzzlewit*'s culpable hero. For Dickens's first plan for Walter was, in effect, to reverse the literary hero's traditional progress entirely, substituting a career begun in happiness and ending in ruin for the familiar journey from adversity to triumph (or rags to riches). Anticipating the protest against lifting heroes out of nature voiced in the *Nickleby* preface, Walter's experience would pit 'that common, everyday, miserable declension of which we know so much in our ordinary life'[14] against the conventional expectations of romance and happy endings. Dick Whittington would turn again indeed and, far from marrying his master's daughter, would keep instead 'some little notion' of her always at the bottom of his ruin. It is, surely, with this design in mind that the rescue of Florence from that genuine wicked witch Good Mrs Brown is surrounded with fairy-tale allusions, allusions that would form a deeply ironic counterpoint to young Gay's subsequent decline:

Walter picked up the shoe, and put it on the little foot as the Prince in the story might have fitted Cinderella's slipper on. He hung the rabbit-skin over his left arm; gave his right to Florence; and felt, not to say like Richard Whittington – that is a tame comparison – but like Saint George of England, with the dragon lying dead before him. (77–78)

It was to be, moreover, a decline of a very particular sort, leaving Walter guilty of far more than selfishness. As with Martin Chuzzlewit and his great failing, Dickens projects here a new relation between 'hero' and theme, making Walter's experience subservient to *Dombey and Son*'s larger design in a way Nicholas Nickleby's life and adventures never are. Explicitly identified by Carker the Junior as a version of his younger self, 'full of the same qualities, fraught with the same capacity of leading on to good or evil' (179), Walter was plainly to have repeated the older man's fall, climaxing his disgrace by stealing from the firm (with Florence, perhaps, playing something of Harriet Carker's angelic role in the life of her fallen brother). After the danger has passed, Carker actually draws out the parallel course Walter might have taken – without ever making it clear why – so that the abandoned fate is, in an odd way, both unrealized and yet present:

'I saw him lightly walking on the edge of an unseen gulf where so many others walk with equal gaiety, and from which . . . one traveller fell . . . who I know set forward on his way, a boy like him, and missed his footing more and more, and slipped a little and a little lower, and went on stumbling still, until he fell headlong and found himself below, a shattered man.' (179)

Assessing Dickens's achievement in *Martin Chuzzlewit*, Forster wrote 'He had scrutinized as truly and satirized as keenly; but he had never shown the imaginative insight with which he now sent his humour and his art into the core of the vices of the time.'[15] (Dickens himself, in a letter of 1843, declared the novel 'in a hundred points immeasurably the best of my stories'.[16]) Arguably, as Forster himself suggests, *Chuzzlewit* is the first of Dickens's 'social novels', the first of those great symbolic documents of which 'the vices of the time' form the imaginative framework. Certainly *Dombey and Son*, which was intended, according to Forster's well-known formulation, 'to do with Pride what its predecessor had done with Selfishness',[17] belongs in their ranks. With its dominant strain of sea and water imagery, its deliberate symbolic patterning and large thematic preoccupations, it clearly anticipates the even greater achievements in the form still to come. And, in the chronology of Dickens's art, the social novel and the culpable hero stand linked. The two emerge, and grow up, together, advancing towards similar 'dark' conclusions. The social concerns which inform *Dombey and Son* are precisely what make the idea of Walter's decline so attractive to Dickens, the one a perfect vehicle to serve the other. In exhibiting, as he had originally planned, 'something of the philosophy of it, in great temptations and an easy nature',[18] young Gay's ruin would provide a sombre and unequivocal answer to the questions which echo so significantly through the novel: '"Papa! What's money?"' (93) and '"I mean, Papa, what can it do?"' (94). *Dombey and Son* revolves around those questions, answering Paul with the example of his father's frozen life. It is an answer in which Walter Gay, as originally conceived, would obviously have played an important part, another life blighted by the all-powerful firm to which little Paul himself is sacrificed.

In the event, of course, this projected design is never realized. The social concerns remain, but Walter does very little to advance them. And yet the abandoned plans do leave their mark. Dickens keeps the shadow of an unhappy future hovering about Walter, as though reluctant to give up the 'good thing' originally conceived for him, rather unfairly raising possibilities he has chosen not to fulfil. Just as Nicholas Nickleby's alternate fate had been enacted by the unfortunate Smike, so Walter too is provided with surrogates: Carker the Junior, a living emblem of bright youth gone wrong; Rob the Grinder, comic parody of a prodigal son. His departure, in the symbolically named *Son and Heir*, forebodes spiritual no less than physical shipwreck, though only the latter materializes: 'The sails shone bright and full above, as Walter watched them spread their surface to the favourable breeze; the water flew in sparkles from the prow; and off upon her voyage went the *Son and*

Heir, as hopefully and trippingly as many another son and heir, gone down, had started on his way before her' (267). Once again, with this last of Dickens's early heroes, the author is glimpsed in uncertain transition, at once embracing and rejecting the traditional model of the 'hero'. Yet one need not turn directly to Richard Carstone, as critics from Forster onwards have done, to find the fulfilment of Dickens's original design, at least in terms of the use to which such a figure might be put. For well before *Bleak House*, in the person of another Richard, hero and theme unite in a manner that eludes Dickens everywhere else in the early novels.

The essential difference between Dick Swiveller and the ostensibly 'natural' young men who come before and after him is, in effect, encapsulated in a passing comment Dick makes midway through *The Old Curiosity Shop*: '"And this," said Mr. Swiveller, with a kind of bantering composure, "is life, I believe. Oh, certainly! Why not! I'm quite satisfied"' (414). For these characteristic reflections denote an involvement, comic yet profound, with life and its implications as developed in *The Old Curiosity Shop*, an involvement holding little place in the conception of Nicholas Nickleby and never successfully realized, notwithstanding Dickens's attempts, in Nicholas's immediate successors. In the final analysis, *The Life and Adventures of Nicholas Nickleby* is about nothing more than the life and adventures of a young man called Nicholas Nickleby as he journeys towards an end most readers anticipate from the start. The world, with its inexplicable cruelties, its suffering and its evil, merely forms a backdrop to this, impinging slightly on the voyage, perhaps, but not upon the goal. Misery, encountered along the way in the teeming schoolroom of Dotheboys Hall – 'What an incipient hell was breeding there!' (88) – and in the desolate London streets – 'How much injustice, and misery, and wrong there was' (693) – never seems to threaten the security of the inevitable happy ending. In *Nicholas Nickleby*, Dickens does not, finally, acknowledge problems the Cheerybles's fairy-tale benevolence cannot solve. Even Smike's death is clearly 'better as it is' (798), since, by his own account, the young sufferer dies contentedly in Eden (763). The problems raised in *Martin Chuzzlewit* and *Dombey and Son* are less easily contained. The life and death of Jonas Chuzzlewit – selfishness finding its logical conclusion in self-murder – cast long shadows, as does the famous outburst in *Dombey and Son* (Chapter 47) which climaxes in the plea 'Oh for a good spirit who would take the house-tops off, with a more potent and benignant hand than the lame demon in the tale, and show a Christian people what dark shapes issue from amidst their homes' (620). And yet, their young male protagonists still follow a similar pattern, ultimately sharing Nicholas Nickleby's special imunity to the deeper meanings of the novel in which he appears.

With Dick Swiveller and *The Old Curiosity Shop*, however, such is no longer the case. Benevolence is not, finally, omnipotent in its design. And the novel has at its centre an essential question: How is one to live in a world where motiveless malignity, cruelty and selfishness apparently run wild, and innocence itself is under siege? Nell supplies one answer, of course, by dying. And the emotional intensity with which her death is rendered can make it seem the only solution the novel offers. But if the comic impulse goes down into the grave with Nell, it will come out again with Dick. He supplies, with his 'bantering composure', the other answer to the question, his union with the Marchioness compensating, if not redeeming, the loss Nell represents. Nicholas's potential to enact a similar thematic function is undermined by his ultimate reversion to the 'hero' type. Martin and Walter come closer in design, yet fail too, for similar reasons. Dick Swiveller alone achieves the desired fusion, uniting the 'natural' and the 'heroic' as none of the three could do, and forging in the process the new relation between hero and theme Dickens still seeks, in vain, elsewhere.

Dick is, essentially, a hybrid figure: natural *and* heroic, serious *and* comic. And it is this fusion of traits that compete everywhere else in the early novels which distinguishes him from his various counterparts, investing him with the varied colour they, in their monochromatic state of 'heroism', lack. It is, moreover, precisely because of these qualities that Dick proves inseparable, as Nicholas, Martin and Walter are not, from the thematic preoccupations of the novel. In Dick kindness and affection still show themselves able, in spite of the lesson of Nell's death, to secure an earthly home. In him too the redemptive powers of the imagination find perhaps their most persuasive embodiment. Faced with a manifestly unsatisfactory reality, Dick counters it with fiction. As with his bookcase–bedstead, so with all the compromises life forces him to make: 'Implicit faith in the deception was the first article of his creed' (53). His is not escapism but an imaginative transcendence which recognizes the grim truths of life, and incorporates them into 'the deception': ' "Marchioness, your health. You will excuse my wearing my hat, but the palace is damp, and the marble floor is – if I may be allowed the expression – sloppy" ' (429). At his most comic Dick possesses a thematic weight Nicholas never attains, and he *is* comic in a way

35

Martin and Walter are never allowed to be. He has a function in the novel, where the others have, in the end, only a role.

Dick's characteristic and truly prodigious 'talent in quotation' (551), his apparently inexhaustible supply of scraps of verse, treated 'as if they were only prose in a hurry' (61), reveal that he too, even more than Nicholas Nickleby, enjoys casting himself in the character of tragic hero. Indeed, life for Dick Swiveller is one continuous melodrama, and he is perfectly content to play all the parts himself, attendant lord as well as prince:

> 'Ha!' said Mr Swiveller, with a portentous frown. ''Tis well. Marchioness – but no matter. Some wine there. Ho!' He illustrated these melo-dramatic morsels by handing the tankard to himself with great humility, receiving it haughtily, drinking from it thirstily, and smacking his lips fiercely.   (429)

Here too Dickens plays, with genuine fondness, with the conventional absurdities of popular drama and fiction. Through Dick he again takes aim, as he had done in *Nicholas Nickleby* and was to do once more in *Martin Chuzzlewit*, at the habits of 'heroes in books' who, from time immemorial, have taken issue with their fate or destiny by addressing themselves in bitter soliloquy to the ceiling, 'which these bodiless personages are usually supposed to inhabit – except in theatrical cases, when they live in the heart of the great chandelier' (254). Nor is Dick above assuming other roles when occasion demands. And it is revealing that Dickens even allows his less-than-sober hero to play with the convention of the homeless waif, and this in *The Old Curiosity Shop* where the figure of the orphan achieves its literary apotheosis. The comic counterpoint Dick provides to the tragic story of the novel's *other* orphan is a measure of the unique imaginative licence he enjoys:

> 'Left an infant by my parents, at an early age,' said Mr. Swiveller, bewailing his hard lot, 'cast upon the world in my tenderest period, and thrown upon the mercies of a deluding dwarf, who can wonder at my weakness! Here's a miserable orphan for you. Here,' said Mr. Swiveller, raising his voice to a high pitch, and looking sleepily round, 'is a miserable orphan!'   (171)

But there is something hopeful and even restorative, as well as absurd, in Dick's endless dramas, in his transformation of the damp, miserable kitchen of Bevis Marks into a baronial hall out of Walter Scott, complete with haughty lord and humble retainer. He has the true imaginative grace and can make a marchioness out of a half-starved little skivvy, knowing that it is indeed 'more real and pleasant' so (427). Much as Sleary and his horse-riding do in *Hard Times*, Swiveller stands for the redemptive power of fancy in a world whose reality is all too pressing. And the Marchioness proves his true consort in this. For she understands instinctively, with her orange-peel-and-water 'wine', the lesson Dick teaches: ' "If you make believe very much, it's quite nice . . . but if you don't, you know, it seems as if it would bear a little more seasoning, certainly" ' (481).

Dick's mode of living, no less than his descriptive powers, may be more remarkable for 'brilliancy of imagination than a strict adherence to truth', (268) but, for all his self-dramatizing, he never loses his sense of the generally unpleasant reality looming just behind his inspired deception. His heroics serve rather as a means of acknowledging, and accommodating, pressures which would otherwise prove intolerable. He too, like the Marchioness, makes believe very much, and for a similar reason. Dick is, moreover, convincingly self-aware in a way Martin Chuzzlewit never manages to be, for all his ostensible self-scrutiny, freely confessing to faults Nicholas Nickleby and Walter Gay are simply never allowed to have: ' "Marchioness," said Mr. Swiveller, rising, "the word of a gentleman is as good as his bond – sometimes better; as in the present case, where his bond might prove but a doubtful sort of security" ' (431). However low their fortunes may ebb, these early 'heroes' always remain within the strict bounds of gentlemanly decorum, their 'naturalness' subordinate to their gentility. They do not, like Dick, owe money they can never pay. They do not get drunk. And they are utterly incapable of joking about either 'low' tendency. Cast initially in a very different mould – comic 'villain' rather than gentleman 'hero' – Dick is free to do all three. He is, in fact, untrammelled by the conventional constraints which do so much to deprive Nicholas, Martin and Walter of genuine imaginative life.

The difference this makes is nowhere more apparent than in the process of change Dick undergoes in the course of *The Old Curiosity Shop*. At his best, Nicholas Nickleby is a static creation. There is no suggestion anywhere in his life and adventures that he is being altered by the experiences they record, still less reformed, no suggestion even that such change might be necessary. Some attempt at the depiction of moral reform is made in *Nickleby* with the figure of Lord Frederick Verisopht, but he never transcends his stock origins to offer anything like a convincingly substantiated transformation. Walter Gay, as originally conceived, is to undergo a gradual decline into moral ruin. As he appears in the novel, however, there is no sense of progress or development about him. His growing up is done, for the most part, off-stage, and what he is when first introduced, he remains to the last: high-spirited, merry, courageous and romantic. Moreover, a letter from Dickens to Forster of October 1846 reveals an emphasis that is now decidedly not on the gradual unfolding of the boy's character: 'Do you think people so likely to be pleased with Florence, and Walter, as to relish another number of them at their present age? Otherwise, Walter will be two or three and twenty, straightway.'[19] And though Martin Chuzzlewit is plainly intended to change, as these other figures are not, he is so unconvincing both before, during and after the process, that he appears in the end as static as either of his counterparts. Their stories are all three, in effect, simply voyages following a familiar pattern through adversity to triumph, journeys from one point to another. But Dick Swiveller's is something more. It is a progress.

Dick begins the novel a 'careless profligate' (179). He is never vicious, only 'thoughtless, [and] light-headed' (57), seldom visited by 'so unwonted a guest as reflection' (179), and apparently incapable of controlling himself. Over the course of The Old Curiosity Shop, however, in a transformation sparked by his growing care for the little Marchioness, Dick himself grows into reflection, emotional responsibility (in contrast to his early playing at love with the unfortunate Sophy Wackles) and even a measure of self-control. His is not an over-night conversion, as Martin Chuzzlewit's effectively turns out to be, but a slow process in which the old flippancy and the new thoughtfulness continually interact:

'Now,' said Dick, walking up and down with his hands in his pockets. 'I'd give something – if I had it – to know how they use that child, and where they keep her. My mother must have been a very inquisitive woman; I have no doubt that I am marked with a note of interrogation somewhere. My feelings I smother, but thou hast been the cause of this anguish, my – upon my word,' said Mr. Swiveller, checking himself and falling thoughtfully into the client's chair, 'I should like to know how they use her!' (272)

The interrupted quotation (Dick 'checking himself' in mid-flight) is the perfect emblem of this process, as reflection steps in to stop Mr Swiveller's usual means of evading responsibility, and leaves him to ponder that one important question.

Early in the course of the novel Dick emerges as something of a holy fool, capable of confronting the melodrama which surrounds him in a manner which shows him wise in his apparent simplicity. Asked by the ridiculous Trent what he thinks will come of a secret marriage to Nell (all of her grandfather's reputed wealth being the expected answer), Dick's reply is succinct: ' "A family and an annual income of nothing, to keep 'em on" ' (56). Dick is a core of normality in the strange, heightened atmosphere of *The Old Curiosity Shop*, cognizant of the unreality with which he is surrounded, yet willing to meet it on its own terms: ' "It's an Arabian Night, that's what it is," said Richard. "I'm in Damascus or Grand Cairo" ' (475). He can mediate between the reader and this Arabian Nights world, with its assorted angels, monsters and other grotesques, precisely because he has a foot in both camps. Participating in the fairy tale, he yet preserves the ability to comment upon it from outside. This duality is perfectly conveyed in Dick's invocation of the Whittington legend – with a final comic proviso – when asked where he would run away to, to make his fortune: ' "Towards Highgate, I suppose. Perhaps the bells might strike up "Turn again Swiveller, Lord Mayor of London." Whittington's name was Dick. I wish cats were scarcer" ' (373).

This essential comic sanity, so much a part of Dick's character, comprehends too a considerable degree of self-knowledge. ' "There is a proverb which talks about being merry and wise," ' Dick informs Trent, and the reader, at an early point. ' "There are some people who can be merry and can't be wise, and some who can be wise (or think they can) and can't be merry. I'm one of the first sort" ' (54). Though his merriness is, ultimately, a higher sort of wisdom, for the first part of the novel it consistently proves Dick's undoing. Assisted by quantities of raw gin, it makes him an easy dupe for the malevolent Quilp, besides losing him a considerable inheritance from his much put-upon aunt in the country. Once reflection has been aroused by the mysterious atmosphere of Bevis Marks, however, Dick gradually begins to turn his self-knowledge to account. It is something he has failed signally to do to this point, as he himself clearly recognizes. ' "Nothing but mysteries in connexion with Brass's house," ' he muses, ' "I'll keep my own counsel, however. Everybody and anybody has been in my confidence as yet, but now I think I'll set up in business for myself" ' (289).

He is, in fact, setting up in business for himself, the universal business of being a concerned and caring adult, participating in the responsibilities of the imperfect world around him, when he first begins to wonder about the three-foot human mystery embodied in 'the small servant' (272): who she is, where she comes from and, above all, how she is treated. For his wonder leads him on, in the most 'natural' manner, to much larger questions, though always with 'the small servant' as their point of departure:

'The Marchioness,' said Mr. Swiveller, folding his arms, 'is a very extraordinary person – surrounded by mysteries, ignorant of the taste of beer, unacquainted with her own name (which is less remarkable), and taking a limited view of society through the key-holes of doors – can these things be her destiny, or has some unknown person started an opposition to the decrees of fate? It is a most inscrutable and unmitigated staggerer!' (432)

But Dick refuses to allow the question of the nameless servant's fate to remain a staggerer. He himself starts an opposition to the decrees of destiny, giving her first a name and then a future: '"Please God, we'll make a scholar of the poor Marchioness yet!"' (502). And the action proves his own salvation no less than hers. His care for her, his kindness and generosity, not least in sharing his gift of imagination, and her loving gratitude in return, not only literally save Dick's life, but win for them both their 'retreat' in Hampstead, in a cottage which is quite rightly 'the envy of the civilized world' (551). His illness, in spurring the Marchioness to run away, is truly the making of them both. Theirs is a retreat from all that has pursued Nell to the churchyard, and from which she has only escaped in death. If there is something magical in the transformation of Sophronia Sphinx, there is yet no sense of unreality about the final union. Though Dick has grown out of his early carelessness, he is not so changed at novel's end as to be above 'an occasional outbreak with Mr. Chuckster' (552). There may be an element of Pygmalion fantasy in the fact, as Dick himself remarks 'at diverse subsequent periods', that 'there had been a young lady saving up for him after all' (551). His own version of the 'hero''s 'happy ending' – playing thousands of games of cribbage with the marchioness he has made – may share something of the 'ever after' stasis of the fairy tale. But, unlike the final tableau of *Nickleby*, with Nicholas's children clustered about Smike's grave, there is nothing disturbing or strained in its implications. Dick has earned his reward and refuge. Nicholas, Martin and Walter simply succeed to theirs as part of the 'hero''s long-established birthright.

For Gabriel Pearson, Dick Swiveller is emphatically the forebear of Dickens's later heroes, evolving, as he puts it, 'through Copperfield into Pip and, by circuitous ways, into one term of a mature human relationship'.[20] Certainly, he anticipates aspects of these later figures, most importantly, perhaps, the way in which the experiences of 'heroes' like Clennam, or Carton, or Pip prove inseparable from the thematic preoccupations and symbolic structures of the novels in which they appear. But Dick has no real successors, being less a forebear than a collateral heir. He too is the product of the same impulses which try, and fail, to create a 'natural' hero in Nicholas Nickleby, Martin Chuzzlewit and Walter Gay, the reflection of that dissatisfaction with convention which moves on to fashion a very different 'hero' in David Copperfield. Yet, recalling Forster's account of the improvised origins of *The Old Curiosity Shop*, it does not seem unfair to call Dick an inadvertent achievement, a happy accident for Dickens, since the whole novel, expanded from an initial 'short half-dozen chapters', is really an accident in its way. And like most happy accidents this will not be repeated.

Significantly, Dick is succeeded not by the mature heroes to whom Pearson relates him, but by the highly conventional figures of Edward Chester and Joe Willett in *Barnaby Rudge*, 'heroes' whose inner life is, for the most part, conspicuous by its absence. There is the potential for something more in Edward's struggles with his heartless father, and the situation itself has an obvious symbolic importance in a novel concerned, as *Barnaby Rudge* so clearly is, with issues of order and rebellion both in public and private life. But Edward Chester is even less convincingly alive than either young Martin or Walter Gay. And the fact that Dickens removes him from the novel for the better part of its action suggests that he himself is not particularly interested in Edward's predicament. Joe Willett is, in the early stages of the novel, considerably more vivid, a function of his lower-class origins, perhaps. His humiliations at the hands of his father and unsuccessful courtship of Dolly Varden individualize him to an extent the pallid Edward never achieves. But Joe too succumbs to the syndrome of the 'hero', disappearing off-stage for long stretches of action, reappearing just in time to rescue his distressed damsel and bring down the curtain on a scene of swarming domesticity. And both these utterly conventional young men are, in turn, followed by the unsuccessfully realized 'natural' figures of *Martin Chuzzlewit* and *Dombey and Son*, a further indication that Dickens had yet to find what he was looking for. Quickly promoted from his original role of mild cockney villain, Dick retains the licence cockney characters enjoy in Dickens to be naturally comic, even ridiculous, at times – a licence not enjoyed by the young men who come after him. That, however, is a function of Dick's origins. The comedy only assumes its later symbolic importance, and Dick his symbolic role, as the novel takes shape, polarizing around celebrations of the grave (in Nell) and the life force (in Dick). The spiritual progress he undergoes is plainly significant. But, in the world of *The Old Curiosity Shop*, what Dick comes to represent (the sustaining, enhancing force of the imagination) is, finally, more crucial than what he experiences, symbolic meaning attaching more to the being than the becoming. For the Dickens hero as he emerges from *Copperfield* onwards, this is no longer the case, nor is his an accidental symbolism. No longer embodying, as Dick essentially does in spite of his regeneration, a fixed thematic value, it is his journey through the increasingly grim world of the novels which becomes, designedly, the vehicle for Dickens's deepest concerns. He is 'natural' in a very different way, with little of Dick's comic joyousness. No longer immune to the social influences surrounding him, as Nicholas and his counterparts are, he is also increasingly incapable of achieving the happy accommodation which is Dick Swiveller's ultimate (if accidental) contribution to *The Old Curiosity Shop*, and to Dickens's early conception of the 'natural' hero.

❧ 2 ☙

David Copperfield and the Emergence
of the Homeless Hero

With the publication in May 1849 of the first instalment of his 'autobiography', David Copperfield joins ranks with Jane Eyre and Arthur Pendennis, two no less determinedly unheroic literary figures whose personal histories had likewise recently been given to the public. Parallels between the trio's stories, not least the coincidence of their meditative, retrospective tone, have often been noted, and so too has the popularity of this confessional mode at mid-century (with 'In Memoriam' and 'The Prelude' appearing the following year). All three novels are tales of initiation and development. All locate their interest in the private world of individual experience, not the public arena of the 'social problem'. And all deliberately call into question conventional notions of literary 'heroism': *Copperfield* with David's celebrated opening, 'Whether I shall turn out to be the hero of my own life' (1), masking a host of other questions; *Pendennis* with the figure of Pen himself, good-hearted and erring, 'who does not claim to be a hero, but only a man and a brother';[1] and *Jane Eyre* with its author's determination to prove, 'in defiance of the accepted canon', that the heroine of a novel could be poor, obscure, plain and little, and still retain the interest of its readers.[2] Thackeray, in fact, in a letter to Lady Blessington of 6 May 1849, detected the influence of *Pendennis* in *Copperfield*'s opening number. And Q. D. Leavis has made a similar claim for influence on Charlotte Brontë's behalf.[3] Yet David Copperfield is neither a passionate rebel, like Jane, nor a reclaimed worldling, like Pen. Nor does he owe much, if anything, to the literary models who feature so prominently in his own childhood reading and populate his early imaginative world, 'heroes' like Roderick Random, Peregrine Pickle, Humphry Clinker, Tom Jones and Gil Blas (48). David is, rather, a figure new to the world of Dickens's fiction. In him appears, essentially for the first time, a fusion of strains familiar, individually, from the earlier works, strains now brought together in distinctive form. It is a combination which will, in the novels to come, increasingly characterize the male protagonists who stand at their heart. Defining the type – a sad, time-haunted and increasingly alienated figure – it establishes the dimensions of the 'Dickens hero'.

For David Copperfield is the first of Dickens's waifs to grow up, the first adult counterpart to the abandoned child whose image haunts the earlier novels, and of whom young David is clearly another version. In perpetual children like Oliver Twist and Nell, the condition of orphanhood draws largely on the religious, folk and fairy-tale associations that cluster about the figures of foundlings and holy innocents. In both the inherent pathos of the young orphan is underscored by the mythic potential of a single image: an unprotected child wandering amid a hostile adult world. David too, in his early experiences in London and on the Dover road, plainly draws on similar traditions. But in him orphanhood goes on to assume an additional, spiritual dimension, becoming a potent symbol of a larger loss. Want of parents, and its corollary the want of a home, mean want of a fixed identity for David, 'home' now functioning as both the source, and the refuge, of selfhood. For Nicholas Nickleby the death of a father had chiefly meant economic vulnerability. For David Copperfield the loss goes infinitely deeper, his resulting homelessness an emblem of the alienation it is the task of his life to overcome.

In effect, Dickens brings together in *David Copperfield* two major, but previously separate, preoccupations of the early novels. David unites the parentless child – victimized and suppressed – represented by Oliver, Smike, Nell and the Marchioness, with the 'natural' hero – imperfect, unliterary and developing – anticipated in Nicholas Nickleby, attempted in Martin Chuzzlewit and abandoned in Walter Gay. What he does not obviously further, however, is a third, equally important strain which emerges at the end of this early period. For *Copperfield* suspends the exploration tentatively begun in *Martin Chuzzlewit*, and temporarily abandoned in *Dombey and Son*, of the possibilities inherent in linking the experience of the recreated 'hero' with the overtly 'social' preoccupations that are now coming to shape Dickens's artistic concerns. And this would appear to have been a deliberate decision. According to Forster, Dickens's completion of the second chapter of the novel ('I Observe') defined to himself 'more clearly than before, the character of the book; and the propriety of rejecting everything not strictly personal from the name given to it'. The introductory words 'The Copperfield Survey of the World as it Rolled' were, in consequence, dropped from the work's title, which then became 'The Personal History, Adventures, Experience, and Observation of David Copperfield the Younger, of Blunderstone Rookery, which he never meant to be published on any account'.[4] There is some doubt as to the accuracy of Forster's dating of this change. Yet the implication is still clear: the character of the book itself was, for Dickens, 'strictly personal', having less to do with the world as it rolls than one individual's 'personal history' in it. And Barry Westburg has noted a further, significant change in the shortened working title Dickens used for the novel's number plans. While the first number is titled 'The Personal History and Adventures of David Copperfield', in the second number and thereafter 'Adventures' is replaced by 'Experiences'.[5] Choosing deliberately to emphasize the internal rather than the external, Dickens moves David still further from the picaresque mode of his childhood reading. It is a change which anticipates the formulation of the 1856 letter and its 'experiences, trials, perplexities, and confusions inseparable from the making or unmaking of all men'. Nicholas Nickleby and Martin Chuzzlewit, it might be recalled, had adventures. David will have experiences.

This is not to suggest, however, as numerous critics of the novel have done, that *David Copperfield* is a work insulated from Dickens's usual 'social' concerns, one in which the critical impulse is entirely suspended to facilitate the accomplishment of an authorial wish-fulfilment. For there are, plainly, a number of very specific 'social' issues addressed in *Copperfield*'s course: the inadequacy of both middle-class and charity schools (Salem House and the foundation that educates Uriah Heep); the rehabilitation of prostitutes (Martha); the obsolescence of Doctors' Commons; the question of penal reform. More generally, as Q. D. Leavis has argued, David's entire history can be read as an exploration of a representative mid-Victorian experience, a testing of the assumptions of 'that buoyant era which believed or held that every man had the prospect of achieving comfort and respectability, even riches and distinction, at any rate happiness, if he would choose the path of thrift, austerity, perseverance in hard work, and self-improvement'.[6] Whether or not one proceeds, as Leavis does, to see in this choice of subject matter and treatment a reflection of Dickens's own growing awareness that self-help and self-made success had failed to bring contentment with them, *David Copperfield* is still clearly, and profoundly, the product of a particular historical moment.

Yet, if David's life is bound up with a specific context, it is not circumscribed by it as the lives of later figures like Richard Carstone,

Arthur Clennam and Pip will be. The world of *David Copperfield* is not dominated by the same sort of explicitly critical, and overarching, framework as that of *Bleak House, Little Dorrit* or *Great Expectations*, a framework that links personal experience – the suffering, loss and self-division David endures – with a larger 'social' cause. In this sense, David's personal history may perhaps be more accurately termed 'universal' than 'social' in its implications. For all the specifically mid-Victorian character of the self-help success story it recounts, *David Copperfield* is, equally, a novel preoccupied with an essentially timeless issue: the growth of the self to full maturity in a world shaped by the eternal cycle of change and loss that defines all human life. David's history is indeed representative in the deepest sense. His early childhood is an Eden of unknowing innocence complete with garden – 'a very preserve of butterflies, as I remember it, with a high fence, and a gate and padlock; where the fruit clusters on the trees, riper and richer than fruit has ever been since, in any other garden' (13) – his subsequent experience a type of the inevitable, but ultimately fortu-nate, fall. It is the continual interaction of its two imaginative dimensions, the timeless and the time-bound, that gives the novel much of its peculiar potency. David is the most time-haunted of narrators, his very act of autobiography an attempt to place himself both within and beyond its influence. And the impossibility of escape is one of the key lessons his narrative will teach him, the sorrowful sense of time past and passing sounding through his prose like the sea that plays so large a part in the story that prose unfolds. *David Copperfield* reflects a vision of the individual in time no less than in society. Interweaving the two to form this 'strictly personal' history, Dickens expands in significant new ways the symbolic potential of its 'heros'' experience, a hero who can now truly be called uniquely Dickens's own.

He is, from the outset, a hero in search of himself. David's opening doubts as to the identity of the 'hero of my life' reflect something graver even than the social malaise or class anxiety to which they are generally attributed. They are, in fact, the residue of a fundamental uncertainty of role, of identity, and of self which first emerges here as the hallmark of the Dickens hero. The first among Dickens's young male protagonists to be homeless in this larger sense, David endures an emotional isolation which Nicholas Nickleby and Martin Chuzzlewit, for all their wandering, never know (though Smike may, perhaps, approach it). His story – part journey of discovery, part spiritual quest – inaugurates a pattern of experience increasingly characteristic of the young (and not

46

so young) men who stand at the heart of the later novels. Walter Gay in *Dombey and Son* marks Dickens's last, abortive attempt to adapt the traditional literary 'hero', and his twin objectives of love and fortune, to his deepening social concerns, an attempt he quickly abandons. With David, the 'hero's' experience undergoes a literal sea-change. More even than an attempt to redefine 'heroism' in moral terms, as *Great Expectations* would redefine gentility, in *David Copperfield* Dickens's thematic preoccupations create a new centre, and give birth to the homeless hero.

In essence, David's prototypal personal history is the story of one who lacks what George Eliot would call in *Middlemarch* 'the centre of self'. And, in many ways, the want seems inevitable, its roots lying in the very circumstances of David's birth. 'I was', he records, 'a posthumous child. My father's eyes had closed upon the light of this world six months, when mine opened on it' (92). Deprived of his father, David is deprived too of the son's symbolic patrimony. There is, for him, no fixed family identity by which to define himself. Lacking his natural guide and social guarantor, David lacks the natural basis for selfhood. He does not even have a name for himself, but takes his various identities as they come: Davy, Brooks, Trotwood, Daisy, Doady. None of these 'corruptions' (514) is of David's own choosing. All are external impositions. And all significantly displace the one name which is truly his own, by right of the dead father he never knew. In view of the legions of inadequate, unloving or parasitic parents peopling the pages of Dickens's fiction, orphanhood might appear as a decided advantage, granting the parentless child a freedom unavailable to an Arthur Clennam or a John Harmon. For the orphan the search for self-fulfilment involves no stigma of selfishness, for he is unencumbered by the ties which go so near to strangling Clennam and Harmon, sons doomed to carry the burden of their fathers' memories, and wills. Yet this very freedom is clearly fraught with dangers. Without a father, David is vulnerable, economically and socially, no less than emotionally. It is a truth the Murdstones understand, and will exploit, and one Clara Copperfield herself recognizes as she prays on her deathbed '"God protect and keep my fatherless boy!"'(114).

But David has more reasons than one for needing special protection. As his narrative increasingly makes plain, he has not been left entirely without a paternal legacy, and it proves a costly inheritance. In the words of his aunt, David is '"as like his father as it's possible to be"' (164). And she is clear what such a likeness entails: '"David

47

Copperfield all over!'' cried Miss Betsey. "David Copperfield from head to foot! Calls a house a rookery when there's not a rook near it, and takes the birds on trust, because he sees the nests!''' (5). The resemblance is underlined again late in the novel in a seemingly inconsequential exchange between the adult David and the doctor who had delivered him: '"There's a strong resemblance between you and your poor father, sir." "I never had the happiness of seeing my father," I observed. "Very true, sir," said Mr. Chillip in a soothing tone. "And very much to be deplored it was, on all accounts!"' (712). As is so often the case in this his 'written memory' (699), few of the details David chooses to record prove utterly without significance. This late 'observation' offers a significant echo of that earlier chapter of his history 'I Observe'. And David's own dreamy timidity and trustfulness, the want of firmness and tendency to be imposed upon which mark him in later life, confirm both his aunt's early judgment and Mr Chillip's passing remark. He is, indeed, his father's son. What is more, he inherits from his father that fatal propensity to fall in love with 'wax dolls' (3) which will lead his undisciplined heart so far astray. When, considerably later in his story, David writes half-jokingly of his instantaneous love for Dora 'All was over in a moment. I had fulfilled my destiny' (333), he writes more truly than he knows, and the effect is deliberately ironic. It is his destiny to repeat this chapter of his father's history. It is his fate to marry a child-wife who is, with her sparkling eyes and clustering curls, her affectionate nature and domestic inadequacy, the exact counterpart of his own child-mother. Given the circumstances of David's childhood, it is, as numerous critics of the novel have noted, inevitable that he should seek to redeem his early loss in the person of Dora Spenlow, the image of his father's Clara.

Though David himself never appears conscious of the patterns he enacts, the ghost of that other David Copperfield, dead six months before his birth, haunts his 'written memory'. Early in his narrative, he associates thoughts of his unknown father with an image which will become one of its dominant emblems, claiming here too an unrecognized legacy:

There is something strange to me, even now, in the reflection that he never saw me; and something stranger yet in the shadowy remembrance that I have of my first childish associations with his white grave-stone in the churchyard, and of the indefinable compassion I used to feel for it lying out alone there in the dark night, when our little parlor was warm and bright with fire and

candle, and the doors of our house were – almost cruelly it seemed to me
sometimes – bolted and locked against it. (2)

For the twin concepts of home and homelessness form in *David
Copperfield* a motif as central as the more remarked upon themes of time
and tide. For David the writer no less than David the character, the
idea of home becomes increasingly inseparable first from the idea of the
absent father, then from the very idea of self, the search for each a part
of the same larger quest. On his coach journey to banishment at Salem
House it is the houses, and their imagined father-owners, which
preoccupy David: 'When we passed through a village, I pictured to
myself what the insides of the houses were like, and what the
inhabitants were about; and when boys came running after us, and got
behind and swung there for a little way, I wondered whether their
fathers were alive, and whether they were happy at home' (60–61). No
less important in his symbolic scheme are images of ruined or
abandoned houses, and, as above, of house-doors locked against the
(houseless) outsider. For David will encounter all three before reaching
his journey's end, and this too is an inheritance from his father. The
white grave-stone in the churchyard is the source, and the sign, of
David's vulnerability to the forces which render him homeless.
Without a father, and without a house, he is easily cast out, and cast
away. The significance of the house motif within the symbolic pattern
David makes of his life story is clearly revealed by his response to the
news of the abandonment of Blunderstone Rookery: 'It seemed as if the
house were dead too, now, and all connected with my father and
mother were faded away' (212).

Given this framework of association, it is virtually inevitable that
David recalls the momentous advent of Mr Murdstone, his hostile
second father, chiefly in terms of the changes made by this new
presence in the 'happy old home' (93) of his childhood: a dog, 'deep-
mouthed and black-haired' like the intrusive stranger chained in the
once empty kennel; David's bed moved from its nook inside his
mother's room to an attic 'a long way off' (37). To his young
imagination, the Murdstones enter his life attended by a blast of cold
air, literally chilling the warmth and brightness of the little house (99).
And it is, of course, Mr Murdstone who sends David away from home,
the symbolic first act in a campaign which will deprive him of place,
identity and, finally, self. The adult David is acutely aware of the
formative influence of his mother's second marriage on that character

which, he elsewhere remarks, 'I shall unconsciously develop, I suppose, in writing my life' (144). He writes of his return 'home' after the wedding in terms that make the connection explicit. And here too the sense of time past, and of opportunity lost not to be recalled, pervades the memory:

God help me, I might have been improved for my whole life, I might have been made another creature perhaps, for life, by a kind word at that season. A word of encouragement and explanation, of pity for my childish ignorance, of welcome home, of reassurance to me that it *was* home, might have made me dutiful to him [Murdstone] in my heart henceforth, instead of in my hypocritical outside, and might have made me respect instead of hate him. I thought my mother was sorry to see me standing in the room so scared and strange, and that, presently, when I stole to a chair, she followed me with her eyes more sorrowfully still . . . but the word was not spoken, and the time for it was gone. (40)

Degraded by the Murdstones' persecutions to the level of an animal – 'He ordered me like a dog and I obeyed like a dog' (103) – David ultimately feels himself reduced to nothing by their systematic hostility. When he returns home for a brief respite from his exile at Salem House, it is to find his mother singing familiar lullabies to another son, with eyes just the colour of David's own, and he himself scarcely more than a blank space 'which everybody overlooked and yet was in everybody's way' (104). David's place, no less than his father's, has been usurped. When his mother's too is emptied, the last vestiges of his identity, even of his existence, appear to David to die with her: 'The mother who lay in her grave, was the mother of my infancy; the little creature in her arms, was myself, as I had once been, hushed for ever on her bosom' (115).

Too young to comprehend inadequacies he has unknowingly observed, David's loss enshrines in his heart what is, in fact, an essentially false domestic ideal. 'From the moment of knowing of the death of my mother,' he writes, 'the idea of her as she had been of late vanished from me. I remembered her, from that instant, only as the young mother of my earliest impressions, who had been used to wind her bright curls round and round her finger, and to dance with me at twilight in the parlor' (114–115). It is an early admission of the necessary, even inevitable, selectivity of the memories he recalls in 'writing his life', an acknowledgement of the way in which need must always condition 'fact'. Cherishing the image of his lost child-mother – forever pretty, girlish and loving – with the memory of that idyllic childhood home vanished so soon, David unwittingly establishes the operative pattern of his adult emotional life. For it is these same bright curls and dancing spirit, the same domestic idyll existing only in memory, he seeks again in his own child-wife. As he truly tells Dora, he could not see her and *not* love her (522). His past experience, the early loss before maturity had brought understanding, has left him no choice.

The child David cannot acknowledge, indeed has yet to learn, what is both plainly evident to the reader and implicit in the narrative his mature self creates, namely the fundamental deficiency of his ideal, its inability to fulfil the needs which underlie it. But the adored mother clearly failed her son. Clara Copperfield's childish affection never shields young David from the Murdstones' tyranny. As Betsey Trotwood later discovers, she makes no provision for her son on her remarriage. At her death, David's legitimate rights are easily superseded, her incapacity leaving him portionless, but for a name, as his father's house is taken from him. David finds in his mother love which provides no shelter for the self he must become, love that is insufficient because it is, ultimately, immature, 'undisciplined'. And in adhering, as he cannot help but do, to a domestic ideal based on his mother's image, David prepares a similar pattern of inadequacy and failure for his own married life. It is a pattern he must break before true selfhood can be attained, and a real home won. A loving heart may have proved 'better and stronger than wisdom' (114) for David's father. For his father's son it is not enough, as his child-wife instinctively knows, and David himself must learn:

> 'It's better for me to be stupid than uncomfortable, isn't it?' said Dora.
> 'Better to be naturally Dora than anything else in the world.'
> 'In the world! Ah! Doady, it's a large place!'   (594)

It is only after long and chastening exposure to the world that this homeless hero can understand what Dora already knows: the true nature of the refuge, the home, he seeks.

The period of David's life between his mother's death and his journey to Dover, that time which, he passionately asserts, 'I can never lose the remembrance of, while I remember anything' (129), marks the Murdstones' last and most nearly successful attempt at suppression, completing the pattern which will shape David's subsequent emotional development. Sent away once more from the home which should now be his, David is stripped of his social no less than his economic birthright. No longer David Copperfield the younger, of Blunderstone

Rookery, he becomes 'at ten years old, a little labouring hind in the service of Murdstone and Grinby' (132). And it is only by the grace of God that the 'shabby child' does not descend into something worse, 'a little robber or a little vagabond' (139), for the Murdstones abandon him entirely, offering, as he himself records, 'not the least hint of my ever being anything else than the common drudge into which I was fast settling down' (148). In this new life new titles are conferred upon him to replace the old, reflections now of a beleaguered genteel status – 'the little gent', 'the young Suffolker' (139) – while David Copperfield himself is all but lost.

So much has been written about Dickens and this episode, such attention paid to the personal obsessions it is held to reveal, it can be forgotten that Murdstone and Grinby's actually forms part of a larger thematic whole. Critics from George Orwell to Philip Collins have objected to the way David insists upon his inalienable gentility throughout the warehouse episode, Collins noting the adult David's complete failure to suggest that such snobbishness might merit the sort of self-reproach Pip will later experience.[7] The prominence of 'the little gent' in these pages may well be attributable, as is often suggested, to Dickens's own intense emotional involvement. Yet, as Forster observed long ago, if nothing else, Dickens understood his calling, and knew that 'to weave fact with fiction unskilfully would be only to make truth less true'.[8] For David the social degradation of his work in the warehouse constitutes self-betrayal. That is its primary function in the symbolic framework of his early experience. It is the culminating attack on a self-image already fearfully undermined, and prompts the decisive act of self-assertion that sets David, literally, on the road to discovery and union. His sufferings there stem from a deeply held conviction, which the reader is never invited to question, that his life as a 'common drudge' (148) denies his best and truest nature, and the uncommon possibilities that nature holds. In his own words, he has been 'thrown away' (132). Though Dickens is clearly intensely engaged (the passage comes, as so many critics have noted, almost verbatim from his autobiographical account, and is referred to in the plans for the number simply as 'what I know so well'), it is David's own anguish over his strangled potential to which he is giving voice:

No words can express the secret agony of my soul as I sank into this companionship . . . and felt my hopes of growing up to be a learned and distinguished man, crushed in my bosom. The deep remembrance of the sense I had, of being utterly without hope now; of the shame I felt in my position; of the misery it was to my young heart to believe that day by day what I had learned, and thought, and delighted in, and raised my fancy and my emulation up by, would pass away from me, little by little, never to be brought back any more: cannot be written. (133)

With David's banishment to Murdstone and Grinby's, the determining pattern of his history is established: a symbolic progress through a series of surrogate homes – inadequate, unacceptable, or ruined – journey's end lying in his discovery of his household angel, and of his true home and self with her. Murdstone and Grinby's warehouse features in David's recollection less as a commercial establishment than a private home perverted and, as it were, gone wrong: 'It was a crazy old house with a wharf of its own, abutting on the water when the tide was in, and on the mud when the tide was out, and literally over-run with rats' (132). The dirt, decay and rottenness of the place live vividly in the adult narrator's mind, 'things of the present instant' (132), as he writes. It is a house fallen away from everything a home should be, offering David, not security or nurture, but a form of social, and therefore spiritual, death. It does so in a manner that recalls the perverted domesticity of Fagin's lair in *Oliver Twist*, where images of hearth and home are diabolically inverted. And the alternative to this debased domestic refuge is, ultimately, no more satisfactory: the Micawbers' house, 'our house, as I suppose I must now call it' (135), being one large monument to their shabby-genteel improvidence. 'The first floor', David remembers, 'was altogether unfurnished, and the blinds were kept down to delude the neighbours' (135), while his own room is a close chamber at the back, as insufficiently provided for as David himself (136).

Makeshift as it is, however, the Micawber household does briefly afford David something of the domestic sustenance he requires, though it can furnish no means of social restoration. (Literal sustenance is offered as well, in the form of Mrs Micawber's innumerable suppers.) And there is, perhaps, a still more insidious social danger in the alternative family the Micawbers supply and the 'curious equality of friendship' (140) which springs up between David and them in this period of his warehouse drudgery. It is for this reason that this refuge too must so soon prove precarious, and David be left alone to 'shift for a lodging' (148) once more. Shifting for a lodging, finding his rightful home, is David's life project. And it is this second, necessary deprivation that spurs him to seek a permanent, and fitting, refuge. And the emphasis must be on *fitting*, for he turns not to Peggotty, of whose love and fidelity he is certain, but to the aunt who is 'the principal magnate of our family' (2), and of whom he has nothing but the most tenuous hopes. David later explains the reasons for his choice to Miss Betsey: 'I broke down as I was trying to say that her [Peggotty's] home was my home, and that all she had was mine, and that I would have gone to her for shelter, but for her humble station, which made me fear that I might bring some trouble on her . . .' (169).

It is not necessary to see in this nothing but a confirmation of that snobbishness with which David has so often been charged. It is, rather, a further expression of the thematic preoccupation with finding one's *true* home that shapes *David Copperfield*. For a home is always more than a physical shelter in the world of the novel. It is a locus of identity, both the refuge and the source of selfhood. It is by consigning David to work in the 'House' of Murdstone and Grinby, and to lodge in the precarious and status-less 'home' of the Micawbers, that Mr Murdstone intends to 'bend . . . and break' (130) David, depriving him of his rightful 'prospects' (131) as a gentleman. To escape from this to Peggotty's humble home, however loving, would be a temporary respite at best, for she is plainly incapable of restoring David to the status that has been so nearly lost. It is his aunt alone, sole representative of his father's family, who can do so. (David's mother, of course, was also an orphan (7) and, consequently, as helpless and status-less as her son is now.) And it is to his aunt that David runs, his nightmare journey to her cottage at Dover dramatically underlining the implications of the isolated, alien and utterly vulnerable state to which he has been reduced. 'Sleep came upon me,' David recalls of his first day's travel, 'as it came on many other outcasts, against whom house-doors were locked, and house-dogs barked, that night' (155), here taking for his own the dominant image originally associated with his father. Having reached the shelter of Miss Trotwood's cottage, and with it the prospect of a new life, David reviews his past experience, concluding with a prayer that is more significant than he knows, the complement to his mother's dying plea for her fatherless boy: 'I remember how I thought of all the solitary places under the night sky where I had slept, and how I prayed that I might never be houseless any more, and never might forget the houseless. I remember how I seemed to float, then, down the melancholy glory of that track upon the sea, away into the world of dreams' (170).

It is precisely at this point, apparently on the verge of entry into a new world, that many commentators on the novel have parted company with David Copperfield. With his status as a gentleman no longer in peril, and the hitherto exclusive focus on his emotional development poised to diverge, David's merit, in their eyes, diminishes significantly. For them, his adoption by Miss Trotwood signals the beginning of that smugly successful self-help career in which a Smilesian doctrine of self-improvement and economic advancement takes the place of Dickens's usual creed. No longer the solitary wanderer in a hostile world of the novel's early chapters, David is seen as an increasingly invulnerable examplar of the self-help creed, a mid-Victorian success story inhabiting a very different fictional universe. But David's journey does not end here. The home he finds with his aunt will not be his final resting place, as her first words to him unwittingly suggest: '"Go away!"' said Miss Betsey, shaking her head, and making a distant chop in the air with her knife. "Go along! No boys here!"' (163).

In fact, David's recovery of his social inheritance through the sponsorship of his aunt compounds rather than resolves his internal divisions. (His 'new life' in Dover begins with the conferring of yet another identity, Trotwood Copperfield, solemnized by Miss Betsey in 'indelible marking-ink' (184).) However benevolently, she too is intent on remaking David, transforming him, as the chapter title proclaims, into 'a new boy in more senses than one'. And there is a limitation implicit in the ideal of self-reliance for which Miss Trotwood speaks. Her desire to make David into 'a fine firm fellow, with a will of your own' (234) carries with it an implicit rejection of both the vulnerability and the associated open-heartedness of his parents: '"That's what your father and mother might both have been, Heaven knows, and been the better for it"' (235). And there is a danger in this. 'Firmness' is, after all, the essence of the Murdstone creed. From that moral scheme softness, even defeat, emerge as positive forces. What David must find is a middle way between the two. It is a disciplined heart he needs, not a dead one. And the search is inevitably complicated, at times frustrated, by David himself. His life in the warehouse, recalled with such pain in the writing, has plainly added further emotional burdens to an increasingly oppressive load, burdens that remain his most lasting inheritance. Past experience is never finished for David, as the very fact of his narrative testifies. Its emotional and psychic legacy continuously conditions his present, forming the chief obstacle to true self-realization, 'in spite of himself'. He is time-haunted in this important sense too. Taking his rightful place as a new boy among the ranks of Dr

Strong's young gentlemen, David is pursued by the spectre of what has become for him a shameful and secret past. His own 'slightest look and gesture' (196) seem to the now self-divided child to threaten betrayal. The threat to identity has become internalized and will prove the more dangerous for being so. The Murdstones can be banished from Dover by Aunt Betsey's intervention. David's psychic divisions are not to be so easily routed: 'My mind ran upon what they [his new school-mates] would think, if they knew of my familiar acquaintance with the King's Bench Prison? Was there anything about me which would reveal my proceedings in connexion with the Micawber family – all those pawnings, and sellings, and suppers – *in spite of myself?*' (195 emphasis added).

This is a more fundamental self-distrust than that which David later confesses has often beset him, 'on small occasions' (243). And it too would clearly be much better away. This psychic division is, presumably, the source of David's subsequent inability to determine on a profession, of his having, as he himself puts it, 'no particular liking, that I could discover, for anything' (233). Divided and uncertain as to what he is, he obviously lacks the means to discover what he will be. When David does arrive at his true 'vocation' of novelist it is as a result of a long process of attempting to discover 'what nature and accident had made me' (592). And the phrase stands equally well as a description of David's larger project in the writing of his personal history. Through all the quiet, secure years with Dr Strong, David remains haunted by the early, and decisive, chapter of loss that effectively begins his life story. His imagination remains possessed by the image of his helpless, hopeless younger self, the ghost of a past that itself becomes a source of further division. At best, David achieves an ostensible distance from the memory, a distance which amounts to little more than self-estrangement. 'I am the head-boy now,' he writes, reliving the earlier time, 'and look down upon the line of boys below me, with a condescending interest in such of them as bring to my mind the boy I was myself, when I first came there. That little fellow seems to be no part of me: I remember him as something left behind upon the road of life – as something I have passed, rather than have actually been – and almost think of him as of someone else' (229). The doubled narrative frame – the mature David recalling his younger self in the process of reshaping memory – is particularly important here. For 'that little fellow' is not, plainly, so easily left behind. He is the companion of David's subsequent journey along the old roads to London, and prompts him to close his first evening there alone retracing the steps, and fortunes, of that other self: 'I turned my face to the Adelphi, pondering on the old days when I used to roam about its subterranean arches, and on the happy changes which had brought me to the surface' (303).

The 'happy changes' of the intervening years have taken David from labouring hind to young gentleman, 'well educated, well dressed and with plenty of money in [his] pocket' (243). But they have not altered the essential pattern of his experience. David's return to London as 'a young man at his own disposal' (233), so different from the orphaned child who once strayed there, is yet prefaced by a comparable loss. For David is old enough, on leaving Canterbury, to recognize the trouble he leaves behind, looming over the home of his restored childhood and blighting its memory, destroying this shelter too. What the child had failed to comprehend in the relations between Jack Maldon and Annie Strong, the young man now knows enough to suspect, and the effect on him is telling. Once again, David sees another home, another in the series of replacements of that long-lost original, being taken from him: 'It was as if the tranquil sanctuary of my boyhood had been sacked before my face, and its peace and honour given to the winds' (241).

The image continues to recur. This 'impending shadow of a great affliction' (241) anticipates others soon to come. Steerforth's treachery not only desolates the home which had twice sheltered David as a child. It also reduces him once more, in his confrontation with Mrs Steerforth on the Peggottys' behalf, to the status of outcast. Once again David enacts a symbolic repetition of his earliest plight: 'At the appointed time, we stood at the door – the door of that house where I had been, a few days since, so happy: where my youthful confidence and warmth of heart had been yielded up so freely: which was closed against me henceforth: which was now a waste, a ruin' (399). When David returns Steerforth's body to this other home he has desolated, he goes through the dreary house and darkens the windows, as though performing its last rites, 'and all the world seemed death and silence' (687). And this dead house too haunts his imagination, joining those earlier images of inevitable loss: 'I thought as little of it as I might. But my mind could not go by and leave it, as my body did; and it usually awakened a long train of meditations' (568), meditations which have their echoes in David's earliest experience of a series of dead houses, and homeless selves.

In similar fashion, Uriah Heep's more insidious evil registers itself in terms of the changes it wreaks in the preeminent surrogate home of David's boyhood, 'the old house, which Agnes had filled with her influence' (241). In its 'old-fashioned' (187) cleanliness and order, the Wickfield house possesses something of the unspoiled, paradisal quality of David's earliest home, with the added benefit of seeming in its tranquillity 'to make the past more indistinct' (196), easing David's burden of memory of the intervening time of suffering. Yet David's first night under its roof had been prophetically haunted by Uriah's intrusive image, a living gargoyle, seemingly part of the house itself. 'Leaning out of window', he recalls, 'and seeing one of the faces on the beam-ends looking at me sideways, I fancied it was Uriah Heep got up there somehow, and shut him out in a hurry' (193). But David does not shut him out. Returning to Canterbury after his first long absence, it is to find Uriah and his mother, 'like two great bats hanging over the whole house, darkening it with their ugly forms' (488). The threat to Agnes, implicit in their constant presence, means David can find no peace in his old sanctuary. And there are deeper threats in this conjunction of Wickfield and Heep which David scarcely recognizes, though Agnes herself has warned him:

'There is such a change at home,' said she, 'that you would scarcely know the dear old house. They live with us now.'
'They?' said I.
'Mr. Heep and his mother. He sleeps in your old room,' said Agnes looking up into my face. (436)

The meaning is clear: as David had predicted long ago, Uriah is coming into partnership, a partnership which should be David's own, dispossessing him, though he has yet to know it, of what he most requires in the 'dear old house'.

It is an emotional pattern the adult David inherits from childhood, and continues to repeat, a pattern of surrogate homes successively lost, with Uriah taking Mr Murdstone's earlier role. But David is not simply a victim now, as his dispossessed younger self had been. His continued experience of loss is complicated, first by his own complicity in its operations, then by the reader's knowledge of the inevitability of this participation – a knowledge the mature narrator shares. In a literal sense David must accept responsibility for Steerforth's 'pollution of an honest home' (388), having been the means of introducing him there. So far his impulse after Emily's flight 'to go down upon my knees, and ask [the Peggottys'] pardon for the desolation I had caused' (388) is a true one. But there is a deeper guilt here that David does not recognize. Steerforth's inclination, on first seeing the Peggottys' boat, to walk in and swear he is David himself 'grown out of knowledge' (257) is symbolically correct. He *is* assuming David's place in his relations with Emily, bringing them to their logical – in social terms – conclusion. As a child, David could love the fisherman's daughter without 'any sense of inequality' (32) between them. He can even return as a young man half expecting to resume the impossibly idyllic relation: 'Whether I had come there with any lingering fancy that I was still to love little Em'ly, I don't know' (269). But, as a 'gentl'man growed' (266), David has grown out of the child's innocent freedom – another loss which he must be brought to 'know'. The genteel status to which he had clung so tenaciously now leaves him only the gentleman's prerogative of seduction, as Steerforth demonstrates.

David never contemplates taking up this class privilege (a Victorian version of the *droit de seigneur*). And it is possible to go too far in assigning both surrogate desire and attendant guilt. It is his failure to recognize the possibility of seduction by others that ultimately makes him culpable rather than any vicarious participation. He has introduced the 'treacherous' (400) serpent into this Eden, incapable of knowing him to be such. Steerforth himself grants David repeated opportunities to understand what he is planning, and there is a host of other warning signs: Agnes's opinion of this 'bad Angel' (313), Rosa Dartle's history, Steerforth's indifference, and worse, to Traddles, a patent moral touchstone, Miss Mowcher's numerous hints. But David will not understand. The child whose need for love and protection, and whose gratitude on receiving them, overwhelmed all other considerations inevitably grows into a man incapable of emotional discrimination. David refuses to see, because he cannot bring himself to see, the heartlessness beneath his friend's fascination until it is too late. A manuscript dialogue between David and Agnes on the subject of David's bad angel, omitted in proof, makes it plain that this is a direct function of David's emotional disabilities:

'Does he look intelligent, gallant, high-spirited?'
'Yes.'
'A gentleman, and a manly handsome fellow?'
'Yes.'
'And do you think it natural, or not, that I should trust in him, and be attached to him, and proud of him?'
'Natural, perhaps,' said Agnes, 'but not wise. No, Trotwood,' raising her

eyes to mine, and looking full upon me while she spoke, 'not wise. It may be only too natural but it is not wise, and not hopeful.'   (313 note 2)

This is a sort of 'naturalness' very different in its implications from that of Nicholas Nickleby. David's blindness and his subsequent inability, once his eyes have at last been opened, to judge Steerforth harshly, plainly have their roots in the formative trauma of his early years and the emotional compulsions it engendered. Being determinedly, and only too naturally, 'blind, blind, blind' (444), David must take a share in the desolation Steerforth has caused, and then mourn this further loss too. For the pattern which shapes his life is a self-perpetuating one. In similar fashion, it is the first critical loss of his child-mother which makes David so fatally blind to the true nature of his relations with Agnes, and allows Uriah Heep to carry his campaign of usurpation as far as David's own bedroom. In this too he is an unconscious, and inevitable, accomplice, an active participant in his own continued homelessness. It is the 'natural' legacy of his childhood.

The adult David's experience is, in essence, a dramatization of the difficulty of overcoming this childhood inheritance in order to achieve a full, and integrated, selfhood. And it is a dramatization in which Steerforth and Uriah Heep play important roles. In addition to serving as symbolic surrogates for David in his relations with Emily and Agnes – and living testaments to David's continued blindness – the two act as thematic counterparts, subtly refracted images of the novel's central figure and situation. All three play out the same basic configuration: fatherless son, inadequate mother, and a formative childhood experience. But Steerforth and Uriah represent a fundamental failure of self, defining through negative example the meaning of David's own, ultimately successful, struggle. It is precisely the sort of thematic reflection/refraction Dickens tries for, but does not achieve, in *Martin Chuzzlewit* with the juxtaposition of young Martin, Tom Pinch, Mark Tapley and John Westlock.

The absence of a 'steadfast and judicious father' (275), an absence that defines Steerforth's life no less than David's, ultimately proves fatal in the former's case. He is himself aware of what this want has meant: '"I wish with all my soul I had been better guided!. . . I wish with all my soul I could guide myself better!"' (274). His present inability to guide himself plainly stems from the earlier lack. Gifted with abilities which might have made him a 'hero' in eyes less partial than David's – the fascination of his manner is well conveyed –

Steerforth is incapable of directing his talents, and of directing, or controlling himself. Indulged since childhood – his mother, David learns at Salem House, 'was a widow, and rich, and would do almost anything, it was said, that he asked her' (86) – he has never lost the child's instinctive tendency to treat other personalities as mere adjuncts to his own. Self, running rampant, prevents truly mutual, and truly human, interaction, as Steerforth's 'love' affairs with Rosa Dartle and Little Emily prove. Each time the woman becomes, in Rosa's words, '"a doll, a trifle for the occupation of an idle hour, to be dropped, and taken up, and trifled with"' (686). Diminishing others to the status of objects, Steerforth equally diminishes himself. He is right to be, as he tells David he is, '"afraid of myself"' (274), for, in the end, the selfishness which is the essence of his nature can lead him to nothing more than a 'heroic' death on the deck of a sinking ship. It has no more positive potential.

And Uriah Heep presents the companion piece to this, the psychological obverse of Steerforth's fatal egotism. Uriah's venomous account of his charity education clearly reveals that society has for years systematically denied him all outward expression of his natural ambitions and needs, insisting instead on a degrading and self-denying humbleness: '"We was to be umble to this person, and umble to that; and to pull off our caps here, and to make bows there; and always to know our place, and abase ourselves before our betters. And we had such a lot of betters!"' (490). The self, so long suppressed in this way, now naturally seeks revenge in the very thing habitually withheld from it, power – as 'naturally' as David seeks confirmation of his genteel status through friendship with Steerforth. Deprived of legitimate psychic fulfilment, Uriah seeks satisfaction in a secret ascendancy, and in doing so twists his already distorted self still further awry.

Both characters function as exaggerated reflections of David's own competing self-images: the status-less charity boy on the one hand, the invulnerable gentleman on the other. The peculiar fascination of repulsion he feels towards Uriah seems rooted in his embodiment of everything David himself feared he would become in the dark days of Murdstone and Grinby, the degradation against which he fought so desperately. That Uriah feels the negative bond in his turn is made evident by his vicious outburst late in the novel, when he is being 'exploded' by Micawber: '"You think it justifiable, do you, Copperfield, you who pride yourself so much on your honor and all the rest of it, to sneak about my place, eavesdropping with my clerk? If it had been *me*, I shouldn't have wondered; for I don't make myself out a gentleman (though I never was in the streets either, as you were, according to Micawber), but being *you!*"' (641). Similarly, something of the fascination Steerforth holds for David obviously resides in his assured possession of the status Uriah, and his example, call into question. Even at Salem House, David is attracted by Steerforth's social image – 'his nice voice, and his fine face, and his easy manner, and his curling hair' (75) – which contrasts so markedly with Uriah's creeping lowness. And when they meet again as adults his admiration for Steerforth's style and manner – his ease with servants, his social grace, his 'gentlemanly' accomplishments – is just as compulsively undiscriminating.

Emblems of a radical failure of self, these distorted reflections embody a fate that clearly threatens David too. But he is not surrounded by negative exemplars alone. If Steerforth and Uriah illustrate the consequences of a fatal self-estrangement, Tommy Traddles, yet another of *David Copperfield*'s fatherless sons, demonstrates the potential of a properly disciplined self to secure a refuge. Where Steerforth and Uriah destroy homes, Traddles creates one. This, surely, is the significance of the house for which he and Sophy work and plan: '"Then, when we stroll into the squares, and great streets, and see a house to let, sometimes we look up at it, and say, how would *that* do, if I was made a judge?"' (725). Traddles functions in many ways as a more convincingly realized version of Tom Pinch in *Martin Chuzzlewit*, minus the explicit moralizing and the rhetoric of insistent pathos. With his genial peculiarities – the comic head of hair and the skeletons – his simple nature and quiet virtues, Tommy offers an alternative to the spurious 'heroic' glamour of Steerforth. Early detecting the selfishness lurking beneath Steerforth's surface charm, Traddles's patience, determination and good sense define the sort of domesticated, moral heroism David himself must embrace, his ability to estimate such heroism at its true worth serving as an index of his own growing maturity. Tommy embodies too the positive answer to Murdstone 'firmness': determination, energy and self-reliance, motivated and softened by love for his 'dearest girl' (347). These are the qualities – 'perseverance', 'patient and continuous energy' – which David's experience will slowly teach him, and to which his older self will look back as 'the strong part of my character' (517). It is, in fact, only by learning the sort of self-denial Traddles represents that David prepares himself to achieve the ultimate self-realization Agnes holds out.

The respective places of Agnes, and Dora too, within the pattern of David's life should by now be evident: one is the true angel in his house, the other the embodiment of David's false domestic ideal. Given the thematic importance of 'home' in the novel, Dora's comic inadequacies as housekeeper assume a particular significance, linking her still more closely to the long-dead mother of David's boyhood. They are the symbol of her inability to provide for David's deepest needs, of her failure to furnish a spiritual no less than a material home. David characterizes their housekeeping by saying 'nothing had a place of its own' (548) and that includes Dora's husband. It is a failure, or rather a lack, David himself soon recognizes: 'I did feel, sometimes, for a little while, that I could have wished my wife had been my counsellor; had had more character and purpose, to sustain me and improve me by; had been endowed with power to fill up the void which somewhere seemed to be about me' (552). This sense of a particular lack is soon assimilated by David to the conviction that it is a universal fate. Acknowledging in his disappointment evidence of his own weakness, of the undisciplined state of his own heart, he sees in it too a natural regret for things lost, or never found, that attends the progress from child to man. Even before her death Dora, like Steerforth, serves David as an emblem of lost youth and promise unfulfilled, as well as of a more personal blindness and unwitting self-betrayal:

When I thought of the airy dreams of youth that are incapable of realisation, I thought of the better state preceding manhood that I had outgrown; and then the contented days with Agnes, in the dear old house, arose before me, like spectres of the dead that might have some renewal in another world, but never more could be reanimated here. (595)

That 'old unhappy loss or want of something' (551) which haunts David is, in fact, a compound of the general loss time brings in its wake, the specific early deprivation of the home he has ever since been seeking, and the want of selfhood attendant upon the quest. And Dora, the inadequate home-maker, can neither compensate for, nor supply, any of these. It is entirely appropriate, perhaps inevitable, that David should forever find himself reading Annie Strong's resonant words – 'the first mistaken impulse of an undisciplined heart' – 'inscribed upon the walls of houses' (595) in dreams. For his own inability to find a home in Dora's 'baby-house' (553) is a clear indication of just how mistaken his own heart has been in choosing a wife who can offer him no more than a 'make-believe of housekeeping' (553).

It is Agnes, the 'little housekeeper' (190) in earnest, who is David's true mate. Long before he learns to recognize his particular love for her, David has cherished the 'general fancy as if Agnes were one of the elements of my natural home' (419). And he himself acknowledges the larger meaning of the role. Agnes is the source of his best self: 'She so filled my heart with such good resolutions, strengthened my weakness so, by her example, so directed . . . the wandering ardor and unsettled purpose within me, that all the little good I have done, and all the harm I have forborne, I solemnly believe I may refer to her' (443). Although Dora holds the pens, it is Agnes and her inspiration which are associated with David's 'growing reputation' (595) as a novelist and his discovery of his true vocation. In this too she consistently serves as his good angel, urging him to work and to a full acceptance of the responsibilities his fame brings with it (698, 721). Agnes is not only the treasury of David's 'earliest and brightest hopes' (699), his muse and his moral guide. In his bereavement she explicitly becomes too 'a sacred presence in my lonely house' (695). In her he finds the 'peace and happiness' (484), the perfect domestic joy he has so long, and so fruitlessly, been seeking and something more: a rock to found his love, and self, upon. David's absence from England not only teaches him the undisciplined nature of his heart, but brings him too to acknowledge his own responsibility for its errors. In his wanderings abroad he learns to give a name to the 'old unhappy loss' and to accept the unalterable fact of its irrevocability:

Home, in its best sense, was for me no more. She in whom I might have inspired a dearer love, I had taught to be my sister. She would marry and have new claimants on her tenderness, and in doing it, would never know the love for her that had grown up in my heart. It was right that I should have to pay the forfeit of my headlong passion. What I had reaped, I had sown. (710–711)

Having made for so long a 'mystery' (699) of his own heart, it is right that that heart should now be a secret to the woman who possesses it. There is a symmetry, a poetic justice to his fate that David the author clearly appreciates: 'I had bestowed my passionate tenderness upon another object; and what I might have done, I had not done: and what Agnes was to me, I and her own noble heart had made her' (700). In acknowledging his own error, David measures too his distance from the conventional 'happily ever after' of the conventional novel 'hero'. He has married his fairy-tale princess and the marriage proved not the end of his story but the beginning of a larger loss, a loss forever present to him in the figure of the 'sister' who could, and should, have been his wife.

Yet, in the end, David is allowed not only to love his 'sister' but to marry her too. In effect, he both acknowledges the lesson time has taught him, the impossibility of retracing the road not taken – 'Home was very dear to me, and Agnes too – but she was not mine – she was never to be mine. She might have been, but that was past!' (701) – and proves it wrong. For Agnes herself embodies a seeming defiance of time and change which coexists uneasily with the insistence on mutability that pervades David's written memory. Where Dora becomes 'the blossom withered in its bloom upon the tree' (598), an emblem of the inevitable law 'of change in everything' (635) David hears sounding in the bells of Canterbury cathedral, Agnes remains frozen in time, forever associated with the 'tranquil brightness' (191) of the stained-glass window in whose frame David first placed her as a child. That is the glory of her final confession to the time-haunted David: she has loved him all her life, and never changed (739). Agnes's intended symbolic function within David's life history seems clear. She fills the void in his heart and mind precisely because she represents 'home in its best sense' (710). Embracing her as his wife, David holds within his arms 'the centre of myself' (740), a centre he has lacked for so long. The homeless hero has overcome his spiritual orphanhood and found in Agnes a home at last. She is the end of a journey begun many years ago, the completion, as David himself indicates, of the circle of his life:

Long miles of road then opened out before my mind: and, toiling on, I saw a ragged way-worn boy, forsaken and neglected, who should come to call even the heart now beating against mine, his own. (739)

As a 'happy ending' it is doubly problematic, in the fact of its presence as well as its form. Is David after all to achieve nothing more or less than the familiar 'heros'' reward? Yet it is important to distinguish here between intentional limitation and imaginative failure. Agnes's apparent immunity to the novel's own laws of change must be the source of some dissatisfaction, for that defies the narrative's very organizing principle. Additionally, to a twentieth-century sensibility, the figure from the stained-glass window, eternally pointing upwards, must be still more unsettling in her capacity as an emblem of mature emotional fulfilment. As Alexander Welsh has demonstrated, the symbolic associations of the angel in the house have a disturbing tendency to become conflated with those of the angel of death.[9] And the stillness and tranquillity so consistently associated with Agnes do carry with them intimations of this ultimate stasis. She represents a denial of energy, her union with David constituting a limitation, a diminution, a loss. But it is a loss that forms part of an essential pattern. Robin Gilmour, in his excellent essay 'Memory in *David Copperfield*', identifies David's movement from child-wife to angel-bride, so inseparable from his own self-discovery – and so unsettling for modern readers – as designedly forming a state of emotional contraction. It marks, in his estimation, a loss of passionate intensity which balances David's increasing material success, and explains his narrative's tone of quiet melancholy.[10] Viewed in this light, Agnes and the depleted domesticity she represents become a part of David's general chastening, a deliberate embodiment of the limits he must learn to accept. Through the medium of his retrospective narration, David does, in fact, resign himself to the inevitable losses time brings in its wake. But that they should be inevitable is itself a source of continuing regret. There is a price to be paid in the substitution of 'domestic joy' (741) for a more spontaneous, freer emotion, a price registered in the voice of David's recollection itself. And there are other shadows qualifying, if not subverting, the 'happy ending' of his history. The very fact of David's narrative suggests a continuity of past into present – the way-worn boy forever toiling on in memory – that resists the closure he attempts to invoke. Why, after all, is David writing his personal history that is never meant to be published on any account? He himself never resolves the issue, but David's last retrospect, his final deliberate act as author, in which the crocodile book and that 'old acquaintance Brooks of Sheffield' (748) turn up yet again, speaks unmistakably of a past that is never truly over, a history never finally ended. Even the Murdstones reappear, by report, at the novel's close, reenacting beyond its confines another *David Copperfield*. Dickens may allow his hero, this once at least, to come home, to achieve a compromised closure, but he pays an emotional price for the privilege. And for his successors the cost will mount steadily higher.

The Dickens Hero and the Social Cause:
Bleak House and *Hard Times*

David Copperfield, the adult waif in search of a literal and figurative home, is the prototype of a literary hero uniquely Dickens's own. As such he sets in motion a progress whose end lies somewhere in the unwritten pages of *The Mystery of Edwin Drood*, or perhaps beyond. The journey David initiates is as much internal as external, the goal being selfhood – identity, role and place – and the means of reconciling the self, once found, with the world in which one must wake to find it. It is the defining preoccupation of the Dickens hero and runs, a common thematic thread, through the novels following *Copperfield*, novels at whose heart the hero stands. If David's personal history establishes the primary pattern, *Bleak House* and *Hard Times* test possibilities his career suggests, but does not enact, extending the potential meaning of the original design. These novels raise the prospect of defeat (encountered by Richard Carstone and Tom Gradgrind) or retreat (Esther Summerson's eventual course) rather than successful accommodation as the end of the hero's progress, and they witness too Dickens's growing interest in uniting that progress, that 'strictly personal' history, with an explicitly 'social' experience. Both are impulses born out of a consciousness of radical disjunction, of an essential wrong at the root of social existence. As the sense of the wrong steadily deepens in the later novels, so too will the meaning of the personal history it informs, for they grow in tandem. *David Copperfield* gives birth to the Dickens hero. *Bleak House* and *Hard Times* establish his place at the centre of the fictional world whose emergence this delivery heralds. And it is at the centre that he stands, his experience an index to the 'darkening' vision which has long been held to shape that world. 'Social criticism' as the structuring principle of the later novels is a well-worn theme in Dickens studies: the relation of the novels' young male protagonists to that familiar principle rather less so. But it is precisely by means of his 'darkening' hero, and that hero's narrowing prospects, that Dickens will register his most profound social indictment: a strengthening conviction that selfhood and society, as he perceives it, are ultimately irreconcilable.

Using a redefined 'hero''s progress as the vehicle for larger concerns is not, in itself, an idea new to *David Copperfield* and the novels that follow it. As the first chapter of this study sought to reveal, there are significant gestures towards this in *The Old Curiosity Shop*, *Martin Chuzzlewit* and *Dombey and Son*. Even *The Pickwick Papers* derives what unity it does possess from the belated introduction of a similar design, with the middle-aged 'hero' Pickwick at its centre. But there is no sense of a unifying, integrating theme to the experiences of these early 'heroes', however far they may stray from conventional type. Theirs is not a search for an identity and role, or for the means of sustaining them in a hostile world which would impose its own definitions. And this is the increasingly elusive goal of the Dickens hero's journey, a journey that effectively takes shape in the pages of *David Copperfield*, *Bleak House* and *Hard Times*.

What *David Copperfield* establishes is a pattern of experience for the Dickens hero, a progress from alienation to self-discovery, that will become inseparable from Dickens's emerging critical vision. But the vision itself, at work in *Martin Chuzzlewit* and *Dombey and Son*, appears suspended in the process. David's history of self-estrangement is given a clear source in the multiple losses he sustains in its early chapters – father, mother, home, status. Like Esther Summerson, he is a virtual case study in the effects of childhood deprivation on emotional development. The symbolic potential of his experience is high but it is also, essentially, a-critical. The retrospective character of David's narrative, the pervasive imagery of ocean and tide, the tone of resigned melancholy, all invest his story with a meaning that speaks through the 'vague unhappy loss or want of something' (430) which haunts his written memory 'like a strain of sorrowful music heard in the night' (594). But what David hears is the music of a past that can never be recaptured; what he loses is the warmth, security and innocence of childhood itself. The incursion of the Murdstones into the idyll of Blunderstone Rookery is a type of the inevitable invasion of the world, with all its attendant limitations and defeats, into the sanctuary of childhood, an invasion to which every life is subject. The forces underlying David's history stem, in the end, from no less a source than time itself.

What this larger symbolism associated with the hero's experience does is, effectively, to insulate that experience from the critical 'social' implications it could potentially possess (and will in succeeding novels). There is simply no overarching institution, or philosophy, or creed, spanning the world of *David Copperfield*, blighting the lives which unfold beneath its shadow, as Chancery and Gradgrind's Utilitarian 'fact' will blight, and shape, the worlds of *Bleak House* and *Hard Times*. There is no dominant vice, like *Martin Chuzzlewit*'s selfishness or *Dombey and Son*'s pride, resting at its core, only time and the inevitable losses it brings in its wake. David's response to his degradation in the wine warehouse, to take a particularly conspicuous example, is characteristically imbued with private rather than public outrage. The point is much less 'Look what society does to its children' than 'Look what society is doing to *me*.' As George Orwell noted long ago, there is a curious omission here and it is telling: though Dickens bitterly denounces David's warehouse slavery, he nowhere suggests that *no* child ought to be condemned to David's fate.[1] Dickens, in the person of David, will go on to attack both the abuses of Doctors' Commons and certain penal practices (in Chapters 33 and 61 respectively), but these are essentially isolated exercises in satire, having little to do with each other, and even less with the established thematic preoccupations of the novel. Nor do they ever quite convince as revelations of David's own characteristic concerns. If topical, 'social' issues are never entirely absent from David's story, they are yet never a primary theme. Mick Walker and Mealy Potatoes are left behind in the warehouse when David escapes, and he is allowed to remain undisturbed by either the fact, the memory, or its implications.

Why Dickens should have chosen at this point in his career to, as it were, turn back and engage in an essentially 'personal' manner with essentially 'personal' material can never really be fully determined, and must remain an open question. Forster has recorded the attempt at autobiography which preceded *David Copperfield*'s composition. And he has documented too the intensity of Dickens's emotional involvement in the writing of the novel with the now famous letter concluding 'if I were to say what *Copperfield* makes me feel to-night, how strangely, even to you, I should be turned inside out. I seem to be sending some part of myself into the Shadowy World.'[2] Plainly, the introspective, 'personal' character of David's history derives at least in part from Dickens's own involvement and needs. But why the material should have proved so powerfully emotive, and the needs so pressing, at this particular time can only be a matter for speculation.

It is this determinedly a-critical strain in *Copperfield* – recall Dickens's early insistence on the 'strictly personal' reworking of the novel's title – which may account for the dissatisfaction its ending has undoubtedly generated. The spectacle of David settling happily at journey's end into the world through which he has travelled so painfully would seem to deny the very lessons that journey taught. The end of David's story – 'I had advanced in fame and fortune, my domestic joy was perfect, I had been married ten happy years' (741) – is not, in fact, simply a catalogue of unmixed blessings. The losses he has encountered on the road to self-discovery are registered in the visit to Ham's grave which closes the novel's penultimate chapter. Yet David does finally achieve a successful, if chastened, accommodation. Perfect domestic joy possesses a particular meaning as the end of this homeless hero's progress. It means integration without radical penalty, a self at home at last within an unchanged world. Such a conclusion – essentially untroubled for David if not for the reader – proves possible only so long as the 'social' is subordinate to the 'personal', the universal and the timeless in the thematic economy of his narrative. Even here there are shadows, however diffuse, cast by the prospect which opens before David's mind of a way-worn, neglected, forsaken boy – his younger self – forever 'toiling on' along an endless road (739). And once the pattern of that boy's experience is united with an explicitly 'social' vision, as it will be in the novels which succeed *Copperfield*, the prospect of accommodation as journey's end will grow increasingly more qualified, and the 'hero''s traditional reward increasingly unattainable.

Bleak House and *Hard Times*, then, mark a transitional phase in the evolution of the Dickens hero, a phase of experimentation with the form, and implications, of the pattern now established. It is the beginning of a process of reformulation that ends only with Dickens's death, for the evolution proves continuous. There are two versions of the hero's experience offered in *Bleak House* (in one of which the Dickens hero is, in fact, a heroine) and together they constitute a significant innovation. Esther Summerson continues the exploration begun in *David Copperfield* of the psychic scars childhood deprivation leaves. Her story, like David's, becomes a chronicle of the self-estrangement and distrust which are now the hallmark of the Dickens hero. Yet there is an important difference between the two. This personal history is conceived as part of a public narrative, a narrative fully involved in issues *David Copperfield* did not choose to address. Esther's search for selfhood will unfold within the explicitly 'social', and explicitly critical, context David Copperfield's did not possess.[3]

But it is not entirely through Esther that the union of internal psychic progress and external 'social' frame is effected. The early, and plainly formative, stage of her history shows something of *Copperfield*'s tendency towards insulation in the essentially private. And it is here that *Bleak House*'s second version of the hero's experience, enacted by Richard Carstone and recorded both by Esther and the impersonal narrator, becomes important. There is a sense in which the specific issue of Esther's illegitimate birth – the source of her characteristic alienation – is tangential to the larger questions the twin narratives explore. The unloved 'love child', emotionally crippled by an inheritance of guilt, plainly has a place among *Bleak House*'s numerous orphan figures – Jo, Charley, Guster, Ada, Richard – children for whom the world makes 'rather an indifferent parent' (72) indeed. But it is, emphatically, the cruelly repressive religion of her aunt which first imposes upon Esther the self-negating definition which will haunt her: '"Your mother, Esther, is your disgrace, and you were hers"' (17). And the relation of this original cause to the novel's principal preoccupations seems less clear, though its effect upon Esther is an obvious illustration of Dickens's concern with the deadening influence of the past, private no less than corporate, upon the living present. In the end, it is through Richard Carstone and Esther Summerson together, dual versions of the hero, through the third- as well as the first-person narrators, that Dickens roots the hero's personal experience in a palpably social cause. In doing so, he lays the foundation for all subsequent reformulations. Together Richard and Esther mark the path subsequent heroes will follow.

For Richard's career of self-destruction is the symbolic complement of Esther's progress, while her story, in turn, provides the final commentary on the implications of his fatal, and fated, course. At the centre of his alienation is Chancery: 'Jarndyce and Jarndyce was the curtain of Rick's cradle' (493), as guilt was the curtain of Esther's. And in this fact the essence of *Bleak House*'s 'social' indictment lies. What Richard presents is a virtual paradigm of selfhood undermined and, ultimately, destroyed by the influence of a society seen here as corrupting no less than corrupt, and one moreover that is inescapably so. The strategic intersection of his experience with Esther's – the account of her illness (Chapter 35) includes Jarndyce's explanation of Rick's own 'terrible misfortune' (492) – links her physical fever with his spiritual infection. Jarndyce's metaphors are more appropriate than he seems to know, if a little tactless, given Esther's recent sufferings: '"Ah, my love, my love," he said, "it is in the subtle poison of such abuses, to breed such diseases. His blood is infected, and objects lose their natural aspects in his sight. It is not *his* fault"' (492). The point has already been made, through the use of Jo, the neglected outcast, as the agent of Esther's infection: the possibility of immunity in, and to, the world of *Bleak House* is becoming increasingly limited. Richard further proves the point, of course, by dying, to begin the world again the only way now open to him. And Esther's progress confirms the bleak conclusion implicit in his experience. Her search for selfhood ends in an accommodation so qualified as to undermine the alternative it might seem, at first, to present. And retreat, rather than integration, now emerges as journey's end for the Dickens hero. Esther's narrative is the supplement to Richard's doomed history, the postscript he does not live to witness, or rather the conclusion he dies to prove.

Critics from Forster onwards have viewed Richard Carstone as Dickens's redemption of an earlier lapse, the author now permitting himself the unhappy ending he had forgone with *Dombey*'s Walter Gay. But for Robert Garis, writing in *The Dickens Theatre*, he is simply another, if different, sort of failure. 'None of Richard's errors is allowed the dignity of being made to seem worth following in detail,' Garis objects, 'as the twisted distortions of an inner life in conflict; pity rules out the possibility, and the necessity, of reproach. But the possibility of taking Richard seriously as a moral being is ruled out too: he is merely a victim, and he takes rather a long time dying.'[4] There is some justice to this last remark, and Garis is certainly not alone in making it. Throughout his history no one who comes into contact with 'poor Rick' (492) – Esther, Jarndyce, Ada, Woodcourt – judges him harshly, or even holds him responsible for his downward course, however much they may warn him off. Jarndyce speaks for all: ' "But again, I say, with all my soul, we must be patient with poor Rick, and not blame him. What a troop of fine fresh hearts, like his, have I seen in my time turned by the same means!"' (492). And this is precisely the point, the point that lies at the heart of *Bleak House*, and renders Richard's fate inseparable from its deepest concerns. He is no more to blame for his infection than Esther is for hers. Each stems from the same festering source – the institutionalized indifference, irresponsibility and worship of dead forms – that makes the world of the novel the deadly place it is. In symbolically supplementary ways, Richard and Esther are both social victims. For these Dickens heroes, that is their meaning as well as their role.

Hard Times, however, begins to probe the implications of this role, calling the very status of social victim into question in a manner that will become profoundly significant. Tom Gradgrind's course through the novel follows closely the pattern consolidated in *Bleak House*, beginning in alienation and ending in ruin. In fact, it is Tom rather than Richard who truly enacts Walter Gay's intended fate, stealing the money that was to have been young Gay's ruin, and deteriorating steadily from then on. Tom provides a case history of a self misshapen and, in the end, destroyed by forces which govern the world of the novel as a whole. But Tom is given none of 'poor Rick''s consistent pathos. The narrative sympathy which invests his predecessor with a certain doomed attractiveness – 'youth, and hope, and beauty' (32) caught in Chancery's fatal web – even at his most wrongheaded, is never extended to him. Typically, he is not 'poor Tom' at all, rather, contemptuously, 'the whelp'. Although it is Harthouse who coins the term, it is the narrator who takes it up and uses it consistently thereafter: 'The appellation was not flattering, but not unmerited' (131). And this deliberate change in narrative stance becomes the more interesting when one considers that Tom's is, in fact, the more complete destruction, and he a more complete victim. For Mr Gradgrind's 'simple arithmetic' (3) has reduced his son's inner life to an endless series of 'calculations relative to number one' (90), and Richard is never brought so low. Gradgrind's 'own mathematical Thomas' (12) has been so utterly denatured as to be capable of no greater self-affirmation than the sullen selfishness which is his 'keynote' (22). And yet the reader is never invited to respond to Tom with the unmixed pity Richard arouses. His whelpishness is far too tellingly documented. He is, indeed, almost as unpleasant as Charley Hexam in *Our Mutual Friend*, another denatured product of a mechanical education system, surely one of Dickens's most unrelievedly hateful creations.

Tom, moreover, stands in a much more complex relation to the 'social cause' of his alienated condition than Richard does to Chancery. Plainly he is the victim of a childhood murdered by the spectre of his father's 'fact, fact, fact' (7), but so too is Louisa, and she experiences nothing like Tom's total degeneration. She remains capable of making a moral choice when her moment of crisis with Harthouse comes. The vestiges of a genuine selfhood survive in Louisa, however mutilated, in spite of an equal imaginative deprivation. Dickens, indeed, makes the difference between Tom and Louisa clear on their first appearance in the novel. She has a crucial spark of inner brightness, he has none:

'There was an air of jaded sullenness in them both, and particularly in the girl; yet, struggling through the dissatisfaction of her face, there was a light with nothing to rest upon, a fire with nothing to burn, a starved imagination keeping life in itself somehow, which brightened its expression' (12). Tom, in contrast, is likened simply to 'a machine' (12). Dickens offers no explanation for the distinction, but it seems an obvious reflection of the belief Michael Slater documents in *Dickens and Women*: the assumption of an innate moral superiority in women allied to their equally innate capacity for unselfish devotion to others. It is a superiority which seems inevitably to insulate them from the sort of moral degeneration their male counterparts may experience.[5] Ada Clare is another case in point. Though exposed to the same disease which consumes Richard, she never succumbs to it herself, though she suffers greatly as a result of his contagion. (The woman's moral immunity never provides protection from involvement, only, in most instances, from corruption.) Whatever the underlying reason for the difference between Tom and Louisa – and it is never made clear – the fact of it serves to make Tom's ultimate moral status somewhat doubtful. How far indeed can one attribute his unequivocally despicable actions – the double betrayal of his sister, first to Bounderby then to Harthouse, his involvement in Stephen Blackpool's death – to a cause that produces no such effects in one no less exposed? How far are they the product of innate limitations that would seem to exist beneath or beyond it? Is Tom even in some oblique way never really explained, an accomplice in his own spiritual ruin?

In a sense, Dickens has already raised similar issues through the troubling figure of Uriah Heep in *David Copperfield*. For Uriah's account of his soul-destroying education at a foundation (charity) school forces David, and the reader, previously equally hostile, to consider the source of his hypocritical '"umbleness"': 'It was the first time it had ever occurred to me, that this detestable cant of false humility might have originated out of the Heep family. I had seen the harvest, but had never thought of the seed' (490). Yet, having occurred to David, the thought still does not mitigate Uriah's sheer loathsomeness, with his fishy hands and his 'galvanic' twistings. The potential implications of the social cause are never investigated, and the mere fact of its existence quickly pales beside the revenge Uriah proceeds to exact: '"I am very umble to the present moment, Master Copperfield, but I've got a little power!"' (491). There is, finally, no sense of the seed which was at the root of Uriah's emotional distortion bearing fruit anywhere else in the novel. But with Tom Gradgrind the case is very different. In him Dickens unites a thematically significant pattern of experience (self-hood strangled by Utilitarian fact) with a complex presentation and an implicit suggestion of personal complicity. Tom is both victim and victimizer, neither entirely pathetic in the one capacity, nor entirely culpable in the other. This ambiguity of status is not an indication of loss of narrative control, as some critics have taken it to be, but the reverse. Tom embodies a deliberate attempt not only to redefine the young male protagonist as social victim, but to create a victim who is both more and less than a much sinned against orphan. What *Hard Times* signals, in fact, is the emergence of a complexity of character and moral status in the Dickens hero to match, and indeed further, the symbolic complexity of experience *Bleak House* has introduced. Together the two novels make possible the transmutation of *David Copperfield*'s homeless hero into *Little Dorrit*'s Arthur Clennam and the other, equally shadowed figures who succeed him.

All of the later protagonists who qualify as 'Dickens heroes' are, essentially, David Copperfield's spiritual heirs. But of the three to be discussed here, Esther Summerson is perhaps the nearest in blood. For she inherits David's role as narrator as well as his characteristic emotional plight. And in her hands the personal history becomes a still more subtle instrument of unconscious revelation. Despite her opening disclaimer – 'As if this narrative were the narrative of *my* life! But my little body will soon fall into the background now' (26) – Esther's 'portion of these pages' (15) is very much the story of her life, her inner life, and more. It is the story of the interrelated impulses which drive her, even here, to seek the 'background' as her natural resting place. Esther's compulsion to insist on her own marginal status is itself revealing, her final disclaimer 'I hope any one who may read what I write, will understand that if these pages contain a great deal about me, I can only suppose it must be because I have really something to do with them, and can't be kept out' (112) carrying a significance she cannot recognize. Esther's own personal history cannot be 'kept out', or kept apart, from *Bleak House*'s other narrative because its very obsession with self – or rather its absence – forms that narrative's primary concern. And it is precisely this unconsciously revealed obsession which qualifies Esther, in spite of her sex, for membership in the fraternity David Copperfield founds. Like Miss Wade, another illegitimate child (mis)shaped by her early experience, though in different form, or Arthur Clennam whom she still more closely resembles,

Esther Summerson too is a 'self-tormentor', and her narrative is her history.

In marked contrast to David Copperfield, Esther has no golden time of early childhood whose loss will forever haunt her written memory. Her ghosts take a different form, her aunt's religious morbidity imbuing the child's first experience with an inescapable sense of 'the fault I had been born with' (18). The idea of her mysteriously absent mother naturally engages the child's imagination: 'I had never heard my mama spoken about. I had never heard about my papa either, but I felt more curious about my mama' (16). Yet her aunt's early training conditions even this imagined relation: '"Oh do pray tell me something of her. Do now, at last, dear godmother, if you please! What did I do to her? How did I lose her? Why am I so different from other children, and why is it my fault, dear godmother?"' (17). Well before the advent of feminist criticism, Dickens highlights the symbolic importance of the mother in a young girl's emotional patterning. The phrasing of Esther's questions, with their instinctive assumption of guilt, is obviously significant, while the answer the child receives will scar the woman for life, forming the basis of a radically divided self intent on suppression. It is at the root of Esther's case history. '"Submission, self-denial, diligent work are the preparations for a life begun with such a shadow on it,"' she is told. '"You are different from other children, Esther, because you were not born, like them, in common sinfulness and wrath. You are set apart"' (17–18). Here, plainly, is the source of the adult Esther's lack of all positive identity, of her acute emotional insecurity, of her desperate craving for approval and attendant inability either to accept it when it comes, or openly to acknowledge the legitimacy of the need. Self-denial, in this deeply destructive sense, truly becomes her preparation for life.

For this childhood trauma – it is nothing less – instils in Esther a conviction that she must somehow 'repair the fault' of which, she writes, 'I confusedly felt guilty and yet innocent' (18). And she resolves in consequence to 'strive as I grew up to be industrious, contented and kind-hearted, and to do some good to some one, and win some love to myself if I could' (18) – a more hopeful formulation, seemingly, than the course her aunt prescribes. But what Esther is actually mapping out is a life-long programme of self-sacrifice in the most literal sense of the word. What she proposes is a consistent denial of her own emotional requirements, a suppression of anything in herself that is ever less than 'contented and kind-hearted', in an attempt to secure the affection of which her aunt's training has taught her to believe she is, in fact, innately unworthy. It is a suppression that extends as far as the telling of her own life history in which she would displace herself, if she could. There is no sense of a legitimate selfhood for Esther in anything but denial, no expectation of mutual exchange. Love, for her, does not come unconditionally, it is 'won'. And her task therefore becomes the construction of a persona, a fictive self, more worthy of winning the precious commodity than 'little Esther Summerson' (16) could ever hope naturally to be, a task she carries beyond the 'end' of her story to the very act of its composition. When Esther steps into her ready-made role of 'industrious' housekeeper at Bleak House, she is, in effect, only completing her original programme of self-effacement: 'This was the beginning of my being called Old Woman, and Little Old Woman, and Cobweb, and Mrs. Shipton and Mother Hubbard, and Dame Durden, and so many names of that sort, that my own name soon became quite lost among them' (98).

Such systematic and sustained repression will, necessarily, exact its toll. And Esther's narrative continually betrays the emotional tensions which lie just beneath 'a cheerful spirit and a grateful heart' (80) so determinedly maintained. Behind Esther's ostensible serenity are strains she cannot openly acknowledge, and yet cannot help registering. The constant habit of speaking to herself as though to some other person, and generally in terms of reproach – ' "Esther! You to be low-spirited. You!" ' (235) – is only one of many indications of a fundamental dislocation that will be expressed. Dickens continues to develop in Esther's narrative the technique of symbolic corroboration employed in David Copperfield's history to reveal much that David would not, or could not, tell. It is a corroboration effected by Esther herself, but one of whose implications she remains unaware. This double narrative is most conspicuous in the account Esther provides of the dreams which trouble her illness. Each detail, as she tells it, is clearly significant, and yet retains the sense of hidden logic which is the essence of the dream experience, allowing Esther to reveal what she cannot herself acknowledge: 'At once a child, an elder girl, and the little woman I had been so happy as, I was not only oppressed with cares and difficulties adapted to each station, but by the great perplexity of endlessly trying to reconcile them' (488). A little later comes a still more nightmarish and, for Esther, incomprehensible time, 'when I laboured up colossal staircases, ever striving to reach the top, and ever turned, as I have seen a worm in a garden path turned, by some obstruction, and labouring again' (488). Esther is here giving voice, in the only way she can, to the increasingly insupportable psychic burdens under which she labours. For hers *is* an endless task of attempting to reconcile her chosen, self-diminishing role of 'little woman' – forever industrious, contented and kind-hearted – with the more demanding, more aspiring self she cannot entirely suppress, the self that would be loved by Allan Woodcourt, if the 'little woman' did not forbid such a possibility.

Given the history of her childhood, with its unexplained but formative loss of mother-love, Esther's discovery of her living, loving mother should interrupt the pattern of self-division that childhood engendered. And, for a moment, it does. For the shock brings Esther to articulate the conviction of guilt and innate unworthiness she has nursed in secret for so long. She becomes, she writes, 'possessed by a belief that it was right, and had been intended, that I should die in my birth; and that it was wrong, and not intended, that I should be then alive' (514). And it is essentially this belief which has shaped, or rather deformed, her entire life. The moment compares to David Copperfield's utter negation when he becomes, in imagination, the dead child buried in his dead mother's arms. The original 'wound' Esther receives on her birthday comes when she reads in the gloom of her aunt's face corroboration of a truth she instinctively knows: 'It would have been far better, little Esther, that you had had no birthday; that you had never been born!' (17). And it is a 'wound' that remains with her for life. The 'augmented terror of myself' (515) she experiences, now seeing in herself not 'little Esther' but the ghost of the Dedlock family legend, is but an extension of her habitual self-estrangement: 'my echoing footsteps brought it suddenly into my mind that there was a deadful truth in the legend of the Ghost's Walk, that it was I who was to bring calamity upon the stately house and that my warning feet were haunting it even then' (515). 'I ran from myself and from everything' (515), she confesses, and so she has been doing, from the earliest days of her history, and so she continues to do to its close. From childhood Esther has been atoning for the sin of being alive by 'running from herself', attempting complete self-effacement. But now, seemingly, she has been freed to come into 'a better condition' (515), to recognize the falseness of her past belief, and disown at last the old childhood fault. And so, she says, she does after her long night of self-communion: 'I knew I was as innocent of my birth as a queen of hers; and that before my Heavenly Father I should not be punished for birth, nor a queen rewarded for it' (516). Like David Copperfield finally penetrating in desolation the mystery of his own heart, crisis brings Esther discovery with it.

And yet insight works no comparable change in Esther's pattern of estrangement. She continues to punish herself, whatever her Heavenly Father may do. Lacking David's ability to move from self-knowledge to fulfilment, hers is a much more qualified progress and, ultimately, a much less hopeful one. Claiming to hold herself innocent of her birth, it is still Jarndyce's indifference to 'my disfigurement, and my inheritance of shame' (611) – twin badges now of a perceived unworthiness – that binds Esther to him in ever-increasing gratitude, and commits her still further to her programme of suppression. For Esther, the circumstances of her birth, like those other wounds the 'deep traces' (612) of her illness with which she now links them, are 'only new reasons why I should be busy, busy busy – useful, amiable, serviceable, in all honest, unpretending ways' (612). And this is only a new formulation of the old 'industrious, contented and kind-hearted' prescription. For Esther herself her physical scarring assumes a symbolic importance, functioning as an emblem of her own disqualification for the romantic love she does not deserve to 'win'. Her proposed marriage to Jarndyce, and final transformation into 'the mistress of Bleak House' (612), simply complete Esther's life-long renunciation of all pretensions to an identity, or even to emotional needs, of her own, offering her, in her own words, 'the undeserved love of the best of men' (612). She has indeed made, as will be suggested later, a religion of sacrifice, and this is to be its last rite. In Jarndyce's words, she ' "will sacrifice her love to a sense of duty and affection, and will sacrifice it so completely, so entirely, so religiously, that you should never suspect it though you watched her night and day" ' (858).

But though Esther tries, she is not, in fact, able to annihilate self completely. Her first response to Jarndynce's letter of proposal is telling: she cries. The self-denying 'sense of duty and affection' which animates her cannot entirely suppress a – in Esther's terms – selfish desire for something other than the fortune Mrs Woodcourt had once predicted for her: a future of passionless, quiet domesticity with a husband many years her senior. ' "That is a good fortune," ' Esther had then remarked. ' "But why is it to be mine?" ' (414). It is this fortune which John Jarndyce now offers and Esther's instinctive recoil is plain, if unacknowledged:

Still I cried very much; not only in the fulness of my heart after reading the letter, not only in the strangeness of the prospect – for it was strange though I had expected the contents – but as if something for which there was no name or distinct idea were indefinitely lost to me. I was very happy, very thankful, very hopeful; but I cried very much. (611)

Like David Copperfield, Esther too is haunted by a 'vague unhappy loss or want of something', a loss to which she will not, cannot, give a name or idea. It is a sense of incompleteness that is the direct result of her compulsive self-sacrifice. Even to herself, and even in retrospect, Esther must not be anything less than 'very happy, very thankful, very hopeful', though she does cry so much. As the wedding approaches, the event which is to crown Esther's career of abnegation, this unacknowledged tension between selfhood and sacrifice takes the cheerfulness that masks it to the borders of hysteria in a parody of domestic duty: 'So I went about the house, humming all the tunes I knew; and I sat working and working in a desperate manner, and I talked and talked, morning, noon, and night' (686). But, of course, this symbolically fraught wedding never does take place. Or rather a different wedding does.

For numerous critics of *Bleak House*, Esther's union with Allan Woodcourt represents the same sort of unintentional problem as David Copperfield's marriage to Agnes, both offering a resolution whose possibility the narrative itself has all along been calling into question. In fact, Esther's progress never achieves a resolution. That is its ultimate meaning. Attendant objections are equally often raised to Jarndyce's manipulative benevolence in stage-managing Esther's future life – providing both husband and home – but she leaves him no choice. For she remains incapable of acting for herself – selfishly in her terms – to secure fulfilment. David Copperfield needed only Aunt Betsey's pious fraud to send him racing to his household angel's side, redeeming the 'vague unhappy loss' which has now taken a very precise human shape. Esther requires a much more elaborate deception before she can be offered, 'a willing gift' (859) in more senses than one, to the man who will make her happiness. And, here too, self-assertion remains impossible. In the end, her happiness consists in the imposition of the 'right' identity. Esther will still be the 'little mistress' of Bleak House. It is only the master who will change. She is, however happily, simply replacing one object of sacrifice with another. There is for her no other way. As Esther herself records, 'I have never lost my old names . . . Dame Trot, Dame Durden, Little Woman! – all just the same as ever' (879). She has never lost the old names, nor learned to reclaim her own. And, just the same as ever, her narrative retains its insistence on her own marginal status to the last: 'The people even praise *me* as the doctor's wife. The people even like *me* as I go about, and make so much of me that I am quite abashed. I owe it all to him, my love, my pride! They like me for his sake as I do everything I do in life for his sake' (880). In winning Agnes David Copperfield wins too the realization of his best self that had so long been lost to him. There is a sense of completion as he draws the circle of his life to a close, though shadows lie along its way. For Esther there is not completion but suspension, and the suggestion – still stronger here than in David's case – of patterns forever repeating themselves. There is, literally, no closure here, Esther 'ending' her narrative in an uncompleted sentence in which she herself, the ostensible subject, is at best only half present: 'But I know that my dearest little pets are very pretty, and that my darling is very beautiful, and that my husband is very handsome, and that my guardian has the brightest and the most benevolent face that ever was seen, and that they can very well do without much beauty in me – even supposing –' (880). In the roll call of her history, Esther is still conspicuous by her willed absence.

With Esther the spiritual end of the Dickens hero's journey proves inconclusive, a fate reflected in the compromised retreat which is the physical consummation of its course. The new Bleak House to which she eventually comes 'home' is removed as far as it can be, but that is not very far, from the contaminating scenes among which the old house stands, while Chancery continues in its perpetual course. Even Allan Woodcourt, the closest thing to a conventional 'hero' *Bleak House* possesses, no longer enjoys the special immunity which is the 'hero''s traditional reward. Significantly, his absence at sea is not, like Walter Gay's, a convenient means of disposing of a character who has no other function but marrying the heroine. It is, rather, the direct result of his inability to find a place within the diseased world of Chancery. He is, moreover, emphatically a working 'hero', not, like Nicholas Nickleby or Martin Chuzzlewit, biding time until reclaiming his gentlemanly inheritance of graceful retirement. His final reward is not a life of untroubled leisure but a career of continuing labour among the poor and suffering who must plainly always be with the inhabitants of Bleak House. And the limited refuge this modest country cottage represents is now the only hope for safeguarding the tenuous selfhood Esther has managed to achieve. The perfect domestic joy of *David Copperfield*'s homeless hero has become elusive indeed. Esther's 'home' is Bleak House.

It is the shadow of Richard Carstone's death that gives Esther's retreat its deepest meaning, the final significant intersection of their parallel careers. Her possession of the new Bleak House depends even more than she realizes 'on Richard and Ada' (859). Mr Pickwick, Oliver Twist, Nicholas Nickleby – all three had ended their adventures by withdrawing to a country refuge, their experience permanently rewarded by a pastoral idyll secure from the realities of wickedness, crime and suffering encountered along the way. But for Esther there is no such recompense, for in the world of *Bleak House* there can be no such immunity. The destruction of Richard's 'youth, and hope, and beauty' by the disease of Chancery – not a 'direct bodily illness' (814) but a sickness of the soul – is the ultimate proof of that. Richard's first exposure to the Court is prophetic. It gives him, he says, '"the headache and the heartache both together"': '"My head ached with wondering how it happened if men were neither fools nor rascals; and my heart ached to think they could possibly be either"' (58). Richard himself, though neither, will not be protected by his already compromised innocence. His is a more explicit, and a more conscious, journey than Esther's, the thematic counterpart to the third-person portion of the narrative with its more overt symbolic design. And 'mad' Miss Flite is only one of many – Jarndyce and Guppy understand them too – who read in him the signs of Chancery's attraction and construe their meaning: '"I saw them beginning in our friend the Ward in Jarndyce. Let some one hold him back. Or he'll be drawn to ruin"' (499).

In fact, the true beginning of Richard's story lies, like Esther's, in childhood, a childhood curtained in its cradle by Chancery. There is in Rick a wild restlessness, 'a carelessness in his character' (113) amid all its natural promise that Esther early observes. 'At the core of so much that is good' (181) there is a constancy wanting, to himself no less than to others. This is Richard's legacy from his 'grim old guardian' the Court (182), part of that larger inheritance of 'protracted misery' (54) which belongs to the wards in Jarndyce. Speaking out of his own bleak knowledge as the heir of old Tom Jarndyce, who 'in despair blew his brains out at a coffee-house in Chancery Lane' (4), John Jarndyce makes explicit the inescapable link between social cause and personal effect:

'How much of his indecision of character,' Mr. Jarndyce said to me, 'is chargeable on that incomprehensible heap of uncertainty and procrastination on which he has been thrown from his birth, I don't pretend to say; but that Chancery, among its other sins, is responsible for some of it, I can plainly see.

It has engendered or confirmed in him a habit of putting off – and trusting to this, that, and the other chance, without knowing what chance – and dismissing everything as unsettled, uncertain, and confused. The character of much older and steadier people may be even changed by the circumstances surrounding them. It would be too much to expect that a boy's, in its formation, should be the subject of such influences, and escape them.' (167)

Richard plainly has no more chance to escape uninfluenced by the 'terrible misfortune' (492) of his birth than Esther does her own. Jarndyce and Jarndyce had begun to unsettle him, he reveals, '"before I quite knew the difference between a suit at law and a suit of clothes"' (322) and has gone on doing so ever since. His years at a public school – an academic equivalent to Chancery in its dedication to outmoded forms – only ingrain the habits of mind so early fostered. There is more than a little of Chancery's systematized futility in the 'education' Richard receives through eight years of learning to make Latin verses. As Esther describes it, 'He had been adapted to the Verses, and had learnt the art of making them to such perfection, that if he had remained at school until he was of age, I suppose he could only have gone on making them over and over again, unless he had enlarged his education by forgetting how to do it' (167–168). (Compare this with the Alice-in-Wonderland-like proceedings of Chancery as Jarndyce describes them: '"Equity sends questions to Law, Law sends questions back to Equity; Law finds it can't do this, Equity finds it can't do that . . . And thus through years and years, and lives and lives, everything goes on, constantly beginning over and over again, and nothing ever ends"' (95–96).) What Richard is never taught, and what he so sorely lacks, is the means of realizing, or even discovering, 'what he was fitted for' (168). His is a career of self-betrayal, a sustained wronging of himself 'every day and every hour' (322), begun in childhood. Incapable of positive self-assertion, conscious of being 'but a worthless fellow' (322) when he might have been so much more, Richard is a victim of Chancery before ever visiting the Court. Esther may wonder whether his is a solitary case. Her co-narrator, and the reader, know better: 'Chancery, which has no wisdom but in Precedent, is very rich in such Precedents; and why should one be different from ten thousand?' (555).

The first real indications of Richard's infection come, in a chapter entitled 'Signs and Tokens', in the form of his carelessness about money, and more particularly in the mental arithmetic he employs to justify his extravagance: '"I have got ten pound more than I expected to have, and consequently I can afford to spend it without being particular"' (114). It is a subtle omen, suggestive of negligence yet inseparable from the buoyancy and lack of calculation which make Richard, at first, such an attractive alternative to the world of Chancery. And its implicit warning is confirmed by Richard's inability to devote himself in sustained earnest to any profession for long. David Copperfield too experiences an obviously symbolic difficulty in determining 'What I would like to be', though his earnestness is never in doubt, coming slowly to the knowledge of his true vocation as he comes to the knowledge of so much else. But Richard's indecision – '"Except that I am quite sure I don't want to go into the Church, it's a toss-up"' (168) – possesses a more sinister significance. For it has its roots in that pervasive moral indifference which has been 'sown broadcast by the ill-fated cause', that 'loose way of letting bad things alone to take their own bad course' (5) which lies at the heart of Chancery's evil. Its manifestation in Richard makes Esther's heart ache much as Chancery had made Richard's such a little time before: 'For I thought how would this end, how could this end, when so soon and so surely all his manly qualities were touched by the fatal blight that ruined everything it rested on!' (324).

It is Richard's passivity in the face of this creeping blight that disqualifies him from tragic status in the eyes of critics like Robert Garis. Too much the quiescent sufferer, too little the struggling man, he has, for them, no inner life, only the rather mechanical pathos of an utterly helpless, and utterly innocent, victim. But this passivity is plainly inseparable from the larger Chancery theme. Richard's inability to resist the fatal attraction is part of Chancery's legacy, part of his own inheritance, part of England's. If Richard is passive, moreover, he is not unconscious, a point Garis overlooks. Esther and David Copperfield are unwitting chroniclers of their self-estrangement, unaware of the significance of much of what they reveal, unconscious of the patterns they repeatedly enact. Their lack of self-knowledge is at once both cause and effect of the divisions that haunt them. But Richard consistently recognizes the moral want Chancery has engendered. He diagnoses his own disease, and traces its progress, as he finds himself '"dragging on this dislocated life, sinking deeper and deeper into difficulty every day, continually hoping and continually disappointed, conscious of change upon change for the worse in myself, and no change for the better in anything else"' (551). Richard possesses from the beginning the knowledge that eludes David

Copperfield for so long and Esther, apparently, for ever. He is capable of contrasting himself with Allan Woodcourt and measuring his own distance from the 'heroic' virtues the young doctor embodies: '"You can pursue your art for its own sake, and can put your hand upon the plough and never turn, and can strike a purpose out of anything. You and I are very different creatures"' (692–693). Woodcourt is indeed an exemplar of the sort of redefined, moral heroism of private life Dickens reaches for in Tom Pinch and achieves more successfully in Tommy Traddles. And Richard is conscious of his own inability to reach that 'heroic' standard. His failure to become such a 'hero' is, in fact, the mark of the estrangement that defines and will defeat him. For Richard is powerless to act upon his self-knowledge, his Chancery legacy having long since sapped all moral will from him, as Miss Flite predicted it would. That is his tragedy. The final lapsing of Jarndyce and Jarndyce in costs leaves Richard 'sitting in a corner of the court . . . like a stone figure' (868), the true 'Monument of Chancery practice' (866), a monument to the spiritual paralysis it breeds.

Together Richard's death and Esther's problematic 'happy ending' mark the beginning of a steady contraction of positive possibilities available to the Dickens hero. Both are caught in a world that seems to make undistorted selfhood impossible, with Richard's the only means of escape. And this is now the hero's predicament, this is the world in which he must seek his home. It is the predicament Tom Gradgrind inherits, and carries to a conclusion already implicit in *Bleak House*. For all Chancery's lurking contagion, Richard yet retains a certain core of human potential, capabilities of kindness, generosity, affection and rectitude, untouched by its blight, much as Esther salvages a capacity to love from the otherwise destructive trauma of her childhood. It is in part what critics like Garis object to. But for Tom Gradgrind there is no such saving grace. His potential is murdered outright. His is a personality warped beyond the pitiful, the point where Richard ultimately rests, to the literally hateful. That is the inevitable conclusion of his progress.

Tom is in this as much a victim as Richard, if not more, given the extent of the moral ruin he suffers. For him too the process of self-estrangement begins at birth, with an imagination 'strangled in his cradle' (132). The 'mathematical Thomas' first appears in the novel 'abasing himself on the ground' (12) to catch a glimpse of Sleary's circus and the world of wonders it represents. He will be brought still lower in its course. When caught, Tom gives himself up to be taken home 'like a machine' (12), a casualty of that arithmetical creed that would 'weigh and measure any parcel of human nature, and tell you exactly what it comes to' (3). The 'social problem' and the hero's experience are identical in *Hard Times*, as they are in *Bleak House*. Both have their source in the Gradgrind philosophy and its attempts to reduce the 'unfathomable mystery' (69) of human potential to a 'mere question of figures' (3). Starving his son's imagination, Gradgrind irretrievably stunts his soul, and the analogy between 'the case of the Coketown population and the case of the little Gradgrinds' (24) is clear. Their imaginative faculty too 'must and would be satisfied aright, or must and would inevitably go wrong, until the laws of Creation were repealed' (25). Like Richard amid the desolation of Chancery, Tom 'no more gathers grapes from thorns, or figs from thistles, than older men did, in old times' (*BH* 814). In his case too the inevitable relation of social cause and personal effect is made explicit, with the narrator now assuming Jarndyce's explanatory function, expounding the 'laws of creation' governing the world of the novel:

It was very remarkable that a young gentleman who had been brought up under one continuous system of unnatural restraint, should be a hypocrite; but it was certainly the case with Tom. It was very strange that a young gentleman who had never been left to his own guidance for five consecutive minutes, should be incapable at last of governing himself; but so it was with Tom. It was altogether unaccountable that a young gentleman whose imagination had been strangled in his cradle, should still be inconvenienced by its ghost in the form of grovelling sensualities; but such a monster, beyond all doubt was Tom.   (132)

Plainly, the more of a 'monster' Tom becomes, the more dissolute, the more sullen, the more selfish, the truer he is being to his monstrous education, and to the soul-destroying philosophy upon which it rests. His very hatefulness, and he is very hateful, becomes the 'natural' index of his victimization, the inevitable result of his most 'unnatural' education. And he too, like Richard, is aware of his plight, self-conscious to the extent of knowing that selfhood is wanting. Tom's self-diagnosis is more than accurate, it is prophetic: '"As to me," said Tom, tumbling his hair all manner of ways with his sulky hands, "I am a Donkey, that's what *I* am. I am as obstinate as one, I am more stupid than one, I get as much pleasure as one, and I should like to kick like one"' (51). It is Tom, indeed, who introduces that recurring strain of animal imagery – donkey, mule, whelp, monkey – suggestive of his own utter debasement. It is at the heart of *Hard Time*'s indictment that the donkey should seek to recompense himself 'for the way in which I have been brought up' (52) by kicking out. It is a still more profoundly damning charge that the recompense should ultimately end in self-destruction.

Tom's proving of his father's 'law' – '"So many people are employed in situations of trust; so many people, out of so many, will be dishonest"' (284) – by robbing Bounderby (a father surrogate) marks a final revenge against the system in which he was brought up. He himself makes the point explicit: '"I have heard you talk, a hundred times, of its being a law. How can *I* help laws? You have comforted others with such things, father. Comfort yourself!"' (284). But it signals too the final surrender of self to the new 'laws of Creation' that mutilated it in its cradle and set it upon this downward course. In Tom's midnight interview with Louisa, after the robbery has been committed, his self-estrangement manifests itself in clear self-hatred, and an attendant rejection of 'all the good in the world' from which he has been cut off, first by his father's system, then by his own act. That the act is both voluntary and inevitable is the essence of his plight: 'Then the wretched boy looked cautiously up and found her gone, crept out of bed, fastened his door, and threw himself upon his pillow again: tearing his hair, morosely crying, grudgingly loving her, hatefully but impenitently spurning himself, and no less hatefully and unprofitably spurning all the good in the world' (191).

Tom is not, clearly, a simple victim. Dickens deliberately qualifies his status from the outset by denying him any of the incidental features that make Richard Carstone almost automatically affecting: the good looks and high spirits, the 'flush and fire and laughter' (535), the romantic interest of a love affair, the residue, in fact, of a conventional 'heroic' persona. Tom is, rather, the deliberate obverse of the conventional figure, and is, moreover, subjected to hostile comment in a way that Richard never is. The account of his drunken evening with Harthouse is merciless in its chronicling of 'the whelp' as he betrays his sister to her would-be seducer, and merciless too in its judgment upon him: 'The whelp went home and went to bed. If he had had any sense of what he had done that night, and had been less of a whelp and more of a brother, he might have turned short on the road, might have gone down to the ill-smelling river that was dyed black, might have gone to bed in it for good and all, and have curtained his head for ever in its filthy waters' (137). This is, of course, an extension of Dickens's willingness, already noted, to make Tom morally reprehensible, even despicable, as a result of his social victimization, something Richard is never allowed to be. What it marks is the emergence of a strain that is latent in the hero's experience in *Bleak House*, but never more than latent.

In a novel as concerned with issues of public and private responsibility as *Bleak House*, Richard's repeated confessions of moral powerlessness – ' "You must know that I have done no good this long time. I have not intended to do much harm, but I seem to have been capable of nothing else" ' (692) – while undoubtedly pathetic, carry with them too a faint echo of Harold Skimpole's self-extenuating plea: ' "I have no Will at all – and no Won't – simply Can't" ' (435). Richard does not trade on his moral weakness. But the very form of his confession raises the question of whether there is not a sense in which he, a 'vexatious and capricious infant' in law (336), is allied to that other 'dear old infant' (521) forever capitalizing on his professed incapacity, allied to Skimpole as well as to figures of 'pure' pathos like his fellow Chancery victims Gridley and Miss Flite. The echoes are unsettling but, ultimately, inconclusive. For the question of Richard's responsibility for his own ruin is never explored. Thematic imperatives – Chancery's function as an *inescapable* social disease; the insistence on the impossibility of social immunity – clear 'poor Rick' from blame as emphatically as Jarndyce does, while the aura of tragedy with which he is so effectively surrounded itself invites a suspension of judgment.

With Tom, however, the case is no longer this plain. His symbolic function as victim depends upon the very hatefulness that victimization is now seen to breed. The inevitability of his moral decline, therefore, will not obscure the nature of his conduct, though it still complicates the issue of responsibility. Gradgrind publishes his son's guilt 'with such extenuation as his years and temptation (he could not bring himself to add, his education) might beseech' (298). And yet that education clearly beseeches a great deal. The completeness of Tom's ruin speaks through every selfish word and worthless action, chronicled by Dickens with a rigour Richard escapes. But unmixed contempt no more proves an adequate response than the simple pity Richard invites. Displays of whelpishness – ' "You have no idea what a state I have got myself into – what a state my sister might have got me out of, if she would only have done it" ' – are punctuated with details that speak of the human cost involved – 'He took to biting the rosebuds now, and tearing them away from his teeth with a hand that trembled like an old man's' (175–176). And the complexity of depiction is maintained to the last. The grotesqueness of Tom's final appearance in the novel, dressed in the 'grimly, detestably, ridiculously shameful' (283) comic livery that is the badge of his utter degradation, ensures that he remains an unsettling figure, resisting resolution into a pathos that blurs but cannot hide his problematic status. Tom dies an exile, moreover, his repentance coming just too late. And his fate proves prophetic for the other, spiritual, exiles who will succeed him.

At the end of *Hard Times* Louisa Gradgrind is able to return, however stricken, to her father's house to be reborn through Sissy's love. But there is no hope of home for her brother, and never has been: '"I can't be more miserable anywhere",' he himself says, '"than I have been here, ever since I can remember"' (285). The whelp may whimper his complaint, 'sulky to the last' (284). It is still a true one, and he most truly injured. The details of that last appearance in Sleary's ring, with Tom perched up high 'remote in the subdued light and strangeness of the place', then descending 'bench by bench, until he stood in the sawdust, on the verge of the circle, as far as possible, within its limits, from where his father sat' (283) have a resonance that Richard's conventional death scene lacks. Tom as unsympathetic victim – part murdered innocent, part implicit accomplice – not only represents a symbolic, thematic problem – the Dickens hero's social dilemma – he embodies one as well, a dilemma of response, status and judgment which involves the reader in its insolubility. It is a problem, and a technique, that anticipates such increasingly compromised 'victims' as Arthur Clennam and Sydney Carton and the qualified 'endings' they achieve. For with Tom, Dickens calls into question the passivity thematic necessity forces on Richard Carstone. More specifically, he begins with Tom to explore the role played by the hero in his own self-estrangement. It is an exploration that will deepen the meaning of the search for selfhood still further, taking Dickens, and his hero, into 'dark' realms indeed.

Arthur Clennam, John Harmon and the Problem of Will

With *Bleak House* and *Hard Times* Dickens moves his hero out of the essentially private world of David Copperfield's personal history, linking his emotional plight to the explicitly 'social' cause the earlier novel had not sought to posit. It is a link profoundly critical in its implications, the focus for an emerging vision of a society fundamentally inimical to selfhood. It is, in fact, the turning point in a progress that will ultimately take Bradley Headstone to death at the bottom of Plashwater Weir and John Jasper, perhaps, to the gallows. For Richard Carstone, whose cradle was curtained by Chancery, and Tom Gradgrind, whose imagination was factually strangled in his, experience alienation as a condition of life in a world grown bleak and hard indeed. Casualties of identifiable and, still more significantly, of representative systems – Chancery in the one instance, Gradgrindian 'Fact' in the other – both are 'symbolic' in a way David Copperfield was never designed to be. The externally imposed roles Richard and Tom, unlike David, cannot escape – 'Ward in Jarndyce', 'Mathematical Thomas' – are *social* constructs, threads of the larger web in which they are, so fatally, enmeshed. More profoundly than young Oliver Twist, they have been 'badged and ticketed' (*OT* 3) in infancy, and there is for them no alternative identity available with which to counter their predetermined fates. Oliver, the 'orphan of a workhouse', will prove to be a gentleman's son and so escape his workhouse destiny. But with Richard and Tom the spiritual orphan is, and remains, a social victim in a much deeper sense, born into estrangement much as Esther Summerson is born into 'disgrace', for no other reason than that of having been born at all. Jarndyce's despairing comment to Esther on the 'Wiglomeration' of Chancery – ' "How mankind ever came to be afflicted with Wiglomeration, or for whose sins these young people ever fell into a pit of it, I don't know; so it is" ' (98) – early establishes the inescapability of Richard's unhappy fate, while his unanswered questions echo through the novel. The dissociation characteristic of the adult waif now emerges as the inevitable consequence of social engagement, and the paradox encapsulates the hero's predicament here taking shape. To be at home in the social world is to be, necessarily, estranged from one's true self. So far has the Dickens hero now come from the prospect of achieving the sort of accommodation in which David Copperfield could, at last, find rest.

For Steven Marcus, 'the discovery of the connections between social and personal disorders' constitutes Dickens's 'chief preoccupation' in all his later writing.[1] And it is precisely this connection which the Dickens hero has come to embody, his private malady, the failure of self, now rooted in the public disease. It is a crucial phase in the evolution of the hero's function, and one inseparable from the simultaneous evolution of a fictional world dominated by forces that undermine, or preclude, positive self-definition: false moral values, dehumanizing institutions, sterile social roles. For it is Dickens's *social* vision, what Marcus calls his 'imagination of society and of its influence on individual life',[2] which now determines the course of his hero's progress. And from *Bleak House* onwards, with the emergence of the world of Chancery, the end of that progress will become ever more problematic, the achievement of selfhood increasingly bringing with it, for those who survive the search, a new sort of alienation.

For these later novels no longer offer a prospect of escape in their final pages as an alternative to the narrowing sphere of their action, a refuge to which the hero may, at the last, withdraw. The untroubled stasis which was the reward of experience for so many of Dickens's earliest protagonists – Pickwick, Oliver, Nicholas Nickleby – has ceased to be possible. It is, rather, 'the noisy and the eager, and the arrogant and the forward and the vain' (*LD* 802) who now go on, uninterruptedly and for ever. Plainly, in a world perceived to be as corrupting as it is corrupt, and one that is, moreover, inescapable, the hero can never be at home. At best he will find, as Arthur Clennam and John Harmon do – and Pip and Eugene Wrayburn in their different ways – the means of coexistence. But the 'Voice of Society' (*OMF* 817) will still drone on, to the same deadly and everlasting tune. In the world of the later novels, the marriage which is the traditional hero's no less traditional destiny has lost much of its ritual power of reintegration and comic triumph. 'Society', as it is now defined, will not admit the alternative moral standard the marriage of the Dickens hero increasingly comes to represent, and 'Society' is omnipotent. Complete integration is no longer open to the divided hero, nor, given the world in which he finds himself, could he desire it. That is his predicament. The 'solutions' a Clennam or a Harmon achieve, the more or less subverted 'resolutions' that end their stories, are, finally, deeply qualified; while for others, for Sydney Carton, Bradley Headstone and John Jasper, the hero's journey leads only to death, as it has done already for Richard Carstone and Tom Gradgrind.

It is not, however, the fact of the hero's victimization alone which preoccupies Dickens in these later novels, but, equally, the form that process takes. Even as he establishes, through the experience of Richard and Tom, the critical sequence of social cause and personal effect, Dickens raises the possibility of a far more complex interaction between the two, with the hero as participant in the alienation that results. The suggestion is just present in the history of 'poor Rick''s decline, a faint shadow cast by his fascination with Skimpole that goes no further. The ultimate status of 'the whelp', however, hateful and pathetic by turns, actively vicious where Richard is merely helplessly weak, is more problematic. For Tom introduces a strain of moral ambiguity into the hero's experience as an accompaniment to the growing psychological complexity David and Richard register, a combination that will, ultimately, lead to the emergence of the Dickens hero as 'villain' in the tormented figures of Headstone and Jasper. The imaginative progress that makes this the logical conclusion of the hero's journey is, as Steven Marcus has put it, the progress of Dickens's 'imagination of society', specifically of the contraction of possibilities within society heralded by the ruined lives and early deaths of Richard and Tom. Raising, as he does with Tom, the issue of the hero's complicity in his own emotional plight, Dickens raises too the prospect of a still more profound form of social victimization. For it will increasingly prove the worst symptom of the 'personal disorder' from which the hero suffers, and the most invidious feature of the larger disease in which that disorder is rooted, that he should be brought to collaborate in its effects. And that is precisely what Arthur Clennam and John Harmon do.

A mature businessman of forty, Clennam might appear an anomaly among Dickens's heroes, on grounds of age if nothing else. Yet the lines of his descent, and Harmon's too, could scarcely be clearer. For both display the characteristic traits of the spiritual orphan first typified by David Copperfield: the emotional dislocation, the lack of positive identity, the self-estrangement. There is, indeed, an obvious kinship between Clennam, the 'Nobody', and Harmon, the 'Man from

Somewhere' who so quickly becomes the 'Man from Nowhere'. Each is the survivor of a childhood as miserable as anything David Copperfield, or even Esther Summerson, ever knows. Each is, in Clennam's telling phrase, 'a stranger in the land' (194), and acutely conscious of being so. Each is an exile – Clennam of twenty years standing, Harmon of fourteen – returning to a home which, by his own account, never deserved the name. Each must confront, on his return, a paternal legacy that lies at the heart of the spiritual burden under which he labours. For Clennam, it is the sense of unpaid reparation, symbolized by his father's watch with its cryptic message of 'Do Not Forget.' For Harmon, it is the arranged marriage that is the literal condition of his inheritance, and the spectre it presents of the baleful influence of his father's money reaching out beyond the grave.

But, underlying all of this, there is a deeper kinship still, one that moves the Dickens hero yet further from the prospect of 'home' at journey's end. For both of these orphan figures are, finally, implicated in the estrangement that marks them so conspicuously. Clennam himself constructs the fiction of 'Nobody', while it is Harmon who initiates the whole series of disguises through which he will eventually pass: Julius Handford, John Rokesmith, Boffin's 'Secretary', Riderhood's 'Captain'. In doing so each symbolically embraces non-identity, seeking the suppression their predecessors could not avoid. Where Richard and Tom were deprived of selfhood, Clennam and Harmon, apparently, simply surrender theirs. Yet this too proves an enforced act, a more profound sort of deprivation that has now become the condition of existence in the world of *Little Dorrit* and of *Our Mutual Friend*. Clennam and Harmon are, not less subject to the social forces that destroy Richard and Tom, but more, as their own co-operation in the process of alienation reveals. The ultimately inescapable 'choice' of self-negation the hero is now seen to make – a choice which increasingly takes the form of role-playing or disguise – far from qualifyng the hero's predicament, here emerges as its essence.

For both men, it quickly becomes apparent, learned early what it means to be 'at home' in a society imprisoned in the dehumanizing values it worships, as Mrs Clennam is imprisoned in her emotional paralysis and Old Harmon in the 'Jail' of his own making. Their present 'choice' of non-identity is the lasting proof of that early encounter. Images of young Arthur, lost in the gloom of his parents' loveless house – 'To sit speechless himself in the midst of rigid silence, glancing in dread from the one averted face to the other, had been the peacefullest occupation of his childhood' (34) – and of miserable little John Harmon, shivering amid the dust and ashes of Harmony Jail (90–91), haunt the recollections of their older selves. And they are as much encapsulations of their present plight as memories of past experience. Long before their terms of exile, Clennam and Harmon were already homeless. That is the spiritual legacy they inherit: life in a world that can offer them no place, a world that has no place, as Arthur recognizes, for anything that cannot be 'weighed, measured and priced' (20). It is a patrimony from which they shrink, retreating into self-negation as a means of escaping the burden it imposes.

In *Bleak House* Richard Carstone's inability to resist the attraction of Jarndyce and Jarndyce was clearly the result of Chancery's fatal contagion, his passivity the mark of a self destroyed by society's pervasive moral disease. In Tom Gradgrind, however, submission to an inevitable social influence includes a dimension of active wrong – betrayal, theft and even, indirectly, murder – that suggests not only a more complete moral collapse but also a degree of complicity in the process. And it is the implications of this equivocal strain that Dickens now begins to explore with the figures of Clennam and Harmon. For in them the hero's passivity is, like his self-suppression, allied to renunciation in a way that suggests both voluntary acquiescence and profound psychic compulsion. From *Little Dorrit* onward, the hero's predicament increasingly takes the form of a problem of will. More specifically, it is the problem posed for the hero by life in a society in which, as Lionel Trilling has most famously formulated it, the negation of the will in death has become the preferred alternative to the death-in-life encountered on every side.[3]

That this is now a condition of existence in the world of the Dickens hero, that retreat into emotional suspension, whether as 'Nobody' or the 'ghost' of one's murdered self, is an instinct of self-preservation bred in acquaintance with that world, is made plain in *Our Mutual Friend*. There the drowned 'Rogue' Riderhood becomes, in his resistance to revival, 'like us all, when we swoon – like us all every day of our lives when we wake' (444), for he is 'instinctively unwilling to be restored to the consciousness of this existence, and would be left dormant if he could' (445). It is a formulation that has its place in *Little Dorrit* too, when Arthur, reflecting on his own troubled life, looks at the quiet river and thinks '–who has not thought for a moment, sometimes – that it might be better to flow away monotonously, like the river, and to compound for its insensibility to happiness with its insensibility to pain' (196–197). *Little Dorrit* and *Our Mutual Friend* explicitly enlarge the experiences of their heroes, moving out of the personal frame and particular historical moment to suggest an unchanging condition of social existence, a condition shared in the reading 'present' and not simply contained by the narrative 'past'. Both Clennam and Harmon would, 'like us all', be left dormant if they could, for the pains that confront them on waking are deep indeed. That is the spiritual reality, and the symbolic problem, the Dickens hero has come both to experience and embody.

It is, for the hero, a problem of 'will' in more senses than one, the relation of wills and will assuming in *Little Dorrit* and *Our Mutual Friend* something of the dimensions of a thematic pun. Both Clennam and Harmon are the heirs, by will, of fortunes that oppress, even paralyse, their own will, the reluctant inheritors of money that is tainted by the remembrance of the misery it has bred, misery to which they early succeeded. Arthur's declaration – '"I have seen so little happiness come of money, it has brought within my knowledge so little peace to this house, or to any one belonging to it, that it is worth less to me than to another"' (47) – is echoed by Harmon's similar avowal. He too knows of '"nothing but wretchedness that my father's wealth had ever brought about"' (366–367). Both speak out of their own experience, the grim houses of their childhood being places of business merely, of money making and hoarding, and no home because of it. For them the material inheritance these family businesses generate becomes the symbol of the larger legacy they know, and dread. For with money comes participation in a world that knows no value but money, in which 'traffic in Shares is the one thing to have to do with' (*OMF* 114), and anything less tangible is nothing: 'Have no antecedents, no established character, no cultivation, no ideas, no manners, have Shares' (*OMF* 114). For all the 'sons of Adam' (*LD* 539) this is now the family business.

Both Clennam and Harmon would escape the consequences of this legacy, if they could, by seeking refuge in renunciation – of money, of will, of self. Arthur, in his obsession with his father's past, looks only too eagerly for any excuse – a secret guilt, an unpaid debt, an old injustice – that would allow him to 'lay down all he had, and begin the world anew' (311), free of the moral taint that hangs over his bequest. Richard Carstone began the world, and ended *Bleak House*, by dying, and Clennam and Harmon now seem to wish only to do the same. Arthur's determination to make himself poor in order, as Pancks tells him, ' "to repair a wrong you never committed" ' (567) is, in fact, an extension of his desire to become 'Nobody', to evade through negation the fact of his social (and spiritual) predicament. And, in first adopting the expedient of disguise that seems to come to him so naturally, John Harmon designs a similar end, seeking in knowledge of his appointed wife a reason for abandoning the inheritance of 'misery-making money' he dreads so deeply, and his own participation in its taint: 'For if he had found her unhappy in the prospect of that marriage (through her heart inclining to another man or for any other cause), he would seriously have said: "This is another of the old perverted uses of the misery-making money. I will let it go . . ." ' (379).

What they propose, however, is only another form of the emotional paralysis each has known, and feared, since childhood. That is their dilemma: seeking to escape the contagion they dread, they compulsively further its effects. Ultimately, Clennam will break the cycle by accepting, in the utter desolation of the Marshalsea prison, responsibility for the self he has sought to negate, and for the part he himself has played in his own estrangement. But Harmon, implicated still more deeply in a more complete negation, will prove unable to free himself in this way. For the hero self-discovery is growing steadily more difficult and the prospect at journey's end steadily more limited. In *Little Dorrit* and *Our Mutual Friend* the progress David Copperfield began in dissociation now ends there too, selfhood bringing with it an inevitable social alienation. For the very qualities that enable the Dickens hero to forge a positive identity at last, qualities of love, truth, generosity and compassion, disqualify him for a place in a world that assigns them no value. Early in their acquaintance Daniel Doyce tells Clennam ' "You hold your life on the condition that to the last you shall struggle hard for it" ' (185), and his words have a larger significance. Both Clennam and Harmon are endowed with a moral life, a soul of humanity, that survives in spite of all – and it is much – a soulless society can do. It is this which enables them to forge an alternate set of values in which money is worthless, and this which allows them to achieve, at last, a self-definition that is more than mere selfishness. But it is now the condition of their existence that they will have to struggle, to the last, to preserve those values and that self intact. Increasingly, from *Little Dorrit* onward, the spiritual journey of the Dickens hero ends in recognition of what Georg Lukács has called, more generally, 'The discrepancy between the interiority and the world'.[4] For some Dickens heroes the recognition leads only to death;

for others to an increasingly uneasy coexistence within limitations they cannot escape.

Virtually the first words Arthur Clennam speaks in *Little Dorrit* make plain his claim to the title of Dickens hero. ' "I am",' he confesses to Mr Meagles, ' "such a waif and stray everywhere, that I am liable to be drifted where any current may set" ' (19). And even at this early stage there is a suggestion of acquiescence implicit in his subsequent explanation – ' "I have no will. That is to say," he colored a little, "next to none that I can put into action now" ' (20) – that anticipates the complexities of voluntary/involuntary co-operation soon to be developed. Like Richard Carstone and Tom Gradgrind before him, earlier victims of pervasive social contagions, Clennam is conscious of his own infection, self-aware to the extent of acknowledging the absence of self. And he too traces his present condition directly to a childhood cause, or rather to a sequence of causes that have together made up the 'uniform tendency' (40) of his life. It is a tendency as inevitable in its effects as that which misshaped the lives of Richard and Tom:

'Trained by main force; broken but not bent; heavily ironed with an object on which I was never consulted and which was never mine; shipped away to the other end of the world before I was of age, and exiled there until my father's death there, a year ago; always grinding in a mill I always hated; what is to be expected from *me* in middle-life? Will, purpose, hope? All those lights were extinguished before I could sound the words.'   (20)

The childhood Arthur then proceeds to describe – ' "Austere faces, inexorable discipline, penance in this world and terror in the next – nothing graceful or gentle anywhere, and the void in my cowed heart everywhere" ' (20) – is, as numerous critics have noted, highly reminiscent of Esther Summerson's formative experience. Both have been traumatized by early subjection to a 'stern religion' (20) presided over by two relentless and, it later emerges, similarly wronged women. Like Esther's aunt, Mrs Clennam compensates personal injury with Calvinist ferocity, demanding life-long penance from the child who is the unconscious product of the 'sin' that has injured her. In the obduracy of her creed, 'veiled in gloom and darkness, with lightnings of cursing, vengeance and destruction' (45), she too looks back beyond *Bleak House*, as Esther's aunt had done, to *David Copperfield* and the life-denying 'firmness' of Murdstone theology.

But there is an important difference between Clennam's miserable childhood and that of either of his predecessors in early suffering.

Where the cause of both David's and Esther's divisions remains essentially personal in its implications, the childhood source of Arthur's estrangement is clearly linked to *Little Dorrit*'s largest thematic (that is, 'social') concerns. With Clennam's parents salvation itself has been subdued to the money ethic that dominates the world of the novel, that spiritual inversion that finds expression elsewhere in the 'worship' (539) of Merdle, 'the rich man, who had in a manner revised the New Testament, and already entered into the kingdom of Heaven' (593). Their very religion, as described by the son who has suffered for it, is a matter of barter and sale, ' "a gloomy sacrifice of tastes and sympathies that were never their own, offered up as part of a bargain for the security of their possessions" ' (20), and the transaction is as fraudulent as any in which Merdle engages. Mrs Clennam has 'reversed the order of Creation, and breathed her own breath into a clay image of her Creator' (754), transforming the 'Majesty of Heaven' (48) into a wholesale dealer in damnation. It is the ultimate expression of the spiritual bankruptcy of a commercial society and she is 'only remarkable in this, for the force and emphasis with which she did it. Thousands upon thousands do it, according to their varying manner, every day' (48). The 'social' implications of her conduct could scarcely be clearer.

There is, moreover, an equally explicit connection established at the outset between this pervasive commercial theology and the imprisonment that features so largely in the novel's metaphoric scheme. Arthur's remembrance of the dreary Sundays of his childhood is of being marched to chapel like a military deserter, 'morally handcuffed to another boy' (30). And in that memory his mother features as both jailer and jailed, 'stern of face and unrelenting of heart', forever barricaded behind a Bible 'bound like her construction of it in the hardest, barest, and straitest of boards, with one dinted ornament on the cover like the drag of a chain' (30). The imagery of incarceration and constriction is so insistent as scarcely to require comment, and the implication it carries seems no less plain. Mrs Clennam is enchained in a state of emotional repression of which her 'mystical religion' (45), so hard and bare and strait, like her physical paralysis, is the outward expression. And her son is no less bound than she, in a self that has been imprisoned and all but suffocated by her distorted, and distorting, creed.

Although Clennam's monstrous education does not destroy him outright, as Tom Gradgrind's had done him, the marks it leaves are deep, a legacy of psychic unease 'peculiar as his life and history' (301). Bred in 'meanness and hard dealing . . . coldness and severity' (158), Arthur does retain, perhaps surprisingly, a belief in 'all the gentle and good things his life had been without' (158). No explanation is offered for his ability to do so, his escape from Tom Gradgrind's fate functioning as a parallel to Amy Dorrit's ability to transcend the prison shadows among which she too is born. Both are, in this sense, equally mysteriously 'blessed'. But if this blessing preserves Arthur's 'warm and sympathetic heart' (158) from the worst effects of his mother's frozen fate, it cannot save him from a crippling paralysis of his own. For it is the 'uniform tendency of this man's life' to make him not only 'a dreamer' (40) but a spectator too, unwilling, indeed unable, to participate fully in the world outside the prison of his mother's house. Clennam's characteristic posture throughout the novel is that of gazer – out of windows (31), into fires (157), along rivers (194) and, frequently, down the perspective of his own overshadowed past. It is how Amy Dorrit sees him, a 'grave gentleman' with an 'attentive and enquiring look' (159), a silent watcher of the life around him.

Throughout the later novels Dickens continues to rework the situation of the abandoned and/or unloved child familiar from his earliest fictions. David Copperfield, Esther Summerson, Clennam, Harmon, Pip all experience childhood desolation that recalls the more spectacular 'orphanhood' of Oliver Twist, Smike, Nell and Florence Dombey. Yet, whatever the psychic strains underlying this compulsive repetition – and they have been very extensively canvassed – it is noticeable that Dickens's interest in the later works increasingly shifts away from the circumstances of abandonment, rejection or lovelessness themselves to the adult legacy they leave behind, and the meaning that legacy can be made to carry. The *story* of childhood experience, though thematically crucial, loses much of its structural centrality until, with figures like Clennam and Harmon, it features only as encapsulated memories, 'flashbacks' to a past that is not itself explicitly narrated. What is more, the very fact that these later figures are adult orphans deprives them of the legitimate passivity of their childish predecessors. In them the helplessness which is the child waif's major source of pathos assumes a much more ambiguous significance. Their failure of will and self becomes itself an issue. Clearly placing the condition of orphanhood, whether literal or figurative, within a larger 'social' context, Dickens moves the centre of interest from the childhood suffering of an Arthur Clennam to his adult recuperation, or its lack, and to his own co-operation in the want.

Plainly, what the emotional starvation and religious terrors of his childhood have induced in the adult Arthur is a state of emotional suspension. Able to recognize the 'gentle and good things' of which his spirit has been deprived for so long, he is yet incapable of acting to secure them. For Mrs Clennam, as for Esther Summerson's aunt, the unsuspecting love child she raises is ' "predestined and lost" ', the sins of his erring parents ' "heavy on his head before his entrance into this condemned world" ' (755). Her relentless doctrine early instils a confused sense of guilt into the child's mind, guilt that will later become an obsession: 'There was the dreary Sunday of his childhood, when he sat with his hands before him, scared out of his senses by a horrible tract which commenced business with the poor child by asking him in its title, why he was going to Perdition? – a piece of curiosity that he really in a frock and drawers was not in a condition to satisfy' (30). Clennam is scared out of more than his senses. As with Esther, the result of his early training is compulsive self-estrangement, a profound conviction that the self is unworthy of the very affection it requires to heal its own divisions. There is for Arthur too no legitimate claim for love, no natural right to affection in his self-definition. Nor does he even seek to 'win' it. He has surrendered such things as he surrenders all else, his upbringing having left him the ability to choose no other course. This is how he begins the novel, in a state of emotional surrender of which both his twenty years in exile in the family business, and his decision to abandon the Clennam 'House' on his father's death, are but further expressions. As he explains to his mother on his return to England: ' "I have given up everything in life for the business, and the time came for me to give up that" ' (37).

It is this same compulsion to 'give up' that determines Clennam's response to Pet Meagles and the prospect of romantic, sexual love she embodies. For his refusal to 'allow himself to fall in love with Pet' (190) is prompted by a reticence that cannot conceal a conviction that he is, in fact, unworthy of being loved. To aspire to win Pet becomes for him mere 'weakness' (194), not because he does not value her, but because he cannot value himself, a man with 'nothing in his favour but his honest love and his general wish to do right' (194). Clennam loses no opportunity to denigrate virtues which are plainly only too rare in the world of Circumlocution and Mrs Gowan's 'Society', seizing every chance to diminish himself in a manner that is the legacy of his childhood guilt. In his own eyes, Clennam is 'Nobody' long before he adopts the title. That is what his early experience has made him, and what he is now constrained to make himself. Nor can he envision any future but negation and the greyness of a shadow life: 'he looked at the fire from which the blaze departed, from which the after-glow subsided, in which the ashes turned grey, from which they dropped to dust, and thought, "How soon I too shall pass through such changes and be gone!"' (158).

It is a measure of the increasing complexity of the hero's predicament that he should now be compelled to perpetuate the estrangement that oppresses him and, moreover, should ally himself with characters of ambiguous moral standing in doing so. In *Bleak House*, Dickens just qualified Richard Carstone's status as social victim by suggesting a potential likeness to the social parasite Skimpole. In *Little Dorrit*, he posits a still more suggestive relationship between Arthur Clennam, of the 'disappointed mind' (158), and both Henry Gowan, self-proclaimed 'disappointed man' (391), and Miss Wade, self-revealed 'self-tormentor' (644). Gowan, in fact, first appears in the novel as 'Nobody's Rival' (197), his relation to Pet forging a link between them Clennam himself will later acknowledge: '"Where are we driving, he and I, I wonder on the dark road of life? How will it be with us, and with her, in the obscure distance?"' (310). And there is a deeper connection still. Clennam may explicitly avoid the 'cruel selfishness' that is Gowan's trademark, never holding, as Gowan consistently does, 'that because such a happiness or such a virtue had not come into his little path, or worked well for him, therefore it was not in the great scheme, but was reducible, when found in appearance, to the basest elements' (158). It is, indeed, the one positive impulse he has been able to salvage from his early experience. But if Clennam's mind is too healthy for such 'unwholesome air' (158), he is plainly not immune to other strains of infection. For he too uses his disappointment, not as an instrument of revenge against 'Society' as Gowan does, but as a means of avoiding participation in a life, and a society, he fears and, on a deeper lever still, as a means of punishing himself for being 'disappointed' at all.

It is this last mechanism, moreover, that allies Clennam with Miss Wade. Inverting her characteristic emotional posture, he too is a self-tormentor, driven by a conviction of unworthiness that is the obverse of her distorted pride. The two meet in a shared compulsion to reject the very love they crave. Embracing a self-definition that denies his deepest needs – a vision of himself as a 'very much older man who has done with that part of life' (327) – Clennam, like Miss Wade, condemns himself to perpetuate the estrangement that haunts him. If she seeks out an alter ego in Tattycoram as a means of observing the course of her own malady, 'as one afflicted with a diseased part might curiously watch the dissection and exposition of an analagous case' (26), Arthur too requires a surrogate on whom to displace the love, and pain, he will not allow himself to feel: 'Why should he be vexed or sore at heart? It was not his weakness that he had imagined. It was nobody's within his knowledge . . .' (194). Plainly, there are important differences between Clennam and Miss Wade, as there are between Clennam and Gowan. Yet both stand as embodiments of that psychic darkness in which Clennam's own 'disappointed mind' is born, reminders of the penalties awaiting those who cannot 'rise into the light, seeing it shine on others and hailing it' (158). If Miss Wade is forever locked in a cycle of self-torment, 'devouring her own heart' (638), Clennam too is caught in a psychic prison he cannot help creating, as he is caught in a society he cannot escape, the one because the other. Liberation will ultimately come to him, as it never does to her, but only through recognition of the self-distortion of which he has indeed been guilty. For it is only then that he can 'hail the light' Amy Dorrit sheds.

In the view of at least one critic of *Little Dorrit*, Clennam in fact achieves this recognition early in the novel's course, resolving his psychic no less than his social dilemma at a stroke, simply by entering into partnership in the firm of Daniel Doyce. For Herman Daleski, the 'active and promising career' (259) this partnership offers effectively liberates Arthur from 'that paralysis of will to which he confessed to Meagles', making him a partner 'as it were, to the Doycean virtues'.[5] Such a simple resolution is, however, plainly impossible, the activity Clennam now undertakes being itself essentially impersonal, an exchange of one self-denying role ('Nobody') for another ('Doyce and Clennam'). Indeed, before he can discover his true self as the lover of Amy Dorrit, Arthur will have to lose not only the partrimony that so oppresses him, but also this new business identity, surrendering his 'active' role in the firm on the collapse of the Merdle speculations, as he has compulsively surrendered everything else: ' "I must retain nothing for myself" ' (693). And though Daniel Doyce will return at novel's end to offer Clennam his former role in the firm – ' "Your old place awaits you, and wants you very much" ' (729) – he will not be seen again in his 'business' capacity.

For it is, quite literally, a life of mechanical energy Arthur takes up when he joins Doyce's 'Works', the new partnership relaunching him on the treadmill of Circumlocution, with its endless round of fruitless activity that is itself a parody of 'business' practice: 'form-filling, corresponding, minuting, memorandum-making, signing, counter-signing, counter-counter-signing' (502). 'Mechanically discharging' (268) his own business duties becomes for Clennam a substitute for the emotional fulfilment he has denied himself, a means of 'compounding with insensibility'. 'Doyce and Clennam' and 'Nobody' are, indeed, born at the same moment, and of the same impulse, the decision to approach Doyce taken on the evening of the resolution *not* to fall in love with Pet (Chapter 16). Arthur's 'little counting-house' (259) at the end of Bleeding Heart Yard, where a low gateway leads into 'a maze of shabby streets' (129), cannot be the termination of his spiritual voyage, for it is itself but another unrecognized form of prison, a further emotional arrest. It is in the maze-like streets that he must find his way, and himself.

Clennam has, in fact, already mapped out the course his progress will take. Retracing his past in an early chapter of the novel, he unknowingly foreshadows the means by which he will, at last, secure the only refuge now available to the hero within the society he can never escape, the society that forms the 'prison of this lower world' (741):

To review his life, was like descending a green tree in fruit and flower, and seeing all the branches wither and drop off one by one, as he came down towards them.

'From the unhappy suppression of my youngest days, through the rigid and unloving home that followed them, through my departure, my long exile, my return, my mother's welcome, my intercourse with her since, down to the afternoon of this day with poor Flora,' said Arthur Clennam, 'what have I found!'

His door was softly opened, and these spoken words startled him, and came as if they were an answer:

'Little Dorrit.'   (159)

The words are, of course, the answer, an anticipation of the 'rain from Heaven' (736) that will revive the blighted tree. In the love of Little Dorrit, the 'vanishing-point' of his 'poor story' (714), Clennam discovers the source of himself much as David Copperfield had done in Agnes, the presiding deity of his personal history. For David recognition of his love is identical with acknowledgment of past 'blindness', the diagnosis carrying with it the means of cure. But Arthur's blindness has more complex roots. His is not merely an error of judgment, but a deliberate rejection of the prospect of romantic love, whether with Amy Dorrit or Pet Meagles. It is the inevitable result of an ingrained compulsion to self-negation, a will to the surrender of will, that continues to shape his history.

Clennam marks, indeed, the recurrence of the technical dilemma first raised by Richard Carstone's career of unresisting self-destruction, and one which will become still more pressing in the case of John Harmon. Developing the paralysis of will as a major strain in the experience of his hero, Dickens effectively limits the possibility of endowing that hero with an active role in his own history. The greater his social victimization, the less of a presence he can be, for the more of an absence the novel's thematic economy must make him. This becomes particularly problematic if the hero is to achieve any other 'resolution' to his story than the ultimate absence of death. The problem is contained in *Little Dorrit* by Arthur's growing awareness of his own displacement. Reclaiming his place in the 'poor story' of his life, and accepting responsibility for the self he has sought so compulsively to negate, Arthur achieves a positive – if strictly limited – conclusion to the narrative he had all but abandoned. It is something John Harmon will prove incapable of doing in *Our Mutual Friend*. And his failure is indeed the logical extension of Clennam's own near-defeat. But it is a failure that will have unsettling effects on the narrative structure that attempts to define it.

Clennam's 'resolution', his compromised ending, is dependent on his acceptance of the fact of his own complicity in the self-estrangement that paralyses him. To find himself, to assume his true identity as Amy's '"dearest and best"' (792), he must, in fact, first become 'the pupil of the Marshalsea' (699), exchanging the emotional jail in which he had lived confined for the literal enclosure of the Marshalsea walls, carrying self-surrender to its logical conclusion. For it is only in prison that he learns the secret he, like David Copperfield, has made of his own heart and understands the consequences of the self-betrayal this represents. For so long only too eager to 'give up', Clennam there finds passivity forced upon him, feeling its bonds at precisely the moment when he discovers a will to act (727). In the desolation he himself has sought – '"I would rather", said Clennam, "be taken to the Marshalsea than to any other prison"' (697) – under the tutelage of John Chivery, he is finally brought to recognize the part he has played in constructing that other prison in which he has immured himself. And with recognition comes release. For self-knowledge transforms renunciation from a method of escape to a means of acceptance, offering 'Nobody' a source of positive affirmation at last.

Clennam's insistence on being taken to the Marshalsea (as a penance
for his ruinous involvement of 'Doyce and Clennam' in the Merdle
speculations) represents, then, both the culmination and the turning
point of that career of self-suppression begun in the gloom of a guilt-
ridden childhood. Imprisonment allows Arthur to do what he has
sought so compulsively for so long, to 'make reparation' (695), and he is
utterly determined in embracing the opportunity it affords. To all the
remonstrances of his 'professional advisor' he makes one reply, ' "I
must take the consequences of what I have done" ' (697), and the
avowal possesses a double significance. For, in effecting this final
surrender – ' "My only wish is, that it should be over" ' (697) – Clennam
recovers the 'settled determination of purpose' (695) he had long
accounted lost. It is a paradox, the discovery of will in the determined
abandonment of freedom, that lies at the heart of this hero's progress,
anticipating its final course when the shadow of the prison wall will
seem to fall 'like light' (737) upon him, a reflection of that greater
transformation that once 'changed the crown of thorns into a glory'
(771).

For Arthur the agent of change is, of course, Amy. She completes the
process of acceptance Clennam's retreat to prison has unconsciously
begun. What the knowledge of her love brings to him is a recognition of
his own self-betrayal in rejecting the positive possibilities that love held
out, a rejection understood, and bitterly repented, when he confronts
her in the prison he has now made *his* home:

'If, in the bygone days when this was your home and when this was your
dress, I had understood myself (I speak only of myself) better, and had read
the secrets of my own breast more distinctly; if, through my reserve and self-
mistrust, I had discerned a light that I can see brightly now when it has passed
far away, and my weak footsteps can never overtake it; . . . if I had so used the
opportunity there is no recalling – as I wish I had, Oh I wish I had! . . .' (739)

Clennam has long been obsessed by the secrets surrounding him,
represented in his mind by that 'grim home of his youth' (525) at whose
heart his mother presides 'firmly holding all the secrets of her own and
his father's life, and austerely opposing herself, front to front, to the
great final secret of all life' (526). And the obsession has prevented him
from penetrating, or even recognizing, the secret he has made of
himself, until now, when it seems to him too late. The fact that Arthur
never does learn the 'secret' of his birth would seem to indicate that this
external mystery is ultimately less important than the other secret he

does come to know, that of the emotional suppression in which he himself has participated for so long. (It suggests too the distance between the world Arthur inhabits and that of Nicholas Nickleby and Martin Chuzzlewit, where, by novel's end, no mystery remains unsolved and no secret untold.)

Though Clennam sees his hard-won self-knowledge, the secret he has finally learned to read, as leading only to further reparation, the insight will form the basis of selfhood: 'It inspired him with an inward fortitude, that rose with his love. And how dearly he loved her, now, what words can tell!' (737). There is indeed a new sense of identity, as well as fortitude, that speaks through his insistence to Amy that she must not sacrifice herself, or her fortune, for him: '"you must see me only as I am"' (739). Having accepted responsibility for what he has made himself, '"a broken, bankrupt, sick, dishonoured, prisoner"' (736), Clennam has ceased at last to be 'Nobody', and is now capable of becoming something more. With the loss of the fortune that separates them, he is free to assume the role that represents true self-fulfilment, that of Amy's husband. As he had earlier acknowledged in the depths of his loss, she is the end of his long journey:

Looking back upon his own poor story, she was its vanishing-point. Everything in its perspective led to her innocent figure. He had travelled thousands of miles towards it; previous unquiet hopes and doubts had worked themselves out before it; it was the centre of the interest of his life; it was the termination of everything that was good and pleasant in it; beyond there was nothing but waste, and darkened sky. (714)

That Amy must lose her fortune before Clennam can act upon this realization is a measure of the limitations that increasingly determine the course of the hero's progress. She too stands in clear opposition to the bankrupt values of a Merdle-worshipping society, values that necessarily form the bounds of her world and influence. For her too money is worth less than to another: '"I have no use for money, I have no wish for it. It would be of no value at all to me but for your sake"' (738). What Amy represents is not integration but community in alienation. For the hero selfhood now brings with it the recognition that beyond the small circle of affection and truth he succeeds in drawing round him there *is* 'nothing but waste and darkened sky'. Amid society's perpetual uproar Clennam and his wife will live, inseparable, blessed and essentially alien, an island of spiritual peace in a noisy world.

If *Little Dorrit* appears to conclude in irresolution, with the only prospect at novel's end one of continual repetition, the effect is entirely calculated, indeed inevitable. For this is precisely what the hero's experience reveals: there is no larger 'resolution' possible, only, at best, an acceptance of the selfhood that is now seen to carry social alienation with it. Arthur Clennam's spiritual journey does not end in the perfect domestic joy David Copperfield ultimately attains, nor even in the much more tenuous happiness of Esther Summerson's new Bleak House. In fact, his journey does not end in a house at all, but in the streets, the collapse of his mother's 'grim home' (525) heralding his final release into them: 'They went quietly down into the roaring streets, inseparable and blessed; and as they passed along in sunshine and in shade, the noisy and the eager, and the arrogant and the froward and the vain, fretted, and chafed and made their usual uproar' (802).

In contrast to this, John Harmon's search for selfhood, in so many other respects an extension of the thematic issues raised by Clennam's, will end in a house, and one far removed from the modest cottage where Esther Summerson ultimately finds her compromised 'happy ending'. Journey's end for him is an 'eminently aristocratic family mansion' (209), and a fortune of some hundred thousand pounds to go with it. Both suggest a departure from the symbolic pattern of Clennam's course: a movement from alienation through self-discovery to a new sort of alienation, a self necessarily homeless in a society inimical to it. For many critics of *Our Mutual Friend*, the story of John Harmon's resurrection, with its dependence on Boffin's assumed degradation, belies the deeper meaning of the imaginative vision that shapes the world of the novel. In their view, Harmon and Boffin both are granted the very immunity Dickens's art has been calling into question throughout *Our Mutual Friend*, Harmon's final accession to fortune, like Boffin's revealed deception, defying the logic of the novel's own repeated explorations of money's inevitably corrupting influence. This is in itself something of a misreading, the point being not that money is necessarily contaminating filth, but rather that 'Society' makes it so. As Boffin early declares and subsequently proves, there are some things that are never to be found 'among the dust' (91), and that fact too is plainly integral to the story-weaver's design. What is more, for all the apparent difference between the symbolic value of roaring streets and luxurious mansion, Harmon does represent an intended continuation of the pattern *Bleak House* initiates. In design, if not in execution, his search for selfhood offers a still more sombre exploration of the problem of will foreshadowed in Richard Carstone, and embodied in Arthur Clennam.

For the 'family building' (771) Harmon and the Boffins found at the close of *Our Mutual Friend* is qualified in a way that suggests a further contraction of possibilities for the hero in seach of selfhood. However 'dainty' and 'tastefully beautiful' (778), however reminiscent of Arabian Nights fantasy or the suspended reality of fairy tale, the 'eminently aristocratic family mansion' is, finally, a shelter provided for Harmon, not a home he himself has won. In a profound sense, Arthur Clennam's descent into the open streets represents a resolution that John Harmon's entry into his 'London house' (778) fails to achieve, for the Boffins bestow that house upon him just as they bestow the 'rightful name' (778) that goes with it. Harmon does no more than acquiesce in the transaction, as he had previously acquiesced in the elaborate deception that made it possible. Unlike Clennam, he never overcomes the passivity into which he had retreated, never replaces self-negation with an acceptance of responsibility. There remains, in the end, a 'dark side' (803) to his story that no amount of light shed from the 'true golden gold' (772) of Bella Wilfer's heart can ever disperse, for it is a story Harmon remains incapable of finishing himself. Bella, like Amy, may be its 'vanishing-point', but it is the Boffins, and not Harmon, who know this to be so, and provide the means of proving it: ' " 'Prove it, John!' we says," repeated Mrs Boffin. " 'Prove it and overcome your doubts with triumph, and be happy for the first time in your life, and for the rest of your life' " ' (773). Harmon's happiness is the gift of others, as is his fortune, his identity and his social role. Unlike Clennam, he cannot take part in winning them himself. In this respect, as well as in the fates of Eugene Wrayburn and Bradley Headstone which intersect with his – the one permanently alienated from a society he must reject, the other rotting in the ooze and scum of Plashwater Weir, the only place he can secure – *Our Mutual Friend* is a novel of still more compromised 'endings' than *Little Dorrit*, of limitations Harmon himself literally embodies.

Harmon's spiritual journey, like Clennam's, begins in a return. And he too brings back with him to England, after a long term of exile abroad, a history of suppression whose childhood source is rooted in a larger cause. 'Constrained, reserved, diffident, troubled' (38), Harmon is an orphan in fact as well as spirit, characterized, as Mrs Boffin remarks with more truth than she knows, by ' "a kind of kept-down manner" ' (332). The origins of his unease are not, as with David

Copperfield, the absence of a father. Harmon's predicament is rather that he is ' "only son of a tremendous old rascal who made his money by dust" ' (13), a ' "growling old vagabond" ', in Mortimer Lightwood's words, whose moral being consisted in ' "anathematising his nearest relations and turning them out of doors" ' (13). Both Lightwood and Boffin provide details of the 'blighted childhood' (184) lived in the gloom of Harmony Jail, a childhood of exile and loneliness, of material no less than emotional deprivation, as Boffin reveals:

'I say he was a child of seven year old. He was going away, all alone and forlorn, to that foreign school, and he come into our place, situate up the yard of the present Bower to have a warm at our fire. There was his little scanty travelling clothes upon him. There was his little scanty box outside in the shivering wind, which I was going to carry for him down to the steamboat, as the old man wouldn't hear of allowing a sixpence coach-money.'   (90)

It is an experience of suffering and neglect climaxed when, at age fourteen, the ' "shocked and terrified boy" ' is anathematized by his ' "venerable parent" ' (15) and turned out of doors.

This, in itself, would sufficiently account for the 'nameless cloud' and 'shadow equally indefinable' (193) that overcast the adult Harmon's face and manner. Like Esther Summerson, like Clennam, his formative memories are of privation, rejection and neglect, all rooted in his father's miserly obsessions. But there is more. For Harmon's 'venerable parent' has left a further legacy to his son, one that drives him still deeper into self-suppression, drives him indeed into complicity in his own 'murder' in an attempt to escape this additional patrimony of dust and ashes. Harmon has learned, early and well, the misery money breeds, and the knowledge renders him afraid of himself no less than of his inheritance. Even the anticipated acquisition of fortune seems, in his divided mind, to bring with it something of the taint that blighted his childhood:

'When I came to England, attracted to the country with which I had none but most miserable associations, by the accounts of my fine inheritance that found me abroad, I came back shrinking from my father's money, shrinking from my father's memory, mistrustful of being forced on a mercenary wife, mistrustful of my father's intention in thrusting that marriage on me, mistrustful that I was already growing avaricious . . . I came back, timid, divided in my mind, afraid of myself and everybody here, knowing of nothing but wretchedness that my father's wealth had ever brought about.' (366–367)

What Harmon fears, the contagion of his father's money, is

specifically represented in his eyes by acceptance of Bella Wilfer as wife, the one condition of his father's will. With a ' "moral timidity" ' (370) he himself dates from childhood strong upon him, the act becomes doubly symbolic, and doubly revolting. It is a transaction that would make him buyer and seller both, prostituting himself in a mercenary marriage to gain a fortune, buying with that fortune a wife who had done the same, utterly degraded in both capacities. And he is conscious of its bitter significance, of the inescapable repetition it represents: ' "What a use for the money, and how worthy of its old misuses!" ' (372). This is Harmon's predicament, and its larger implications seem clear: his ' "fine inheritance" ' carries with it an inevitable condemnation to perpetuate ' "the fate that seemed to have fallen on my father's riches – the fate that they should lead to nothing but evil" ' (370). His father's memory and his father's money are inextricably linked for Harmon. Claiming his identity as his father's son means a return to imprisonment in Harmony Jail, to spiritual death in a house desolated by worship of money, 'bare of paint, bare of paper on the walls, bare of furniture, bare of experience of human life' (183). This now is the paternal inheritance of all the 'sons of Adam'.

Harmon's response to this dilemma, and to the larger social predicament it represents, is to seek refuge, as Clennam had done, in renunciation and disguise. As revealed in a protracted session of self-communion (Book II, Chapter 13 'A Solo and a Duett'), his intention on returning to England ' "was to be lost" ' (367) for sufficient time to encounter, unrecognized, the wife his father had willed him. Had she proved unhappy in her appointed fortune, he would have renounced the 'misery-making money' conditional on their marriage and so escaped the fate he dreads, that of perpetuating the money's 'old perverted uses' (379), of becoming, in fact, like his own ' "unhappy, self-tormenting father" ' (787). It is a design born out of the 'uneasiness of mind' (367), the desperation and distrust, his self-described 'wretched childhood' (379) has engendered, a product of that psychic legacy that has become the source of his own self-torment. For it is distrust of himself, no less than of his father's wealth, that is demanding expression in this literal self-denial.

The actual plan, however, is vague and, as recounted by Harmon himself, more than a little improbable: ' "So the plot was made out of our getting common sailor's dresses . . . and throwing ourselves in Bella Wilfer's neighbourhood, and trying to put ourselves in her way, and doing whatever chance might favour on the spot, and seeing what came of it"' (367). And it is here that one becomes acutely conscious of a disparity between thematic design and imaginative execution that will increasingly undermine Harmon's story. It is a disparity most tellingly revealed in the lengthy 'solo' he executes, carefully expounding his psychic dilemma apparently for his own special benefit – and incidentally clarifying the mystery of his identity at precisely the moment when it is most necessary to do so. This technical failure is symptomatic of a more general inability to find an appropriate or convincing mode for Harmon, a means of bringing his thematically resonant experience to life. No matter how self-divided this 'living-dead man' (373), no matter how central the meaning of his mystery, his inclination to 'think in explanatory prose for seven or so pages' cannot but strain narrative licence – and credulity – to the breaking point, as a recent editor of the novel has very reasonably pointed out.[6]

Some critics of *Our Mutual Friend*, and of the other novels of Dickens's last decade, both in their own day and since, have viewed them largely in the light of the 'sensation' fiction so popular in the 1860s. And this does suggest one possible means of approaching the problem posed by Harmon and his 'plot'. The 'sensation' form, exemplified by such best-selling titles as *East Lynne* and *Lady Audley's Secret*, relied for its interest on secret guilt and domestic intrigue, bringing violence out of the safely distanced Gothic castle or underworld den and into the 'respectable' English home. With their elaborate machinery of mystery, coincidence and revelation, they placed a premium on plotting in both senses of the term, with an accompanying tendency to subordinate character to situation, larger meaning to local effect. John Harmon, with his secret return from the dead – a favourite 'sensation' device – his assorted disguises and mysteriously murdered double, could certainly qualify as a 'sensation' hero. His story bears, in fact, a certain resemblance to the disguised heroine's in *East Lynne*. And the example of this highly successful mode might explain something of his undeniably under-realized character. But the formula provided by Mary Elizabeth Braddon, author of *Lady Audley's Secret*, for the 'right-down sensational' style could apply equally well to any number of Dickens's novels, including those written well before the 'sensation' vogue. Braddon's list includes 'floppings at the end of chapters, and bits of paper hidden in secret drawers, bank-notes and title-deeds under the carpet, and a part of the body putrefying in the coal scuttle'.[7] Ignoring for a moment the very complicated plots of *Bleak House* and *Little Dorrit*, with their secret documents, suppressed wills and long-concealed family crimes – pure 'sensation' material – one might recall the very high body count of *Martin Chuzzlewit*, or even the macabre inset tales of *The Pickwick Papers*. 'Sensation' plotting, and all its accompaniments of violence, mystery, detection and extreme characterization, is indeed a constant of Dickens's fiction from the outset. There is nothing new, or necessarily limiting, about its presence in the later work, where it is often put to highly sophisticated technical use. It is precisely the 'sensation' apparatus of violence, mystery and detection which provides the narrative structure of *Bleak House*, the formal expression of its thematic principles of interconnection and entrapment. And the 'sensational' origins of Pip's great expectations play a similar role in his narrative.

The problem in *Our Mutual Friend* seems to lie less in the presence of such materials than in the thematic preoccupations they are intended to serve and the structure such preoccupations impose. The trouble stems particularly from the complete suspension of selfhood Harmon is plainly intended to embody. For it is difficult, perhaps impossible, to design an action that will convincingly enact *absence*, and that is what Harmon's story attempts to project. Dickens comes very close in Harmon's chosen existence as the 'living-dead man', but the situation never loses the sense of mechanical design, or Harmon the impress of the thematic programme. Other divided heroes in the later novels, figures whose self-estrangement includes a dimension of *active* wrong-doing – whether directed against themselves or others – prove much less problematic. It is almost as if the utter depletion of energy this hero is meant to experience carries with it an imaginative depletion too. Certainly, one can never lose sight of the gap which exists between the character as he develops in the novel and the intended design informing his history.

Having said which, however, there is no doubt the design itself is revealing, if essentially unrealized, carrying the implications of Arthur Clennam's inevitable passivity to their logical conclusion. And there are moments when its resonance is undeniable: Harmon looking into the churchyard and finding there his rightful place (366); the 'Man From Nowhere' revisiting his desolate home and hearing the story of his own unhappy past (189); the 'living-dead man' carefully preserving the placard proclaiming his death (451). For Harmon the surrender of identity, the wish to be 'lost' which is at the heart of his 'plot' in more senses than one, is as much the inescapable result of his estrangement as Clennam's 'choice' of the role of 'Nobody'. In fact, as the highly complicated series of events stemming from this initial suppression unfolds, the element of choice disappears completely. When the body of the murdered George Radfoot is recovered from the river and identified as Harmon's own – this as a consequence of Radfoot's murderous designs upon him – Harmon is instinctively drawn to acquiesce in this ultimate negation, 'confusedly accept[ing] the aid that fell upon him' (379). And as he does so he discovers his identity is no longer his to claim:

> 'Next day while I hesitated, and next day while I hesitated, it seemed as if the whole country were determined to have me dead. The Inquest declared me dead, the Government proclaimed me dead: I could not listen at my fireside for five minutes to the outer noises, but it was borne into my ears that I was dead.'   (371)

As Harmon recounts the circumstances leading to it, his 'death' is unwittingly revealed to be as much suicide as murder, a willed abandonment of will that is the culmination of a lifetime of emotional suppression. For his own words seem designed to attest, however improbably, that he is lost to himself no less than to the outside world that so insistently proclaims his demise. His extraordinary 'solo' owes much of its awkwardness to the fact that it is an elaborate profession of negation: ' "This is still correct? Still correct, with the exception that I cannot possibly express it to myself without using the word I. But it was not I. There was no such thing as I within my knowledge" ' (369). And this is the essence of his predicament. There is no such thing as 'I' within his self-definition. For Harmon, thrown into the river, drugged and almost insensible, oblivion has become the only course, a fate in which the very world around him appears to conspire, as he does himself: ' "Looking over the black water, I saw the lights racing past me on the two banks of the river, as if they were eager to be gone and leave me dying in the dark" ' (370).

Some deeper instinct of self-preservation does survive in him, as it survived in the warm heart of Arthur Clennam, in spite of his freezing childhood. But it proves significantly limited in its redemptive powers, sufficient now only to make the one identification needed and no more: ' "This is John Harmon drowning. John Harmon, struggle for your life. John Harmon, call on Heaven and save yourself" ' (370). Even here there is no 'I'. Though he can just pull 'John Harmon' from the water, Harmon cannot, in fact, save himself. The struggle which is the condition of existence for Clennam is now beyond him. When he emerges from the river, it is to life as the 'living-dead man' (373), to continued renunciation as the 'ghost' of his true self. Like Clennam, he embraces negation, '"I am nobody . . . and not likely to be known"' (95), envisioning no other acceptable alternative. For Harmon can find no reason to 'come to life' (372), the woman whose love could resurrect him having proved that she cares for nothing but the fortune the dead man would bring back with him from the grave (372). On the night of his long self-communion, in fact, after reenacting the events that first brought him to it, Harmon embraces once more his initial resolution. It is all to be given up: 'It was all over now. No ghost should trouble Mr. and Mrs. Boffin's peace: invisible and voiceless, the ghost should look on a while longer at the state of existence out of which it had departed and then should for ever cease to haunt the scenes in which it had no place' (379).

What Harmon proposes for himself is a life of complete suppression, an existence more shadowy even than Clennam's, rendering himself 'invisible and voiceless'. It is a negation symbolized by Harmon's presence at the deathbed of his small namesake Johnny, a witness to John Harmon's second 'death', and by his subsequent rejection of his own unlucky name: '"The name has always been unfortunate. It has now this new unfortunate association connected with it. The name has died out. Why revive it?"' (333). He is, it would seem, speaking to himself here as much as to Mrs Boffin. Unlike Clennam, Harmon will not, cannot, participate in his own revival. The identity Arthur wins so painfully, through acceptance of responsibility for the self he had sought to deny for so long, must be bestowed upon Harmon by means of the Boffins' 'pious fraud' (771), for he is incapable of claiming it himself. So deep are the divisions from which he suffers, so ingrained the compulsion of denial, that recognition and affirmation must come entirely from external sources – '"I know you now! You're John!"' (770) – and so too must the means of acceptance. It is the Boffins' 'little scheme' (775), rather than any new-found strength in Harmon, that ultimately provides the basis of selfhood. For it is only their vindication of Bella's worth that enables him to abandon self-suppression and assume his true identity at last, to come back to life by claiming Bella, substituting the terms of Johnny's will – '"A kiss for the boofer lady"' (330) – for those of his father's.

Given the implications of Harmon's earlier embrace of passivity, his declaration at novel's end, '"I owe everything I possess to the disinterestedness, uprightness, tenderness, goodness . . . of Mr. and Mrs. Boffin"' (788), assumes a particular significance. For what this utter reliance on others would suggest is a necessity of being endowed with a selfhood he cannot win. With Harmon, in other words, the hero's limited possibility of a purely personal integration is designed to appear still more qualified. Clennam required the assistance of Meagles and Doyce to free him from his physical prison, though it was Arthur himself, with Amy's love, who had finally broken the spiritual bonds that had so long confined him. But for this hero, who does not merely make himself 'Nobody', but actually connives at his own 'murder', such self-liberation would no longer seem possible. Harmon's continued resistance to being brought back to life, recounted by Mrs Boffin in his own words – ' "I can't afford to be rich yet" ' (774) – speaks indeed of a fear of social involvement that not all the evidence of Bella's love, proved several times over, and the Boffins' fidelity has been able to overcome.

For within the world of *Our Mutual Friend*, for all the fairy-tale trappings of John and Bella's homecoming, there remains serious doubt whether anyone can ever 'afford to be rich'. It is a doubt Bella expresses, and one Harmon can only answer with a hope that is plainly less than certain:

'But all people are not the worse for riches, my own.'
'Most people?' Bella musingly suggested with raised eyebrows.
'Nor even most people, it may be hoped.'   (680)

Some people, as the Boffins prove, may not be the worse for exposure to what Harmon has so often called 'misery-making money'. But his own experience has shown just how much misery it can work, and how rare such exceptions are. And Harmon is, finally, unable to be rich on his own initiative. It is Boffin who must make him so, incidentally accomplishing the renunciation he himself had sought, as Harmon goes on to reveal: ' "The conditions that he made with me, before parting with the secret of the Dutch bottle, were, that I should take the fortune, and that he should take his Mound and no more" ' (788).

Harmon receives his identity, then, as he receives his fortune, as a gift from the one man who has proved immune to that fortune's taint. And it is, significantly, only an external pressure, the unexpected recognition by Lightwood, that finally forces him to acknowledge his true self. The resistance to being brought back to life is not so much abandoned as overcome by circumstances. It is entirely appropriate that Harmon should be, however briefly, under threat of arrest for his own 'murder' as a result of Lightwood's recognition. There can be no doubt that he is deeply implicated. Harmon never achieves the personal solution to the problem of will Clennam's acceptance of responsibility represents. Journey's end is for him, not the roaring streets, but a barricade against them of another's providing. It is a still more restricted prospect in every sense, and as central to the meaning of *Our Mutual Friend* – in design if nothing else – as the intersecting fates of Wrayburn and Headstone will prove. All three are, indeed, extensions of the pattern that shaped Clennam's course. For Stephen Gill, a recent editor of the novel, the 'Harmon Plot' is simply the 'albatross around Dickens's neck', a 'disguise story, which has, in itself, no interest at all'.[8] And he is by no means alone in his judgment. But this is to dismiss entirely the potential implications of a symbolic problem of will designed to remain essentially problematic; of a spiritual journey that can never end but must rather be brought to a close; of a history that remains, in its deepest sense, endless.

ぉ5と

Will and Gentility: *Great Expectations* and the Problem of the Gentleman

For Arthur Clennam and John Harmon the surrender of will is an inevitable consequence of the social engagement that lies at the heart of the Dickens hero's predicament. Their complicity in self-suppression, at once involuntary and self-willed, is a measure of the distance that hero has travelled from David Copperfield's unqualified rejection of the externally imposed role of 'labouring hind' and the self-betrayal it represented. Where David acted to defend his social birthright, Clennam and Harmon embrace passivity in an attempt to escape theirs. For him the paternal legacy was gentlemanly status – 'David Copperfield the Younger, of Blunderstone Rookery' – an identity as well as a heritage. For them it is implication in a society whose deadening influence they have known since childhood. Both retreat from the spectre of this larger 'social' inheritance into self-denying indentities they themselves create. Cooperating in their own suppression, they do no more than substitute one form of emotional sterility for another, fostering the very paralysis they fear. Like Clennam and Harmon, Pip too is made a participant in his own self-estrangement, but through acceptance rather than rejection of the spiritual bankruptcy society propagates. The agency of his co-option is nothing less than that most cherished Victorian social ideal, identified by a recent commentator as one of the most important of Victorian notions,[1] the idea of the gentleman. Inverting David Copperfield's experience still further, coupling it with a passivity that now brings complicity in self-division with it, Dickens creates in *Great Expectations* an ironic revision of the Victorian self-help fable, exposing the falsities upon which it rests. For David genteel status had provided the only means of self-definition for much of his life journey. Amid psychic and emotional dislocation, it formed the foundation of a conviction of what he was and should be – not 'labouring hind' but gentleman's son – in this sense if in no other. But for Pip gentility is itself the source of alienation, whether despairingly wished for or uneasily possessed in the false shape society venerates, or painfully earned at last in the true form it does not recognize. That, indeed, is the essence of *Great Expectations'* social indictment. At novel's end Pip is left an exile from a world that affords no status to a 'gentle Christian man' (439), and no home to a gentleman conscious of its failure.

Robin Gilmour, writing in *The Idea of the Gentleman in the Victorian Novel*, has demonstrated very clearly the importance of Pip's 'historical situation' to the implications of the spiritual progress he undergoes. For him Pip's predicament is, first and foremost, representative of a social class in transition. More specifically, it represents the experience of the Victorian middle class in its emergence from its own primitive, eighteenth-century origins.[2] And this gives *Great Expectations* a special status in his eyes, separating it from the great social satires *Bleak House*, *Little Dorrit* and *Our Mutual Friend*. For Gilmour, the novel is unique among Dickens's fiction, concerning itself less with specific social abuses (Chancery, Circumlocution) than the dilemma of Victorian civilization itself. Behind Pip's personal history stands the social experience of the first generation of the Victorian age as it struggles towards maturity.[3] Illuminating as this reading is, however, and important the insights it offers, it scarcely does justice to the still larger concerns informing 'the great social satires'. As previous chapters have argued, the real subject of these novels is nothing less than the social experience of which the specific series of related abuses they address have become representative. The fate of Richard Carstone, Arthur Clennam and John Harmon – of the Dickens hero generally – increasingly emerges as the inevitable condition of social existence, their life journeys functioning as a type of the individual's inescapable experience in an increasingly inhuman and alienating world. Gilmour's elucidation of the social/historical context of *Great Expectations*, his relation of Pip's particular aspirations to the concerns of a culture emerging with difficulty from the shadow of its own violent past, is utterly convincing.[4] Yet his inevitable emphasis of the time-specific nature of Pip's experience – the repeated insistence on dating and chronology – seems to discount, perhaps unintentionally, a further range of implication that experience carries.

For the predominance within *Great Expectations'* symbolic landscape of elemental imagery – fire (Joe's forge, the blaze that consumes Miss Havisham); water (the Thames); earth (the marshes of Pip's childhood home); air (the mists rising from the marshes, the vapour of the lime kiln into which Pip himself is so nearly dissolved) – suggests a broader context still for Pip's life journey, one that encompasses without difficulty the specific 'historical situation'. Like Dickens's earlier retrospective first-person narrative, Pip's story is both time-bound and timeless, a representative Victorian case study *and* a universal history of the losses, errors, regrets and compromises that now inevitably accompany the progress towards selfhood in the world of Dickens's 'social' novels. It is Magwitch who, during the course of his river journey with Pip, makes explicit this imaginative strain which runs through the novel like the river itself: '"I was thinking through my smoke just then, that we can no more see to the bottom of the next few hours, than we can see to the bottom of this river what I catches hold of. Nor we can't no more hold their tide than I can hold this. And it's run through my fingers and gone, you see!"' (415). Pip's written memory, like David Copperfield's before him, is as much concerned with 'the deep of Time' (*DC* 635), and its eternal tides of change and loss, as with a particular historical moment. For Pip self-discovery will bring not only a recognition of the hollowness of society's gentlemanly ideal, and of his own self-betrayal in subscribing to it, but, equally, a knowledge of the truth Magwitch plainly has learned, a sense of the impossibility of bending the past 'out of its eternal shape' (432). And the lessons are inseparable. For the past errors Pip must come to acknowledge, errors which, being past, can never be undone but only redeemed, are themselves the fruits of his willing participation in a society which excuses the gentleman criminal Compeyson while hunting the wretched 'warmint' he so ruthlessly exploits, and society itself has made.

Pip's progress from rags to riches, country to city, innocence to experience, plainly has archetypal patterns underlying it. They are patterns familiar from the *Bildungsroman* form yet carrying with them a specific historical relevance for an age of upward mobility and hardening class distinctions, the two symbolic dimensions continually interacting within the narrative Pip supplies. For if the world in which Pip wakes to consciousness is, as Robin Gilmour amply demonstrates, both as carefully dated as *Vanity Fair*, and in much the same period,[5] it is also dateless, as old as the Fall whose image lies behind the closing lines of *Great Expectations*, with their echoes, so frequently noted, of *Paradise Lost*. In this larger sense, Pip's world represents the ruined garden in which every man must, with more or less of pain, make his way. He comes to self-awareness as 'the small bundle of shivers growing afraid of it all' (1) in an encounter with violence, crime and guilt (and cruelty and injustice) that appear as elemental as the earth, air, fire and water that dominate the landscape of the child's experience. In his terrified eyes, Magwitch springs up inexplicably from the earth itself – 'A man started up from among the graves at the side of the church porch' – an extension, and victim, of the natural world – 'a man who had been soaked with water, and smothered in mud, and lamed by stones, and cut by flints, and stung by nettles, and torn by briars' (2). And similar language will, a little later, establish 'Old Orlick''s no less primal associations: 'There started up from the gate, or from the rushes, or from the ooze (which was quite in his stagnant way), Old Orlick' (124). An emblem of the inexplicable, irruptive evil that has its own inevitable place in the ruined garden, Orlick is old indeed, with a pedigree that extends, as Pip recognizes, back to 'Cain or the Wandering Jew' (105). As a balance to this, Magwitch's Christian name is Abel – an equally fitting title for a figure who increasingly becomes the novel's preeminent social victim. The 'taint of prison and crime' (294) which encompasses Pip, and which he first encounters 'out on our lonely marshes' (294) on Christmas Eve, is his inescapable legacy, as the double burden of money and guilt was Clennam's, and money and self-distrust Harmon's. The first bequest of his self-described 'second father' (304), it is the condition of existence in the world in which Pip must, in a double sense, find himself.

And it is precisely the interweaving of this aspect of Pip's experience with his more explicitly 'social' – in the historically specific sense – aspirations that gives Dickens's ironic fable for his times its timeless imaginative power. The linking of the two forms is, indeed, the basis of the novel's thematic structure. For Pip's 'gentility', understood in society's terms of money and the genteel appurtenances money can buy – education, fine clothing, appropriate accomplishments – represents a means of repudiating the fellowship in error and guilt his early encounter with 'his' convict had brought. It is a way of rising above the 'guiltily coarse and common' experience of being 'on secret terms of conspiracy with convicts' (73), of separating himself from implication in the 'common' human condition. To be a gentleman, for Pip, is to adopt without question society's dictum that 'gentlemen' have nothing to do with convicts, in any sense. True gentility, however – moral sensitivity, compassion, gentleness of spirit – comes when Pip accepts the connection, finding in the experience of his own 'sore mistakes' (377) the basis of fellowship with 'his' convict. It comes when he not only recognizes in Magwitch, as Joe had done long ago, a 'poor miserable fellow-creature' (36), but when he can go further still and see in him a better man than he has been. In the end, the 'warmint' does make a gentleman out of 'the small bundle of shivers', for he makes him a truly gentle man. And in doing so he renders him forever homeless in a world that has no value for either. That too is part of Pip's legacy.

Pip makes his journey from alienation through self-discovery to a new sort of alienation – the journey of the Dickens hero – in a world where innocence no longer enjoys the almost miraculous immunity that hedges it about in *David Copperfield*. (It is, in David's words, 'the mercy of God' that prevents him becoming, in the Murdstone and Grinby days, 'a little robber or a little vagabond' (*DC* 139).) David's experience leaves him deeply, divisively ashamed of his premature 'knowing'-ness, of his precocious familiarity with 'some of the meanest phases' of London life and London streets (*DC* 196). But for Pip knowledge of a much more profound and inescapable sort, of social cruelty, injustice and guilt, is inseparable from his first coming to consciousness of both the self and the world, and of the disjunction between the two. The compensatory life of the imagination into which David can retreat, shielding his romantic innocence from 'such strange experiences and sordid things' (*DC* 145), becomes in Pip a 'secrecy of . . . terror' (12) which imbues even the inanimate world about him with an accusatory and hostile life. Yet his 'fancy' is a 'pitying young fancy' too, as David's often is not, and can see reflected in the paleness of a winter afternoon something of his own instinctive sympathy for his 'fugitive friend on the marshes' (29).

Socially, morally, imaginatively, the world of Pip's experience is more complex, more compromised, more essentially ambiguous, than the one David inhabits. Like Clennam and Harmon, he is made forcibly aware of its dark shadows (as embodied in 'his' convict) in childhood, and the knowledge shapes irreversibly his subsequent development. He too has never known a home in David Copperfield's sense of the word, his earliest memories, like Clennam's and Harmon's, dominated rather by the experience of inadequate refuge and emotional dearth. Pip's very lament for his later lost faith in the domestic rites of his sister's house reveals the insufficiency, the limited and limiting nature of the shelter it provided:

Home had never been a very pleasant place to me, because of my sister's temper. But, Joe had sanctified it, and I had believed in it. I had believed in the best parlour as a most elegant saloon: I had believed in the front door, as a mysterious portal of the Temple of State whose solemn opening was attended with a sacrifice of roast fowls; I had believed in the forge as the glowing road to manhood and independence. Within a single year all this was changed. Now, it was all coarse and common, and I would not have had Miss Havisham and Estella see it on any account.   (100)

Beneath the child's ingenuous vision of domestic splendour, as the adult Pip recounts it, another reality can be glimpsed. Although the Gargery household is materially prosperous – there is no lack of food or shelter, however grudgingly doled out – Pip yet experiences a continued starvation. He is deprived of the intellectual food he plainly requires. Once his curiosity and ambition are aroused by a glimpse of a larger life, the deprivation makes his 'home' into a place of frustration and constraint. And the agency that works the change is itself represented in the other dominant non-home of Pip's early years. If Satis House awakens in Pip aspirations to a life beyond the narrow existence he knows 'at home', the spiritual nourishment it supplies is far from wholesome. Although his sister's house offers him little intellectual sustenance, Pip's physical needs are met there, in spite of the pins and needles from Mrs Joe's impregnable apron front which occasionally mingle with the bread and butter. Satis House, in contrast, feeding Pip's imagination with its weird and morbid glamour, is yet a house fallen away from all natural nurturing functions, a house defined in terms of lack rather than domestic plenitude, in which there are 'no pigeons in the dove-cot, no horses in the stable, no pigs in the sty, no malt in the storehouse, no smells of grain and beer in the copper or the vat' (58)

Both houses are, in effect, compromised refuges, emblems of the increasingly complex moral world in which Pip must make his way. They have their human counterparts in the three inadequate or compromised father figures – Joe, Jaggers, Magwitch – who preside over the 'stages' of his progress. There is an almost ritual formality to their succession. The first stage of Pip's expectations closes with the transfer of the young apprentice from his 'master' Joe to his 'guardian' Jaggers; the second with the reappearance of his 'benefactor' Magwitch and the end, in its turn, of Jaggers's tenure. Unlike John Harmon, blighted by the shadow of the deceased warder of Harmony Jail and rescued by Boffin at novel's end, Pip possesses a surrogate 'good' father from the beginning of his life journey, but a father limited by his own acknowledged incapacities. From childhood Pip must 'overlook short-comings' (45): Joe cannot protect him from the domestic tyranny of Mrs Joe or the persecutions of Pumblechook. Equally importantly, he holds no clue to the moral and emotional labyrinth into which Pip is so helplessly drawn. He too is incapable of understanding why the child's first encounter with the 'incomprehensible' (61) world of Satis House should result in 'stunning and outdacious' (66) lies, or in misery and self-disgust. The simple moral guidance he can offer fails to meet the 'metaphysics' (65) of Pip's need: '"If you can't get to be oncommon through going straight, you'll never get to do it through going crooked. So don't tell no more on 'em [lies] Pip, and live well and die happy"' (66). Joe's response to the actual spectacle of Miss Havisham and Satis House reveals his own vulnerability. He is first confounded – 'When we stood in the daylight alone again, Joe backed up against a wall, and said to me, "Astonishing!" And there he remained so long, saying "Astonishing" at intervals, so often, that I began to think his senses were never coming back' (96) – and is then led into some very efficient, if less 'outdacious', fiction making of his own.

Though Joe undoubtedly represents a moral touchstone in *Great Expectations*, the one type of gentlemanliness, in Gilmour's estimation, Dickens will at the end unequivocally affirm,[6] his ability to 'live well and die happy' is clearly a function of his distinctive, childlike simplicity and of the essentially limited nature of the world he is content to inhabit. It is a truth Joe himself recognizes: '"I'm wrong out of the forge, the kitchen, or off th' meshes"' (212) he tells Pip, and in this too he is 'simply right' (443). This 'gentle Christian man' has no place in the confused, and confusing, world that lies beyond the forge, the kitchen and the marshes. But for Pip the price of selfhood is precisely participation and, ultimately, a recognition that if he too has no place in society's larger world he yet cannot return to the 'home' Joe's simple innocence circumscribes. The little world of the forge does not constitute an alternative to the larger world beyond. At most it offers a coexistence made possible by an acceptance of limits Pip must challenge. For all his simplicity Joe possesses a clear sense of his own inadequacies, and of the part they have inevitably played in making Pip what he is: '"Supposing ever you kep any little matter to yourself when you was a little child, you kep it mostly because you know'd as J. Gargery's power to keep you and Tickler in sunders, were not fully equal to his inclinations"' (444). The world of the forge is a world of voluntary acceptance of the limitations that serve to keep Joe 'simply right', an acknowledgment of the good man's essential marginality, and helplessness, in the complex world where Pip must find his way.

For Pip, then, there is no all-sufficient father to guide him, untainted, through the moral mists that close about him. That is an essential part of his predicament. Nor are Jaggers and Magwitch – his 'bad' fathers as Joe is his 'good' – simply 'false' preceptors luring the fatherless boy – who is by no means reluctant to go – from his 'true' spiritual parent. Jaggers, as the presiding deity of Little Britain, is fully implicated in its darkest taints, a man reputed to be 'more in the secrets' (255) of Newgate than any in London, and one who has grown powerful upon them. But he knows other secrets as well, knows, like Magwitch, the inevitable cycle of injustice and crime, the inescapable 'atmosphere of evil' (391), that lurks beneath the surface of Great Britain's social façade. It is a knowledge he will share with Pip, as he shares the awareness of the price of his own complicity – ' "You know what I am, don't you?" ' (205) – a complicity he can never wash away. And the criminal Magwitch, the most compromised of Pip's spiritual fathers, has still more profound lessons to teach. From the ultimately limited fellowship of Joe – 'I always treated him', Pip records, 'as a larger species of child, and as no more than my equal' (7) – through the guardianship of Jaggers, to the discovery of his convict benefactor, Pip's progress towards selfhood is inseparable from an increasing identification with the 'hunted, wounded, shackled creature' (423) who has become by novel's end the type of the social outcast. And the resulting alienation proves an inheritance unlike his 'expectations', for it can never be lost.

Pip himself begins his history on the 'memorable raw afternoon towards evening' (1) of his first meeting with this 'terrible patron' (315). It is the moment of his 'first most vivid and broad impression of the identity of things' (1), an impression inseparable from an awareness of the solitude and lack of identity which alone define the 'small bundle of shivers' (1) that is Pip. For many critics of the novel, it is the 'memorable' encounter following so closely upon this first awakening which initiates Pip into an inevitable self-estrangement, establishing the symbolic pattern of his narrative just as it prepares its central mystery. But Pip's self-division is antecedent even to the meeting on the marshes, a meeting which becomes indeed the more insistently 'memorable' because of it. As his own words attest, his is a childhood shaped by a twin consciousness of guilt and injustice that dates, quite literally, from birth, the interaction of the two conditioning his self-perception, or rather its lack. 'As to me,' Pip records, 'I think my sister must have had a general idea that I was a young offender whom an Accoucheur Policeman had taken up (on my birthday) and delivered over to her, to be dealt with according to the outraged majesty of the law' (20).

In the eyes of this 'all-powerful' (12) sister, Pip's guilt is, like original sin, identical with his birth: 'I was always treated as if I had insisted on being born, in opposition to the dictates of reason, religion, and morality, and against the dissuading arguments of my best friends' (20). Her hostility is inexplicable, and inescapable, a condition of existence in the 'little world' (57) of his childhood. In fact, in his sister's 'fearful catalogue', Pip's existence itself constitutes a perpetual offense, her long list of his crimes culminating with 'all the times she had wished me in my grave, and I had contumaciously refused to go there' (24). Joe, the gentle Christian man, suffers the little child as his wife emphatically does not: ' "God bless the poor little child," I said to your sister, "there's room for *him* at the forge" ' (44). But this same 'tender simplicity' makes him choose not to compete for status in the domestic world she rules, a world where Joe holds indeed no 'station and influence' (23) at all. Pip never associates him with any of the 'housekeeping property' (10), but only Mrs Joe. And it is Mrs Joe's vigorous abuse – 'I came to myself (with the aid of a heavy thump between the shoulders, and the restorative exclamation "Yah! Was there ever such a boy as this!" from my sister)' (38) – rather than Joe's ultimately powerless love, which proves formative for the persecuted Pip, bringing him to the guilt-ridden and divided self who opens the narrative:

Within myself, I had sustained, from my babyhood, a perpetual conflict with injustice. I had known, from the time when I could speak, that my sister, in her capricious and violent coercion, was unjust to me ... Through all my punishments, disgraces, fasts and vigils, and other penitential performances, I had nursed this assurance; and to my communing so much with it, in a solitary and unprotected way, I in great part refer the fact that I was morally timid and very sensitive.   (57–58)

It is this early conditioning which determines Pip's response to the encounter on the marshes, rendering him truly 'helpless' (3) in the face of the moral and social complexities Magwitch represents. Together the two establish the pattern of alienation and self-condemnation which will dominate his emotional life, to culminate in a complete surrender of self with the embrace of his 'great expectations'. For Pip, as for Arthur Clennam and John Harmon, childhood experience makes participation in his own self-estrangement inevitable. Like Clennam and Harmon, Pip encounters within the 'little world' of an unhappy childhood reflections of the forces governing the larger world beyond.

There too goodness seems essentially marginal and injustice all pervasive. For the domestic tyranny that so irrevocably conditions Pip, there is the social oppression inexorably determining the life, and death, of *Great Expectations*' other orphan figure. Mrs Joe is, in Joe's phrase, 'given to government' (44), and her methods of maintaining order plainly have larger parallels. Pip's 'personal' history of perpetual durance – 'punishments, disgraces, fasts and vigils, and other penitential performances' – has a 'social' equivalent in the still grimmer experience of young Abel Magwitch: '"I've been carted here and carted there, and put out of this town and put out of that town, and stuck in the stocks, and whipped and worried and drove . . . I've been took up, took up, took up, to that extent I reg'larly grow'd up took up"' (328). Magwitch is, indeed, the living and dying proof of the 'case' Jaggers will later put to Pip, the case of those born into 'Little Britain's' atmosphere of evil, children habitually '"imprisoned, whipped, transported, neglected, cast out, qualified in all ways for the hangman, and growing up to be hanged"' (391).

This is the world in which Pip comes to himself to receive his inheritance of estrangement. If his sufferings at the hands of his all-powerful sister breed an instinctive identification with the outcast who becomes, for Pip, 'my particular convict' (30), the fellowship seems too to confirm her direst predictions of guilt and crime: '"I tell you what, young fellow," said she, "I didn't bring you up by hand to badger people's lives out . . . People are put in the Hulks because they murder, and because they rob, and forge, and do all sorts of bad; and they always begin by asking questions"' (12). To the 'morally timid' Pip the personal application of the case appears indisputable: 'I was fearfully sensible of the great convenience that the Hulks were handy for me. I was clearly on my way there. I had begun by asking questions, and I was going to rob Mrs. Joe' (12). For all the humour of the adult Pip's recreation of the unbending logic of childhood, this is Magwitch's first legacy to 'his' boy: a conviction of guilt to compound the internal divisions he has known, by his own account, since babyhood; a 'wicked secret' (20) the possession of which leaves him 'in mortal terror' (12) of his own guilty self. Pip's subsequent reports of the remorse 'with which my mind dwelt on what my hands had done' (20) and of the discomposure of what he calls 'my inner self' (37) confirm the psychic split.

The 'secret burden' (10) of conscience the encounter with Magwitch generates proves indeed doubly crippling, alienating the 'very

126

sensitive' boy from his one source of comfort no less than from himself. Fear of losing Joe's confidence keeps Pip from confessing the guilt that oppresses him. And it is a fear that both reflects and reinforces a habit of self-condemnation now well ingrained: 'It was much upon my mind (particularly when I first saw him looking about for his file) that I ought to tell Joe the whole truth. Yet I did not, and for the reason that I mistrusted that if I did, he would think me worse than I was' (37). Pip's tongue is 'tied up' by his own insecurities. He is, effectively, helpless here too, divided from Joe by an instinctive reserve and from himself by a conviction of moral weakness, a conviction which then serves as a further source of self-reproach: 'In a word I was too cowardly to do what I knew to be right, as I had been too cowardly to avoid doing what I knew to be wrong' (37). In time the divisive secret itself becomes a part of Pip's uneasy inner life, forming a 'spell of . . . childhood' (114) that precedes, and in a profound sense prepares for, the 'stronger enchantment' (226) of Estella and Satis House. When the old stain, 'faded but not gone' (249), starts out once more with the use of 'his' convict's leg-iron in the attack upon Mrs Joe, confession has become a virtual physical impossibility, envisioned as a further self-division: 'The contention came, after all, to this: – the secret was such an old one now, had so grown into me and become a part of myself, that I could not tear it away' (114).

It is this secret conviction of crime which would seem to animate Pip's relationship with the real culprit of the attack. Much has been made of the presence of Orlick in Pip's personal history, and more particularly of the role he plays in the psychic drama that history unfolds. Julian Moynahan, in his influential essay 'The Hero's Guilt: The Case of *Great Expectations*', has developed very extensively the idea of this other orphan/apprentice as a double, or more precisely, an extension of Pip himself, what he calls 'a shadow image of the tender-minded and yet monstrously ambitious young hero'. For Moynahan, *Great Expectations* – and it is unclear whether it is Pip's ostensible or Dickens's actual narrative he refers to here – attempts to displace criminality from the hero on to 'a melodramatic villain' but, 'on closer inspection, that villain becomes part of a complex entity – we might call it Pip–Orlick – in which all aspects of the problem of guilt become inter-penetrant and co-operative'.[7] This is undeniably suggestive as to the nature of the peculiarly intense bond between the two. Yet the implications Moynahan goes on to develop cannot really be contained within the structure of the novel as it exists, for they call into question the status of the narrative Pip supplies in ways the text itself scarcely sanctions. If Orlick is, in Moynahan's terms, a product of Pip's own unacknowledged hostile urges, an instrument for punishing those who injure him, the identification necessarily implies that Pip's entire story operates on the same 'psychological' level, that it too is enacted solely within the world of Pip's unconscious and/or repressed emotional life, with no other 'reality' beyond. But is this the novel Dickens wrote?

It might be as helpful here to recall David Copperfield's equally charged relationship with Uriah Heep, and the fascination of repulsion informing it. For Orlick too, like Uriah, presents to the divided hero an exaggerated reflection of his own negative self-image. In his coarseness, ignorance and brutality, Orlick embodies everything Estella despises in Pip, and teaches him to despise too. This is the source of his instinctive hostility, for Orlick is the fate he fears, the antithesis of all he longs to become. The capacity for violence latent in his physicality is a constant reminder of the criminal secret Pip himself harbours, a living manifestation of his concealed 'stain'. That Orlick is no less conscious of the bond between them, and reciprocates the instinctive antagonism, is made evident in his much-analysed attack upon his 'enemy' late in the novel: '"You was always in Old Orlick's way ever since you was a child. You goes out of his way, this present night. He'll have no more on you. You're dead"' (403). Orlick has his own 'great expectations' which Pip has thwarted and, like Uriah Heep confronting David at last, hates his 'rival' for his very unconsciousness of the injuries he has repeatedly inflicted. But what Pip hates in Orlick has still deeper roots, being nothing less than everything he hates about himself, everything Estella and his early experience have taught him to condemn.

For numerous critics of *Great Expectations* it is central to the understanding of the novel's thematic logic that Pip possesses his self-destructive aspirations long before he acquires the expectations that make them possible. But it is his self-division, going before both, which makes the two inevitable. Like Clennam and Harmon, he is caught in a cycle of voluntary/involuntary self-suppression, suppression which climaxes in his eager submission to the will of the 'mysterious patron' (135) who is to make him a gentleman. Haunted by alienation, joint legacy of his sister's tyranny and 'his' convict's guilt, Pip is emotionally preconditioned, almost indeed compelled, to embrace aspirations and expectations alike as a means of escaping a self he distrusts. The confusions and falsities they entail, the self-contempt and social shame – 'What would it signify to me, being coarse and common, if nobody had told me so!' (121) – the neglect of Joe and obsessional love for Estella, all have their ultimate source in the predicament of the lonely child in the graveyard confronting the injustice and guilt which define his world. There is nothing 'monstrous' in Pip's ambition, notwithstanding Moynahan's assertions, for it is rooted in his own early experience and the legacy of self-division that experience has left behind. Pip is as helpless at Satis House as on the marshes, defenceless in the face of the taint it breeds: 'What could I become with these surroundings? How could my character fail to be influenced by them? Is it to be wondered at if my thoughts were dazed, as my eyes were, when I came out into the natural light from the misty yellow rooms?' (89). The questions echo throughout Pip's history, while the recurrence of mist is no less significant, recalling the marsh mists which had earlier hidden Pip's 'fugitive friend'. Nor is this the only link Pip's narrative makes between that other 'memorable' encounter and the 'memorable day' (67) of his first visit to Miss Havisham.

At the gate of Satis House, and of the 'unnatural' world whose influence will prove so far-reaching, stands Estella. It is she who, emblematically, admits Pip inside: '"This is Pip, is it?" returned the young lady, who was very pretty and seemed very proud; "come in, Pip"' (50). His 'conductress' through the dark passages of the desolate house, where the light of her candle shows 'like a star' (54), Estella is also, of course, the false star who leads the 'dazed' village boy into a labyrinth of self-destructive yearning, of love persisted in 'against reason, against promise, against hope, against happiness, against all discouragement that could be' (219). She is, in fact, as Pip himself will later explicitly acknowledge, inseparable from his emotional and moral bewilderment, 'from all those wretched hankerings after money and gentility that had disturbed my boyhood – from all those ill-regulated aspirations that had first made me ashamed of home and Joe' (223). Under her scornful influence Pip's early self-estrangement deepens to something little short of self-hatred and in this too she is, as he says, impossible of separation from 'the innermost life of my life' (223), that 'inner self' already so discomposed. If Estella's coldness is, as she tells Pip, '"in the nature formed within me"' (343), his destructive passion has been no less inexorably bred in him.

The ethereal girl, seemingly so unattainable in her pride and beauty – 'I saw her pass among the extinguished fires, and ascend some light iron stairs, and go out by a gallery high overhead, as if she were going out into the sky' (59) – is the other pivot of Pip's childhood, the opposite pole to the shackled, earth-bound convict he succours. It is, of course, one of the shaping ironies of the novel that it is the outcast hunted to 'death and dunghill' (16) who has fathered this star-like lady. Through Estella Pip's emotional predicament assumes its explicitly 'social' dimension. She awakens in him the first desperate longings for the 'gentility' that will bring nothing but futher discontent with it, a false ideal based on 'fortune and prospects' (223) that discounts any other less tangible values. She is, in effect, the necessary preparation for the complete surrender of will and self which attends Pip's acquisition of his 'great expectations'. And this too is part of an inevitable progression. For it is Pip's own early experience which makes Estella's contempt no less 'irresistible' (219) than her 'beauty and pride'. She 'beggars' him emotionally with their first game of cards together, her disdain depriving him of the little that remains of an extremely tenuous self-worth:

'He calls the knaves, Jacks, this boy!' said Estella with disdain, before our first game was out. 'And what coarse hands he has! And what thick boots!'

I had never thought of being ashamed of my hands before; but I began to consider them a very indifferent pair. Her contempt for me was so strong, that it became infectious, and I caught it. (55)

What Pip catches, being highly susceptible to the infection, is Estella's literally self-denying perception. In her eyes he is barely an individual, merely 'a common labouring-boy' (55) whose heart is scarcely worth the breaking. Her most frequent name for him is, simply, 'boy'. And Pip automatically assimilates the self-diminishing image along with the very language of her contempt: 'I took the opportunity of being alone in the court-yard, to look at my coarse hands and common boots. My opinion of those accessories was not favourable' (57). She wounds him and Pip can respond in no other way than by adding to the injury, wringing his own hair after Estella has, as he recalls, 'wrung my heart' (380). In subsequent encounters it is her anonymous terms which Pip will use to define himself in a form of verbal self-effacement that recalls Arthur Clennam's 'Nobody': 'I kissed her cheek as she turned it to me. I think I would have gone through a great deal to kiss her cheek. But, I felt that the kiss was given to the coarse common boy as a piece of money might have been, and that it was worth nothing' (86). For Pip there is no sense of deserving, no sense of self, beyond 'the coarse common boy'. It is a formula he returns to repeatedly under Estella's influence – 'I fancied, as I looked at her, that I slipped hopelessly back into the coarse and common boy again' (222) – participating with each repetition, as he cannot help but do, in his own symbolic negation.

Pip's expectations come as the culmination of this process of estrangement, as he willingly resigns his 'restlessly aspiring discontented' (101) self into the hands of an anonymous patron, to be 'made' along with his fortunes. If the intervening years of his apprenticeship to Joe had been a time of 'dull endurance' (100) haunted by uncertain longings – 'What I wanted, who can say? How can *I* say, when I never knew?' (101) – those longings are at once defined and fulfilled with the appearance of Mr Jaggers and his momentous communication: 'My dream was out; my wild fancy was surpassed by sober reality; Miss Havisham was going to make my fortune on a grand scale' (130). What Jaggers brings to 'the little child' (133) Joe had so often blessed before is, as Joe clearly recognizes, a new identity: ' "Pip's a gentleman of fortun' then," said Joe, "and God bless him in it!" ' (135). But it is an identity that is as much of an imposition as any of Estella's most contemptuous epithets, acquiesced in equally compulsively, and carrying no more positive means of self-definition. In allowing himself to be 'made', and the fate is, by Pip's own account, long wished for, he effectively abandons all responsibility for himself. Embracing a passivity that anticipates the sort of paralysis John Harmon will experience, Pip eagerly surrenders his will to the vagaries, as he thinks, of a 'fairy godmother' (149) who is clearly more than half witch. And, in doing so, he surrenders too all vestiges of a fixed identity, losing even the negative ability to define himself through rejection of the self and role Estella has taught him to despise. No longer 'a blacksmith's boy', he will find that he has yet become nothing else. ' "You call me a lucky fellow," ' he remarks to Herbert Pocket. ' "Of course, I am. I was a blacksmith's boy but yesterday; I am – what shall I say I am to-day?" ' (234). Like virtually everyone else Pip encounters, Herbert offers his own definition in return: ' "Say a good fellow, if you want a phrase . . . a good fellow, with impetuosity and hesitation, boldness and diffidence, action and dreaming, curiously mixed in him" ' (234). It is not a definition Pip recognizes, but, characteristically, he does not think it 'worth disputing'.

From the first night of his 'bright fortunes' (137), Pip discovers that they bring not identity but only new disquiet with them. Lonely even in his own familiar room, silently but irrevocably cut off from Joe and Biddy, Pip's analysis of the change, so 'sorrowful and strange' (137) to him, is telling: 'Dissatisfied with my fortune, of course I could not be; but it is possible that I may have been, without quite knowing it, dissatisfied with myself' (136). The dissatisfaction grows as Pip becomes conscious of the aimlessness and wastefulness, the sheer emptiness, of his life as a 'gentleman', a life consisting of foolish expenditure, debt, and 'the Finches of the Grove'. It will grow deeper still as his new 'gentility' draws him inexorably into neglect of his old home and friends. If Pip knows the shame which prompts him to be false, he yet proves, once again, unable to resist. These are the fruits of his great expectations: 'restlessness and disquiet of mind' (258), new sources of guilt and self-reproach to replace the old:

I lived in a state of chronic uneasiness respecting my behaviour to Joe. My conscience was not by any means comfortable about Biddy. When I woke up in the night – like Camilla – I used to think, with a weariness on my spirits, that I should have been happier and better if I had never seen Miss Havisham's face, and had risen to manhood content to be partners with Joe in the honest old forge. (258)

Pip's uneasiness is, as J. Hillis Miller has noted, an integral part of the very condition of being a gentleman in the world of *Great Expectations*. And it must be so when the title can mean, as it does with Bentley Drummle, nothing more than the possession of 'money and a ridiculous roll of addle-headed predecessors' (296) or, in the case of Compeyson, a public school education and the manner it supplies. For Hillis Miller, Pip's problem is that in being transformed into a 'gentleman', he necessarily loses all ability to define himself by means of some externally imposed duty or code, gentility offering no more positive value.[8] In fact, the predicament goes still deeper. Having embraced the externally imposed role of 'gentleman', Pip has discovered that it brings nothing but compounded self-division with it. What he must do is, in effect, become his own creator, reclaiming the will he has surrendered and fashioning an identity based on a gentility that does not equate human worth with social status. That such gentility must, necessarily, leave him estranged from a society that knows no such values is the true gentleman's problem, a larger uneasiness that remains chronic indeed. What Pip must do is accept responsibility for his own selfhood, and accept a new alienation with it.

The actual process of self-discovery begins for Pip with the appearance of his true patron, born out of the negation in which his great expectations inevitably culminate. With the return of 'his' convict to reverse their original relation and claim the 'brought-up London gentleman' (306) he has made, Pip's 'uneasy' social identity collapses. And there is nothing to take its place. The shock of the revelation may delay the knowledge, but the ruin is complete: 'For an hour or more, I remained too stunned to think; and it was not until I began to think, that I began fully to know how wrecked I was, and how the ship in which I had sailed was gone to pieces' (307). Magwitch claims kinship no less than possession – '"Look'ee here, Pip. I'm your second father. You're my son – more to me nor any son"' (304). He embodies, literally, the old taint of crime and guilt that had proved so divisive, the 'lowness' Pip had sought to escape for so long. In the eyes of his appalled creation, 'there was Convict in the very grain of the man' (319). If Pip reflects on what seems to him the abyss between 'Estella in her pride and beauty, and the returned transport whom I harboured' (335) – he will soon learn, of course, how closely the two are connected – it is an abyss into which he himself has fallen. For the prospect of renewed fellowship with 'his' convict drives Pip back beyond the small bundle of shivers of their first encounter to a state of complete non-identity:

> When I opened the shutters and looked out at the wet wild morning, all of a leaden hue; when I walked from room to room; when I sat down again shivering, before the fire, waiting for my laundress to appear; I thought how miserable I was, but hardly knew why, or how long I had been so, or on what day of the week I made the reflection, or even who I was that made it. (311)

But Magwitch brings more than the 'gold and silver chains' (307), and the wretchedness, with which Pip feels himself bound. The convict 'father' awakens in his 'son' a consciousness of his own errors, a sense, as Pip puts it, of 'my own worthless conduct' (308) to Joe and Biddy which is the beginning of true self-knowledge. For, according to the by now familiar pattern, though this proves a source of enduring regret – 'I could never, never, never, undo what I had done' (308) – it also marks a new affirmation.

Turning from his real to his supposed patron, Pip now discovers among the 'old strange influences' (222) that had worked so fatally upon him the basis of his own identity. With all her perverse pretences, she too confers a lasting legacy. Confronting Miss Havisham, all mists dispelled by Magwitch's return, Pip finds himself amid the ruins of his long-cherished hopes:

As I stood compassionating her, and thinking how in the progress of time I too had come to be a part of the wrecked fortunes of that house, her eyes rested on me. She started, and said in a low voice, 'Is it real?'

'It is I, Pip.' (374–375)

And with this discovery comes the moral strength to refuse Miss Havisham's subsequent offer of money. He can, indeed must, accept her aid in order to help Herbert Pocket and to complete what Pip himself describes as the 'only good thing' (394) he has done since first being apprised of his great expectations. It is one of the many signs of his own social helplessness. But he will take nothing more. When Miss Havisham makes the highly significant enquiry, '"Can I only serve you, Pip, by serving your friend? Regarding that as done, is there nothing I can do for you, yourself?"', Pip's reply is unhesitating: '"Nothing. I thank you for the question. I thank you even more for the tone of the question. But, there is nothing"' (376).

It is the completion of a circle. Pip's childhood dream, clung to for so long and but recently shattered, is being renewed: Miss Havisham will make his fortune. And Pip refuses. Though the offer is tendered with affection as it would not have been before – she seeks to serve Pip, not to use him – Pip will no longer grant the role of creator to anyone else. The new resolution, and the compassion and sense of self which attend it, grow out of an acceptance of responsibility, a recognition of community in error that will unite Pip with Magwitch no less than Miss Havisham. Pip leaves Satis House having forgiven his 'false' patron the wrong she has done him. And the forgiveness is inseparable from an admission of his own equal need of it: '"There have been sore mistakes; and my life has been a blind and thankless one; and I want forgiveness and direction far too much, to be bitter with you"' (377). The moment is an important anticipation of the epiphany on the river soon to come.

Like this changing relation to Miss Havisham, Pip's deepening attachment to Magwitch is at once an agent and a reflection of his deepening sense of self. With the acknowledgment of his own need for 'forgiveness and direction', Pip finds the clue to the 'dreadful mystery' (319) Magwitch first presents, a mystery solved for ever in the moment of identification on the river. Slowly shedding the 'frenzy of fear and dislike' (313) which is his immediate return to his benefactor – Pip is 'softened' (357) and 'improved' (384) no less than Magwitch – he sheds too the solipsistic self-pity underlying it: 'Nothing was needed but this; the wretched man, after loading wretched me with his gold and silver chains for years, had risked his life to come to me, and I held it there in my keeping!' (307). For Pip self-discovery brings the ability to transcend self, to substitute fellowship for isolation, and to find in self-forgetfulness the means of affirmation lacked for so long. As he prepares to aid Magwitch's escape, Pip leaves behind the concern for 'wretched me' as he leaves the other trappings of his old, uneasy life of expectation: 'Where I might go, what I might do, or when I might return, were questions utterly unknown to me: nor did I vex my mind with them, for it was wholly set on Provis's safety' (412). Pip accepts the prospect of an uncertain exile with his devotion to Magwitch. The two are indeed inseparable in a deeper sense than he knows. For his very commitment to 'his' convict will bring, inevitably, social and emotional exile in its wake. Yet the feeling brings too a moment of spiritual location – 'When I took my place by Magwitch's side, I felt that that was my place henceforth while he lived' (423) – born out of a newly acquired self-knowledge:

For now, my repugnance to him had all melted away, and in the hunted, wounded, shackled creature who held my hand in his, I only saw a man who had meant to be my benefactor, and who had felt affectionately, gratefully, and generously, towards me with great constancy through a series of years. I only saw in him a much better man than I had been to Joe. (423)

But with this discovery Pip finds too an inescapable alienation. His alliance with the criminal outcast places him beyond the social pale, and it is a dissociation in a double sense. For, having substituted true moral values for great expectations, Pip can have no place in a society that does not recognize their worth, a world where gentlemanly status forbids human community. It is a social fact explored too in the parallel career of Herbert Pocket, the 'pale young gentleman'. Herbert is a touchstone of true gentility among the Bentley Drummles and Compeysons. But the 'natural incapacity to do anything secret or mean' (167) which establishes him as such, also proves a natural incapacity for making his way in a world where secrecy and meanness predominate. Pip is correct in his judgment. Herbert will never be 'very successful or rich' (167) on his own initiative. His very gentlemanliness makes that impossible. His career too inverts the Smilesian self-help myth of material success as an index of moral virtue. It is only Magwitch's money, the 'criminal' outcast's wealth, that can buy the gentleman opportunities he himself can never naturally win.

Magwitch's and Miss Havisham's equally compromised fortunes are necessary to secure Herbert's future. What their spiritual legacy buys Pip is, as he himself recognizes, the knowledge that he possesses no such hope, that he has 'no home anywhere' (428). Selfhood and alienation prove, once again, inevitably allied. After Magwitch's death, Pip falls into an illness that is obviously symbolic, an expression of his social dilemma. For his fever brings with it a dissolution of self that recalls Esther Summerson's dream experiences. Pip's illness not only causes him to confound 'impossible existences with my own identity' (438) but allows him to return, for a time, to his childish self and to the old relations to Joe so soon, and so thanklessly, abandoned, 'as if I were still the small helpless creature to whom he had so abundantly given of the wealth of his great nature' (442). And this too is an 'impossible existence'. He seeks now the other sort of wealth Magwitch has taught him to prize. But the prospect of return is itself a deception. The old roles, like the expectations that had displaced them, have passed irrevocably away. When Pip regains his strength, and the adult consciousness illness had temporarily suspended, he does go back to the forge. He attempts to return 'home' in a conscious retreat to the haven of truth and goodness Joe and Biddy now seem to represent: 'I went towards them slowly, for my limbs were weak, but with a sense of increasing relief as I drew nearer to them, and a sense of leaving arrogance and untruthfulness further and further behind' (452). But Pip can no more leave arrogance and untruthfulness behind than Arthur Clennam could. The forge offers him no permanent refuge. As he himself realizes, the place he once held there can never again be his: 'Dear Joe, I hope you will have children to love, and that some little fellow will sit in this chimney corner of a winter night, who may remind you of another little fellow gone out of it for ever' (454).

Pip had left the forge, so many years before, drawn by the promise of self-fulfilment his great expectations appeared to hold out. Now, having discovered the falseness of that promise, and his true self by doing so, he must inevitably leave once more. For some critics of the novel, this second departure from the forge constitutes an essential betrayal of the 'social problem' Pip's self-destructive career of 'gentleman' was designed to explore, testifying to a residual snobbishness in Pip's creator that will not allow the gentleman hero to become at the end anything more than a village blacksmith and husband of the local schoolmistress. For them it is this same failure of imaginative conviction which produces *Great Expectations* double ending, in both instances muffling meanings the narrative itself has generated. But Pip's separation from the forge and Biddy is clearly intended to be registered as a loss, an inevitable – and irretrievable – restriction of future prospects that is the accompaniment, and price, of his true gentility. Unlike David Copperfield, who sees among his children at novel's close a small replica of his 'old acquaintance' Brooks of Sheffield, Pip has no child of his own, and no chance of rewriting his own history to a happier end. It is Joe and Biddy's son who presents to him another version of his younger self, a self to whom it will be 'natural' to grow up a better man than he has been (455). It is, finally, impossible for Pip to remain in the safely insulated, and limited, world Joe and Biddy's truth and goodness define. That would indeed have constituted a betrayal of his problem, a problem that is, and must remain, insoluble.

When Pip returns again to the forge, eleven years later, it is as a self-described 'wanderer' (459), such being the identity he has achieved, the only identity available to him. And this surely is the real significance of Pip's life of exile in the East, an exile both voluntary and utterly inescapable. Pip lives out of England because he can no longer live in it, and this is what selfhood has brought him. The true gentleman is, necessarily, also truly a 'wanderer'. That is his perpetual problem. The reunion with Estella, achieved on this second return, and the source of so much critical discussion, does not, ultimately, affect the alienation to which Pip's spiritual journey inevitably leads. *Great Expectations*, like *Little Dorrit*, does not end with an image of domestic enclosure. And this is as true of the published second ending as of the cancelled first. Pip's self-discovery is, rather, accompanied, like Clennam's, by the destruction of one of the dominant houses of his childhood, while his old place at the other (the forge) is taken by his own small namesake. Leaving the ruins of Satis House behind them, Pip and Estella go out into the evening mists, as Arthur Clennam and Amy Dorrit had gone down into the roaring streets, houseless, and homeless, forever. (In the first version of the ending, he re-encounters her walking along Piccadilly, literally in the streets.) Together they face an undefined future which offers in its very irresolution the fitting 'end' to Pip's progress as gentleman, and Dickens hero, and the more so for carrying with it the possibility of a still more sombre conclusion. Once again, the problem of closure itself possesses a significance inseparable from the hero's social experience, and closure could scarcely be more problematic than in a novel with two written endings. As numerous critics have pointed out, Pip's ambiguous final words – 'I saw no shadow of another parting from her' (460) – may point not to permanent union with Estella, but to a separation he had yet to envisage, yet which would come (a third possible 'ending' to add to the other two). If they do, then Pip is left, at last, alone with his recovered selfhood in an alienation still more complete than any we have yet seen the Dickens hero experience. And that is now journey's 'end'.

❦ 6 ❦

The 'Dandy' Vindicated: Sydney Carton, Eugene Wrayburn and the Reclaimed Self

At first glance, 'dandy' must seem an inappropriate title for Sydney Carton and Eugene Wrayburn both, the one so conspicuously slovenly in dress and manner, the other with an appearance never particularized beyond the general facts of a beard and a handsome face. But, as Ellen Moers has shown in her study *The Dandy: From Brummell to Beerbohm*, from its first embodiment in 'Beau' Brummell himself, the idea of the 'dandy' involved issues of social attitude no less than questions of fashion or style. Indeed, as Carlyle would most famously demonstrate in *Sartor Resartus*, the two were inseparable. The relevant chapter comes in Book Three, 'The Dandaical Body', which opens with the definition of the 'dandy' as 'a Clothes-Wearing Man, a Man whose trade, office and existence consists in the wearing of Clothes'. Carlyle's entire 'philosophy of clothes' has, of course, an obvious relevance to the question of spiritual, and social, dandyism. And if it is a bastardized version of the 'dandy' style which Dickens first draws upon in earlier fiction like *Nicholas Nickleby* and *Martin Chuzzlewit*, it is the underlying social attitude which increasingly interests him in the later novels.

For the 'dandy' as exemplified by Brummell elegance of mode was an extension of elegance of manner, the ideal being a detached poise well above any suspicion of the sort of earnestness, enthusiasm and high seriousness that would prove so sacred to the heart of Carlyle. According to Moers, the 'dandy' represented above all a consummate irresponsibility, a dedication to the external and the superficial admitting no higher law or cause than 'taste'.[1] Uncommitted, essentially unconcerned, the 'dandy''s self-chosen role was that of the disengaged observer, never the ardent participant. It is this perversely attractive freedom from commitment which provided the groundwork for both the Victorian hostility to, and lingering fascination with, his elegant, irresponsible image. It is a fascination Dickens shared, incorporating the 'dandy''s deliberate dissociation into the social vision embodied in his own distinctively alienated hero.

Although the 'dandy''s characteristic pose of cool disengagement might be attacked as selfish, unmanly and even un-Christian by eminent Victorians like Carlyle and Thomas Arnold, his spectre continued to haunt the imagination of many a writer throughout the period. However strong the reaction, the 'dandy' remained a Regency ghost who refused to be laid. In Moers's estimation, the novelists could not avoid him.[2] Certainly Dickens does not. A type of debased 'dandy', compounded of whiskers, jewellery and impossible waistcoats, appears in *Nicholas Nickleby* in the person of Mantalini. And he is followed in *Martin Chuzzlewit* by the equally splendid, and more sinister, Tigg Montague. In fact, as Moers makes clear, extravagant costume was never a feature of 'Beau' Brummell's own elegant simplicity of style, coming rather to be associated with the 'dandy' through subsequent figures like Bulwer-Lytton, Disraeli and Alfred D'Orsay.[3] The parasitic Turveydrop, *Bleak House*'s model of deportment, is a more genuine 'beau', appropriately superannuated, complete with perfectly formed 'surface' and an unfortunate son named for the Prince Regent. Dickens's interest with all three is primarily in the external phenomenon, Carlyle's thing made by a tailor, and, in the case of Tigg and Turveydrop, the ease, indeed the willingness, with which society is brought to take the sham article for the genuine. A late version of the type, used for similar thematic ends, reappears in *Our Mutual Friend* in the specious Lammle, he with 'too much nose in his face, too much ginger in his whiskers, too much torso in his waistcoat, too much sparkle in his studs, his eyes, his buttons, his talk, and his teeth' (10).

From *David Copperfield* onward, however, it is the other, as it were internal, aspect of the 'dandy' which increasingly preoccupies Dickens. Turning his attention from sartorial to spiritual dandyism, he creates a gentleman of a new dandy tradition: polished, poised and essentially amoral. With figures like Steerforth and, more particularly, James Harthouse in *Hard Times* and Henry Gowan in *Little Dorrit*, Dickens begins to explore the idea of the 'dandy' as disengaged observer, possessed in his detachment of a peculiar insight into the workings of a society he may profess to despise, but never actually rejects. It is an exploration that culminates in a yet more ambiguous version of the divided, alienated Dickens hero, embodied in the 'careless and slovenly if not debauched' (*ATTC* 69) Sydney Carton and the 'utterly careless' (*OMF* 286) Eugene Wrayburn, emotional 'dandies' both.

It is, specifically, the 'dandy' strain of graceful nonchalance that Dickens takes up with Harthouse and Gowan. They transform the elegant self-possession of the 'beau' into a distinctive blend of negligence, 'genteel listlessness' (*HT* 126) and a studied avoidance of all enthusiasm. Steerforth, with his condescending appreciation of David Copperfield's 'daisy'-like freshness and his own self-confessed lack of purpose, occasionally exhibits similar qualities. But it is in James Harthouse, 'who had tried life as a Cornet of Dragoons, and found it a bore; and had afterwards tried it in the train of an English minister abroad, and found it a bore; and had then strolled to Jerusalem, and got bored there; and had then gone yachting about the world, and got bored everywhere' (95), that they first receive sustained attention. Steerforth is, in fact, a compound of the emotional dandy and a sort of domesticated Byronic hero, his death as a result of passions he could not control distinguishing him from the essentially passionless Harthouse. Unencumbered by David Copperfield's compulsive hero-worship, the presentation of Harthouse – like his predecessor a seducer, but unlike him unsuccessful – is, moreover, overtly critical as the presentation of Steerforth, mediated through David himself, could not be. And Dickens now makes clear the previously implicit connection between the unshakeable ease of manner and the fundamental moral indifferentism of men of the Harthouse type, 'fine gentlemen who, having found out everything to be worth nothing, were equally ready for anything' (94). There is a definite class dimension to the charge. Both Harthouse and Gowan are offshoots of what Dickens calls 'good family' and their habitual negligence carries a discernible flavour of class contempt. Beneath this consistently graceful exterior, Harthouse is plainly hollow, 'a thorough gentleman, made to the model of the time, weary of everything, and putting no more faith in anything than Lucifer' (91). His ultimate moral status, suggested here, is indeed early and unambiguously established:

When the Devil goeth about like a roaring lion, he goeth about in a shape by which few but savages and hunters are attracted. But when he is trimmed, smoothed, and varnished, according to the mode; when he is aweary of vice, and aweary of virtue, used up as to brimstone and used up as to bliss; then, whether he take to the serving out of red tape, or to the kindling of red fire, he is the very Devil.   (137)

For the most part Henry Gowan shares a similar pose of well-bred indifference, though with the pernicious variation in his case of an occasional enthusiasm reserved strictly for the contemptible and the second-rate. An artist by profession, he maintains 'a slight, careless, amateur way with him – a perceptible limp, both in his devotion to art and his attainments' (201) designed to suggest the absurdity of such a man having any profession at all. In the shrewd estimate of Daniel Doyce, '"he has sauntered into the Arts at a leisurely Pall-Mall pace . . . and I doubt if they care to be taken quite so coolly"' (201). As with Harthouse, his moral status is early established. Gowan is, in fact, one of Dickens's more sinister creations who yet never actually does anything unequivocally villainous. There is an undercurrent of sadism that attends him from his first appearance in the novel, wrenching stones into the quiet water of a river and 'spurning' them with his heel, a sadism that recurs in his savage beating of his dog. And Miss Wade's revelation of the devilish part he has played in her history of self-torment confirms the sense of latent menace with which Gowan is imbued.

Yet for all their 'dandy' cynicism, indeed because of it, Harthouse and Gowan display an insight into the falsities of their respective social worlds, an insight that goes well beyond the opportunism of a Tigg or a Lammle. And it is this feature particularly which forms the basis of Dickens subsequent reworking of the figure. Though far from representing any form of moral alternative, the two men yet stand, in their very disengagement, as types of the social critic. Steerforth too has his moment of critical vision, reflecting on the 'very pleasant profitable little affair of private theatricals' (293) that is 'Doctors' Commons. But such commentary is not a developed feature of his character, nor does he articulate a sustained social vision, however negative and self-serving, as Harthouse and Gowan do. With Steerforth the centre of interest is his fatal self-indulgence rather than the cultivated cynicism his successors display. For all the studied enervation of Harthouse's manner, there is the sense of an ironic consciousness lurking beneath his fatigued gentility. At the very least, his encounters with the overblown Bounderby are marked by a quiet insolence that effectively undercuts the self-made mannerisms of that 'Bully of Humility':

'Don't you deceive yourself by supposing for a moment that I am a man of family. I am a bit of dirty riff-raff, and a genuine scrap of tag, rag, and bobtail.'
If anything could have exalted Jem's interest in Mr. Bounderby, it would have been this very circumstance. Or so he told him.   (97)

Gowan's responses are more directly rendered. Indeed, it is one of his most invidious features that he revels in the social hollowness he reveals, finding nothing in 'the market' but impostors and rejoicing in the fact: "'Give almost any man I know, ten pounds, and he will impose upon you to a corresponding extent, a thousand pounds – to a corresponding extent; ten thousand pounds to a corresponding extent. So great the success, so great the imposition. But what a capital world it is! . . . What a jolly, excellent loveable world it is!"' (302). Both Harthouse and Gowan plainly thrive on the spiritual bankruptcy they anatomize so coolly. There is no suggestion with either that they seek anything better, or indeed believe in the possibility of its existence, no suggestion that their own moral emptiness is a consequence of their recognition of society's sterility. It is, however, precisely this strain that Dickens goes on to develop as he takes the type of the disengaged, sauntering cynic and reshapes it into the alienated, self-divided figures of Sydney Carton and Eugene Wrayburn.

What the two represent is, in effect, a fusion of the spiritual dandy and the spiritual waif, a further darkening of the figure of the Dickens hero and of the prospects of integration open to him. As with Clennam, and John Harmon, and Pip, there lies at the heart of their experience a compulsive emotional negation now taking the form of cynical indifference. In the view of John Gross, Carton belongs primarily to 'the line of the cultivated wastrels who play an increasingly large part in Dickens's novels during the second half of his career', a line which includes Richard Carstone in *Bleak House* and culminates in Eugene Wrayburn.[4] Yet Carton and Wrayburn both possess significant counterparts beyond the succession Gross traces. For the indifference they profess as a function of their 'cultivated wastrel' role also constitutes a self-suppression no less deliberate, and no less inevitable, than Clennam's fiction of 'Nobody', Harmon's existence as the ghost of his murdered self, or Pip's life as a 'gentleman'. Indeed, it is precisely the sense of a better nature, a *true* nature, concealed beneath the careless mask they assume which distinguishes the two from figures like Gowan and Harthouse, who are simply wastrels and nothing more. The point forms the essence of Carton's curious interview with Lucie Manette in the chapter entitled 'A Fellow of No Delicacy'. It is, in fact, explicitly made by Sydney himself as he briefly lifts the mask for Lucie's pitying eyes. '"Within myself,"' he then declares, '"I shall always be, towards you, what I am now, though outwardly I shall be what you have heretofore seen me. The last supplication but one I make to you, is, that you will believe this of me"' (145). If the terms of the appeal are more than a little obscure, Lucie yet understands its import, as her own subsequent plea to her husband on 'Poor Carton"s (201) behalf makes clear: '"I would ask you to believe that he has a heart he very, very seldom reveals, and that there are deep wounds in it. My dear, I have seen it bleeding"' (198). With Wrayburn it is not a wounded heart but a genuine feeling self that lies buried beneath the apparently impenetrable façade of 'that unmoved barrister-at-law' (159): a self capable of an all-consuming passion for Lizzie Hexam, and one which can have no place in a society that, in the words of its arbiter Podsnap, does not 'admit' the emotion.

Both men are divided from their true selves, divided by the very indifference which separates them too from a world offering that self no home. Lizzie Hexam's words apply to Carton no less than Wrayburn. Each is 'like one cast away, for the want of something to trust in, and care for, and think well of' (349). It is a something Carton will find only in death, Wrayburn in a marriage which puts him for ever beyond the social pale. They are not moral cynics, of the Harthouse/Gowan type, but rather failed idealists, retreating into negligence as a refuge. Like Clennam and Harmon in their different ways, they too suffer a double alienation, caught in a cycle that has become increasingly difficult to break. Each inevitably substitutes the negation of self-suppression for that of social engagement. For Wrayburn's consummate carelessness, a carelessness which manifestly includes himself – '"I am in a ridiculous humour," quoth Eugene. "I am a ridiculous fellow. Everything is ridiculous. Come along"' (166) – stands as a response to the 'good society' (14) of 'Podsnappery' and veneer in which he drifts. Eugene plainly possesses intelligence, and moral discernment, enough to despise the 'Society' that claims him, as his own satirical comments to Lightwood reveal. Similarly, Carton's drinking and the squandering of his talents have their roots in a bitter consciousness, barely concealed, of the emptiness of the world around him. And, once again, it is Sydney himself who makes the point explicit early in the novel's course in an emblematic encounter between the recently acquitted Charles Darnay and his 'Double of coarse deportment' (78):

'Do you feel, yet, that you belong to this terrestrial scheme again, Mr. Darnay?'
'I am frightfully confused regarding time and place; but am so far mended as to feel that.'
'It must be an immense satisfaction.'
He said it bitterly, and filled up his glass again: which was a large one.
'As to me, the greatest desire I have, is to forget that I belong to it. It has no good in it for me – except wine like this – nor I for it.' (77)

With both Carton and Wrayburn their self-surrender to recklessness and negligence constitutes a form of social indictment, an arraignment of the society whose hollowness provides nothing 'to trust in, and care for, and think well of'. Carton indeed takes the 'social criticism' implicit in the Dickens hero's characteristic progress (from alienation, through self-discovery, to alienation once more) to its final form. His ability to find his best self and best rest only in death stands as the ultimate condemnation for it signals acquiescence in the ultimate estrangement. And there is a significant echo of 'Poor Carton''s far, far better thing in Wrayburn's wedding day speculation '"whether it is not the best thing I can do, to die"' (754). Knowing the price of social engagement to be a form of spiritual death, conscious of his own self-described 'trifling, wasted youth' (754) and the self-betrayal it represents, Eugene doubts whether he can ever be truly recalled to life, even by Lizzie's love, and the alternative self-definition it provides. '"There is a sharp misgiving in my conscience,"' he tells her, '"that if I were to live, I should disappoint your good opinion and my own – and that I ought to die, my dear!"' (754). Though Wrayburn does not, in fact, embrace death as his journey's end, as Carton does, his self-discovery carries with it an acceptance of perpetual estrangement, a recognition of the need to '"fight it out to the last gasp"' (813) with and for the woman he has defied the conventions of 'good society' to marry. For Angus Wilson, in the line of development of Dickens's later heroes, Wrayburn marks the 'redemption' of the type of the 'somewhat stray villain' first embodied in Steerforth.[5] Yet there is a sense, with Carton and Wrayburn both, that in them the figure of the spiritual dandy is as much vindicated as redeemed. Neither can achieve a place for the true selves they ultimately reclaim within the society in which they must live. And the fact carries with it an implicit justification of the impulse, however perverted its form, which first sought retreat from that society's deadening influence. Their fates point towards the final metamorphosis the Dickens hero will undergo into the 'villainous' shapes of Bradley Headstone and John Jasper, men whose socially induced self-suppression leads inexorably to literal self-destruction.

From its opening sentence, from its very title, *A Tale of Two Cities* declares itself to be constructed on a principle of polarity, a polarity which, in psychic form, marks other figures in the novel no less than the self-estranged Sydney Carton. In their different ways, Charles Darnay and Dr Manette too struggle with divided identities which carry an undeniable symbolic weight. While Manette balances precariously between the skilled scientist, the Doctor of Beauvais, and the haunted Bastille prisoner 'One Hundred and Five, North Tower', his son-in-law moves from the aristocrat Evrémonde to the new self he has attempted to create in the citizen Darnay, only to be forced back once more. It is the essence of his predicament that he cannot escape the legacy of the past symbolized by the family name, one '"more detested"', in Darnay's words, '"than any name in France"' (116). With both men the identities which thus supplant or, in Darnay's case, threaten their true selves are external, political constructs. 'One Hundred and Five, North Tower,' is the creation of the injustice of the old regime; 'the aristocrat Evrémonde', 'the emigrant Evrémonde', products of the inevitable vengeance of the new. And it is precisely through the efforts of Manette and, more particularly, Darnay to overcome the roles imposed upon them that Dickens develops *A Tale of Two Cities'* explicitly 'historical' themes, the 'prophetic' vision of regeneration and redemption which attends Carton to the guillotine finding concrete expression in the union of the last of the Evrémondes with the daughter of the Bastille prisoner. Indeed, of all Dickens's young male protagonists, Darnay most closely resembles the figure Alexander Welsh has labelled 'The Hero of the Waverley Novels' in his book of the same name. Like so many of Scott's 'heroes', Darnay is a young man caught between the opposing forces of old and new, past and future, with emotional ties to both, a figure whose experience ultimately represents an historically inevitable reconciliation of the two.

In contrast to the stories of Darnay and Manette, the experience which leads Carton himself to death and the attainment of his final vision is not placed within an explicitly historical or political frame. In many ways, Carton conspicuously lacks the sort of 'significant' past Darnay so plainly possesses, a past significant in thematic terms and as an explanation of his present response. In this, as also in his death-wish, Carton looks forward to John Jasper, the relation of whose past experience to his present predicament, though plainly important to an understanding of the full meaning of his dilemma, is still less explicitly established. Yet the fact does not, as has been suggested, necessarily undercut the resonance of 'Poor Carton''s progress towards his ultimate self-suppression, reducing him to a simple victim sacrificed for calculated effect at novel's end. For Carton's predicament, unlike Darnay's, exists essentially independently of *A Tale of Two Cities'* 'historical' concerns. Carton is not the representative of a new order struggling against the deadening weight of the old. He is not, like

Darnay, a Waverley figure caught between that epitome of aristocratic tyranny 'Monsieur the Marquis' and the revolutionary 'Jacques' of Saint Antoine. He is, rather, a figure familiar from the pages of Dickens's non-historical, 'social' novels, reworked towards a still darker end: a spiritual wanderer forever homeless in a world he can neither accept nor escape. His is a timeless plight, as relevant to 1859, the date of the novel's publication, as 1789, a personal history of alienation that transcends 'historical' limitations. Several critics of *A Tale of Two Cities* have identified in Charles *Evrémonde* Darnay, with his almost diagrammatically symbolic adventures and suggestive name, a form of Anglo-French 'Everyman'. But, in a still more profound sense, it is to Carton that the title truly belongs. Darnay's experience, very much like Edward Waverley's, constitutes a virtual parable of the process of historical change, reflecting successive phases of repression, reaction, new repression and reform. But Carton's life journey stands as a still larger type, that of the social Everyman adrift in a world grown increasingly hostile to true selfhood, the world of the Dickens hero. His is the characteristic dilemma of the morally sensitive individual caught in a society which holds no value for him. In many ways Carton's real thematic opposite within the world of the novel is not Darnay but Stryver, the ironically titled 'Fellow of Delicacy' in contrast to Sydney, the fellow of none. For Stryver is everything Carton is not, the manipulating impostor being also 'a glib man, and an unscrupulous, and a ready, and a bold', (80) blustering his way to success on society's terms, and the pickings of Carton's brains.

That these are terms Carton was long ago driven to reject is, notwithstanding the lack of detail concerning his 'significant' past, at least implied by the less than sober 'jackal' himself, in conversation with his overbearing 'lion'. '"You were always driving and riving and shouldering and pressing,"' he tells Stryver, '"to that restless degree that I had no chance for my life but in rust and repose"' (84). If Carton lacks the sort of representative childhood experience with which Arthur Clennam, Pip and, to a lesser extent, John Harmon are endowed, it is yet clear that he too has made an inevitable 'choice' of self-suppression. Like them he embraces an alternative identity and finds in it, not escape, but rather a more profound estrangement. In place of Clennam's 'Nobody' or Harmon's 'living-dead man', Carton assumes the role of the self-described 'disappointed man' (79), reckless, indifferent and beyond recall. '"I care for no man on earth,"' he early informs Darnay, '"and no man on earth cares for me"' (79). The title

147

'disappointed man' is not new to Carton. Henry Gowan too had claimed it, but with him it had functioned as nothing more than a mask for frustrated self-interest. With Carton the 'disappointment' goes much deeper, constituting his own critical response to a world that failed to provide sustenance to the 'youth of great promise' (298) he once had been, a world that early left him no chance for his life but in 'rust and repose'. The difference between the two marks the point of separation between the mere 'cultivated wastrel' and the figure of the spiritual dandy/waif as Dickens now develops it. So much at least would seem to be implicit in Carton's recollections of the self-betrayal into which he has, apparently inevitably, been drawn.

Carton's professed carelessness conceals, in fact, a double alienation. Beneath the social contempt of his 'fully half-insolent manner' (77) – a curiously ambiguous description – there lies an estrangement that goes beyond the self-distrust from which Clennam and Harmon suffer, anticipating the utter self-contempt Pip will later experience. Where Pip's self-division stems from a compound of guilt and social inferiority, Carton's has its roots in a consciousness of moral weakness and potential unfulfilled. The point is made most strongly in the set-piece which follows Carton's first meeting with his 'counterpart' (77) Darnay, an abbreviated 'solo' which carries a psychic symbolism comparable to John Harmon's much more extended meditation (with considerably less of its technical obtrusiveness). Addressing his own reflection in bitter soliloquy after the departure of his morally superior alter ego, Carton appears surrounded by refracted images of his own divided self – as he once was, might have been, and is. The sense of unstable, multiplying identities is indeed so strong that the speaker's final words seem directed as much to himself as to their ostensible object, that self's more fortunate 'double':

'Do you particularly like the man?' he muttered, at his own image; 'why should you particularly like a man who resembles you? There is nothing in you to like; you know that. Ah, confound you! What a change you have made in yourself! A good reason for taking to a man, that he shows you what you have fallen away from, and what you might have been! Change places with him, and would you have been looked at by those blue eyes as he was, and commiserated by that agitated face as he was? Come on, and have it out in plain words! You hate the fellow.'   (79)

Carton will, of course, change places with 'the fellow' and so fulfil his own estrangement. He is caught, in effect, in an emotional trap, driven to seek in the self-negating identity he has created – ' "a dissolute dog who has never done any good, and never will" ' (197) – justification of the self-destructive impulse which first led to its adoption. ' "Now you know me," ' he appeals almost eagerly to Darnay, ' "you know I am incapable of all the higher and better flights of men. If you doubt it, ask Stryver, and he'll tell you so" ' (197). It is as if he cannot bear to contemplate the true nature of the self he has denied for so long. Like Arthur Clennam before him, and Pip and John Harmon after, Carton retreats into a passivity which is itself another form of suppression. He too is a participant in his own estrangement, deliberately and also, seemingly, inevitably embracing a negation that will render him less than 'Nobody'. Even when revealing to Lucie Manette the existence of that other self of great promise never yet fulfilled, Carton does so with a 'fixed despair of himself' (143) that speaks of complete surrender, a despair that will reappear most conspicuously in John Jasper and his resignation to the impossibility of integration. In a still more profound sense than Harmon, Carton exists in a state of emotional suspension as the shadow of his real self. Lucie weeps to think 'how much he had thrown away, and how much he every day kept down and perverted' (145). But though she perceives his own part in the betrayal, she fails to acknowledge the dimension of inevitability that runs through his history. His is the tragedy of one 'self flung away' (143) for want of a goal worth dedicating that self to, a goal society has never provided and even Lucie cannot supply. Like John Harmon once more in this, Carton too proves unable to break free from the negation in which he has co-operated for so long. He too fails to discover for himself an alternative identity, a means of positive self-definition.

Not even the love of a good woman can restore the self-described ' "wasted, drunken, poor creature of misuse" ' (143) to life, as Bella Wilfer will resurrect the 'living-dead man' Harmon, and Amy Dorrit free the prisoner Clennam. Carton's love for Lucie is, in his own words, a fire ' "inseparable in its nature from myself, quickening nothing, lighting nothing, doing no service, idly burning away" ' (144). If Lucie is the object, the something to trust in, and care for, and think well of, Carton had sought for so many years, she has been found too late. And he remains, until his apotheosis at the guillotine, 'the man of good abilities and good emotions, incapable of their directed exercise, incapable of his own help and his own happiness, sensible of the blight on him, and resigning himself to let it eat him away' (85). He is in this an important anticipation of the fate of Bradley Heastone and, perhaps,

John Jasper, one of whom at least will die without even the tenuous comfort of Carton's conditional consolation. In all three, good abilities and good emotions have become irretrievably perverted.

Throughout *A Tale of Two Cities* Carton exists, essentially, in a state of spiritual death, a condition he himself repeatedly acknowledges. '"I am,"' he tells Lucie Manette, '"like one who died young. All my life might have been"' (143). The declaration comes as the culmination of the series of self-negating identities he has embraced: the 'disappointed man', the 'dissolute dog who has never done any good, and never will', the 'wasted, drunken, poor creature of misuse'. And the words spoken here will be echoed significantly much later in the novel, as Carton meditates on the end he has chosen: 'Long ago, when he had been famous among his earliest competitors as a youth of great promise, he had followed his father to the grave' (297–298). The literal meaning of the phrase is obvious, of course, as he hears again in memory the words of the burial service. But, in a deeper sense, Carton had followed his father to the grave, living since that time as the shadow, or ghost, of the youth he once had been, his promise dissipated in drink and other more insidious self-betrayals. What Carton goes to at the guillotine is, in effect, a second death designed to put this first one right. He too, no less than the Bastille prisoner, must be 'recalled to life'. But at the heart of his history there lies the paradox that will, in modified form, shape Pip's experience too. For Carton discovery, or rather recovery, of the true self comes only with self-abandonment. It is the essence of his predicament that self-fulfilment can be found only in the ultimate self-sacrifice. He is, finally, resurrected *into* death, not from it.

Viewed in the light of his history of determined self-destruction, Carton's final sacrifice scarcely presents the sort of victory of life and love against the forces of darkness so many commentators have taken it to be. The utter resignation, the sense of complete self-surrender with which he abandons himself to his far, far better fate, fatally undercuts any suggestion of redemptive significance. Even the regenerated society Carton foresees on the scaffold remains suspended in the curious conditional past of a dying man's potential vision: 'If he had given utterance to his [thoughts], and they had been prophetic, they would have been these' (357), a possibility not once but twice removed. What the guillotine offers is oblivion to one who had long sought it by other means, convinced, as he himself says, that '"I have no business to be, at all, that I know of"' (133).

Carton's manner on the eve of his self-willed death is, significantly, that of a 'tired man, who had wandered and struggled and got lost, but who at length struck into his road and saw its end' (297), and this is precisely the point. Death is the only journey's end for him, the only refuge and rest his world offers. As he remarks to Mr Lorry, in a phrase that could stand as his own epitaph, '"my young way was never the way to age. Enough of me"' (296). Carton has had enough of himself. He will not grow old because he does not seek to. For this Dickens hero the acceptance of an inevitable alienation takes its final form in the acceptance of the ultimate alienation of death. For him positive selfhood can only be achieved vicariously – and conditionally – in a namesake yet unborn who will reclaim in life the self Carton can only fulfil in death:

'I see the child who lay upon her bosom and who bore my name, a man winning his way up in that path of life which once was mine. I see him winning it so well, that my name is made illustrious there by the light of his. I see the blots I threw upon it, faded away.' (358)

Carton's sacrifice, while it exalts his recovered generosity, devotion and fortitude, establishes beyond doubt the vulnerability of such values in the world he leaves behind. Indeed, the recovery and the sacrifice are inseparable, the one impossible without the other. Neither through his own exertions, nor anyone else's, can Carton find a refuge other than death. He remains, in fact, deliberately problematic in a way which marks a further deepening of the Dickens hero's predicament, for he remains a self-suppressed, self-divided wanderer unable at last to overcome his own negation. His predicament is suspended for ever by his act of self-sacrifice, not resolved. That is the only 'end' he can hope for. It is a symbolic legacy shared to some extent by all his successors, though not all will die to realize its implications.

In apparent contrast to the self-doomed Carton, Eugene Wrayburn ends his spiritual progress in a determination to '"fight it out to the last gasp"' (813) within a world that can now be escaped only by 'Poor Carton''s means. Yet the battle, and its implications, remain essentially the same for both. For Wrayburn too is divided between a true self and an assumed/imposed identity which betrays it. With Carton the 'dandy' pose of professed indifference had emerged as a response to a society offering no more positive role, a form of silent indictment. With Wrayburn its function becomes yet more complex. To see in him merely a reworking of the idle gentleman Steerforth is to miss the double significance with which Dickens invests 'this utterly careless

Eugene' (286). His assumption of indifference constitutes, in fact, both a social response *and* an externally imposed role, and carries a doubly inescapable estrangement with it. For Wrayburn moves in a 'good society' which has reduced impressibility to the level of weakness or solecism. Like his friend and imitator Mortimer Lightwood, he is capable of a feeling, human response to the story of the wretched Harmon children Lightwood tells. But, as a member of 'good society', he suppresses the inadmissable emotion as he manifestly suppresses so much else:

There is that in the indolent Mortimer, which seems to hint that if good society might on any account allow itself to be impressible, he, one of good society, might have the weakness to be impressed with what he here relates. It is hidden with great pains, but it is in him. The gloomy Eugene, too, is not without some kindred touch . . .   (14)

It is, indeed, at the cost of 'great pains' that Wrayburn conforms to the dictates of a society in which the specious Veneering, 'sly, mysterious, filmy' (10), stands as 'representative man' (244). The identity he embraces, or at least accepts – '"a young man of very fair family, good appearance, and some talent"' (817) in the words of Lady Tippins – is a definition based solely on externals, one which necessarily denies the inner man who must not, 'on any account', be revealed. A society based on surface and sham can 'admit' nothing more genuine. Eugene is 'buried alive' (11) in the world of Podsnap, Veneering and Tippins, and in a double sense. For, acquiescing in his own self-estrangement, Wrayburn retreats too into a determined isolation which is his response to the 'good society' that has made such estrangement a condition of membership. In effect, he turns his socially approved posture of insolent carelessness against society itself. And yet, in doing so, he only compounds his own psychic divisions. Capable of any number of small demonstrations of scorn and indifference – 'ferociously' (14) trifling with his dessert-knife in a parody of self-assertion at the Veneering table; eating the man's dinners but refusing to talk – Wrayburn is unable to free himself entirely from the paralysing conventions of 'good society'. He exists in a state of emotional suspension, withdrawn into a private world shared only by his soulmate Lightwood, contenting himself with the contemplation of his own cool superiority. Mortimer's worried comment to his immovable friend on the worsening state of his affairs – '"You have fallen into the hands of the Jews, Eugene"' – elicits a declaration of wilful isolation that suggests less a concession of defeat (as in the case of Carton) than a refusal to engage: '"My dear boy," returned the debtor, very composedly taking up his glass, "having previously fallen into the hands of some of the Christians, I can bear it with philosophy"' (535).

Taking Fascination Fledgeby as a specimen of 'some of the Christians' who populate the world of *Our Mutual Friend* – '"As to Christians," proceeded Fledgeby, "look out, fellow Christians, particularly you that lodge in Queer Street! I have got the run of Queer Street now, and you shall see some games there"' (432) – Wrayburn's contempt appears increasingly justified. As with Carton's preference for 'rust and repose' to the blustering self-advancement of Stryver, Eugene's very embrace of dissociation suggests a moral sensitivity for which society has no value, and no outlet. And yet, as with Carton too, the pose of 'reckless indifference' (286) with which he effects his disengagement constitutes a betrayal of the self he would save. 'Poor Carton' had proved incapable of discovering a means of positive definition on this side of the grave, and Wrayburn fares little better. If Sydney was a self-described 'dissolute dog', Eugene is a 'bad idle' one (235). Indeed Wrayburn has all but abandoned the attempt to become anything else, having long ago resigned himself to being a 'riddle without an answer' (238) and no more:

'You know what I am, my dear Mortimer. You know how dreadfully susceptible I am to boredom. You know that when I became enough of a man to find myself an embodied conundrum, I bored myself to the last degree by trying to find out what I meant. You know that at length I gave it up, and declined to guess any more.' (286)

With Harthouse, 'boredom' had functioned as a badge of social cynicism and class contempt. With Eugene it goes much deeper. He is being, as Lightwood perceives, true to his 'utterly careless' (286) self in this. For he carries that carelessness to its logical conclusion, professing indifference even to the self that must take its place in a world demonstrably not worth the caring for. It is the paradox that lies at the heart of his experience: in being true to himself he betrays himself. If there is an underlying despair, a consciousness of emptiness below the surface flippancy, Wrayburn is yet plainly an active participant in the estrangement that results. Like Clennam, Harmon and Pip, as well as Carton, he is driven to co-operate in his own suppression.

What is more, Wrayburn actively exploits his avowed lack of self-knowledge, using it as a means of evading the moral implications of his pursuit of Lizzie Hexam, further complicating the mechanism of his own divisions. When Lightwood first learns of his friend's continued involvement with the waterman's daughter, he confronts him with the questions to which such conduct must inevitably give rise. And Eugene shuffles off the questions, as he does the reproach they convey, by renouncing all control over self and circumstances alike:

'Eugene, do you design to capture and desert this girl?'
'My dear fellow, no.'
'Do you design to marry her?'
'My dear fellow, no.'
'Do you design to pursue her?'
'My dear fellow, I don't design anything. I have no design whatever. I am incapable of design. If I conceived a design, I should speedily abandon it, exhausted by the operation.' (294)

Eugene is telling the truth: he does not know what the final outcome of his passion will be. Indeed, he never knows. Beseeched by the worried Lightwood to '"Look on to the end"', his confession of weakness is explicit: '"Ah! See now! That's exactly what I am incapable of doing"' (537). He has no fixed objective beyond pursuit. But there is a sense in which he seems to speak as much for his own benefit as for Mortimer's, avoiding the admission of his own potential, if not yet actual, wrongdoing. In him passivity now amounts to a surrender of moral responsibility. If he designs nothing then he cannot be at fault and need not blame himself, whatever consequences ensue:

'I am bent on finding Lizzie, and I mean to find her, and I will take any means of finding her that offer themselves. Fair means or foul means are all alike to me. I ask you – for information – what does that mean? when I have found her I may ask you – also for information – what do I mean now? But it would be premature in this stage, and it's not the character of my mind.' (537)

Self-estrangement here combines with self-deception to become a form of moral escapism, and the result is yet deeper division. Eugene draws on the lack of self-knowledge in which he has so long acquiesced to hide himself from himself, and in so doing further suppresses the better nature that requires to be so deceived.

Wrayburn's predicament, his division between a social identity he will not, cannot, overcome and the true self that identity displaces, comes increasingly in the course of *Our Mutual Friend* to crystallize around the figure of Lizzie Hexam. She represents the only possibility of self-discovery and self-fulfilment for him, as Agnes Wickfield, Amy

Dorrit and Bella Wilfer had done for other Dickens heroes. Yet, for all her ability to lift the dying Betty Higden 'as high as Heaven' (514) in her loving arms, Lizzie is no simple, sexless saviour, no Agnes forever pointing upward. For before he is thrown into the river, all but dead, to be rescued by Lizzie's love, Wrayburn's passion for her has led him to an ever-increasing self-estrangement, to manifest cruelty, even sadism, and to the brink of seduction. She stirs, of course, still greater depths in the suffering Bradley Headstone. The feelings Lizzie awakens in both her lovers, far from redeeming either, actually take on increasingly perverted, and self-destructive, forms. Deprived of Lizzie's presence by her own determined flight, Wrayburn relieves his disappointment by tormenting the wretched Headstone in a manner which, for all its negligence, falls little short of the wilfully sadistic. The class dimension of the conflict between them could not be more clearly established than by the elaborate parody of fox-hunting Eugene devises, with himself as the gentleman sportsman and the miserable Headstone the quarry. The coolness with which he undertakes the 'pleasures of the chase' (543) makes the carefully planned torture these nightly excursions represent all the more hateful. Even Lightwood is astonished 'that so careless a man could be so wary, and that so idle a man could take so much trouble' (544). And, in his gratuitous cruelty, Wrayburn closely approaches – perhaps even outdoes – his dandy forebear Gowan. Eugene is, in fact, vicious here in a way that has surprised critics of *Our Mutual Friend*, another index of how far the Dickens hero has travelled from the innocent vulnerability and helplessness of young David Copperfield. For his hatefulness becomes much less surprising when it is viewed within the context of the hero's deepening moral ambiguity, even culpability, itself inseparable from the shaping vision of the increasingly inimical, and increasingly invasive, world the hero inhabits. And yet Eugene is never simply a wicked aristocratic predator. His refusal to confront the true meaning of his attraction to Lizzie also recalls Clennam's own inevitable self-deception over Pet Meagles. Certainly, in the ensuing rivalry with Headstone, he seems no less determined to punish himself for his '"most ridiculous position"' (696) than Clennam does for his own 'weakness'. Eugene's deliberate goading of the desperate schoolmaster suggests more than class contempt. It carries too a dimension of self-destructive yearning, a compulsive provocation of the other man's violence which further qualifies the first effects of Lizzie's love upon him. There are disturbing undercurrents to his relations with the tormented Headstone that go beyond the undeniable cruelty of his gentlemanly 'sport', impulses sparked into life by the gentleman's unsettling, and highly ambiguous, passion for the waterman's daughter. The two men are, indeed, united in a love that threatens the only self-definitions they possess, a love that will ultimately make one a murderer, the other his victim, binding them even here.

For if Lizzie finally resurrects Eugene to a new life, she first innocently precipitates his near-death, morally and spiritually no less than physically. Her first influence upon him is not redemption or reform, but rather an 'intensification of all that [is] wildest and most negligent and most reckless' (166) in his character. She introduces, in fact, 'something new and strained in him' (166). Their relations unfold within a framework of conventional social expectations early outlined by Mortimer Lightwood – '"Do you design to capture and desert this girl?"' (294) – acceptance of which would signal not only moral collapse for Wrayburn but, equally, a submission to the deadening creed of the 'good society' he so rightly scorns. It is, after all, James Steerforth's adherence to the class conventions of capture and desertion that leads to his own watery death, an adherence Wrayburn must, and does, strain against. And yet to reject such norms outright is to abandon the only identifying role Eugene possesses. Young men of 'very fair family, good appearance, and some talent' do not love or marry watermen's daughters, though they do seduce them, as Steerforth has demonstrated. 'Society' can no more admit the possibility than Mrs Steerforth could: '"I am sorry to repeat, it is impossible. Such a marriage would irretrievably blight my son's career, and ruin his prospects. Nothing is more certain than that it never can take place, and never will"' (*DC* 401). To compound the division still further, there are in operation here too the somewhat nobler conventions of class honour for which Lightwood is spokesman, conventions which yet constitute a denial of the genuine emotion Wrayburn feels. For Lightwood too the emotion is inadmissible. In his estimation, if Eugene truly loves Lizzie, then the difference between them makes it all the more necessary for him to renounce her. This is the most the gentleman's love can do in the world of 'good society': '"But if you do care for her, so much the more you should leave her to herself"' (536). It is a claim Lizzie herself will later raise. And against this assumption too Wrayburn struggles. He is torn between the gratification of a selfish passion in the socially sanctioned manner and the rejection of that heartless society through an act of deeper love. Lizzie has shaken the very foundations of his self, stripping him of his customary defences and deceptions, as he himself passionately avows:

'Lizzie! I never thought before, that there was a woman in the world who could affect me so much by saying so little. But don't be hard in your construction of me. You don't know what my state of mind towards you is. You don't know how the cursed carelessness that is overofficious in helping me at every other turning of my life, WON'T help me here. You have struck it dead, I think, and I sometimes wish you had struck me dead along with it.'   (692)

Deprived of the carelessness which has insulated him for so long, Wrayburn is brought at last to confront his own essential division. His encounter with Lizzie by the riverside takes him, as he himself will recognize, to the crisis point, and the issue seems genuinely in doubt. For there is a part of Eugene which struggles against the self-knowledge that forces itself upon him even as his better nature struggles towards it. As he walks by the river its flowing water becomes a reflection of his own fast moving thoughts, showing him the direction to which they inexorably tend: 'As the ripple under the moon broke unexpectedly now and then, and palely flashed in a new shape and with a new sound, so parts of his thoughts started, unbidden, from the rest, and revealed their wickedness. "Out of the question to marry her," said Eugene, "and out of the question to leave her. The crisis!"' (698). At the very moment when Wrayburn is attacked he is balanced uneasily between seduction and renunciation, divided between the competing versions of the self they represent. Like Pip, he faces a moment of absolute choice, but lacks the moral strength to choose correctly. In fact, the choice will be made for him. Before Eugene can reclaim his true self, the social identity which suppresses it must be destroyed, and so it is. He is beaten almost to death and thrown into the river.

It is not Wrayburn that Lizzie rescues from the water but a thing scarcely to be recognized as a person, a thing without name, sense, or motion. There is no Eugene at all, only a shattered object floating in the river: 'It was insensible, if not virtually dead; it was mutilated, and streaked the water all about it with dark red streaks. As it could not help itself, it was impossible for her to get it on board' (700). This is what the 'immovable' Eugene has come to, the symbolic fulfilment of his socially induced negation. And it is from this utterly helpless 'wreck' (753) that the real self is at last to rise. Yet it now seems possible that selfhood will prove to have come too late, that self-discovery, identical with death for Carton, will here be forestalled by it. For Eugene emerges from the river to a state of suspension likened to another drowning, an ironic reenactment of his original division. Fading in and out of consciousness, he repeatedly loses and as often regains his identity and knowledge of himself. Estrangement takes on a new form as Eugene despairingly finds himself withdrawn from his own world and sent to wander in unknown places, oppressed all the while by a longing to return. His very struggles against this enforced separation – struggles he would not, indeed could not, make before – only compound its effects: 'As the man rising from the deep would disappear the sooner for fighting with the water, so he in his desperate struggle went down again' (740). The once indolent Eugene has discovered in the ruins of his old self a new sense of purpose. He is buoyed up now by the spiritual energy he had lacked so conspicuously for so long, and yet it scarcely seems to be enough, for it cannot prevent him from sinking. The 'gloomy Eugene' (13) who had sat in silent contempt at the Veneering dinner-table now seeks desperately to break his silence, and the impulse marks the beginning of self-recovery: '"Don't tell me not to speak, for I must speak. If you knew the harassing anxiety that gnaws and wears me when I am wandering in those places – where are those endless places, Mortimer? They must be at an immense distance!"' (737–738).

The anxiety which so oppresses Eugene in his 'wandering' is his desire to return and make reparation, and it is in the wish that the source of true self-fulfilment lies. For, as with Arthur Clennam, the act of 'reparation' proves equally an act of identification and an acceptance of responsibility. After endlessly losing himself in the distant worlds where he is now forced to wander, Eugene returns long enough to communicate a resolution to Lightwood: his attacker, Headstone, is not to be pursued or brought to justice. His 'murder' (738), and Wrayburn himself terms it so, must be subordinated to the protection of Lizzie from the slander prosecution would generate: '"Lizzie and my reparation before all!"' (739). The situation effectively reworks John Harmon's connivance at his own 'death', with Eugene an accomplice in his own 'murder'. Yet here the act signals not self-negation but recovery. Willing now to sacrifice the last remnants of himself for Lizzie's sake, surrendering even the just retribution for his death to protect her name, Eugene assumes at last responsibility for his own self and all that self had once designed:

'Her innocent reputation would be ruined, my friend. She would be punished, not he. I have wronged her enough in fact; I have wronged her still more in intention. You recollect what pavement is said to be made of good intentions. It is made of bad intentions too. Mortimer, I am lying on it, and I know!'   (738)

As with Carton, it is through self-sacrifice that self-recovery is achieved. The riddle has now found an answer and it speaks through Wrayburn's last words, 'I know.' But there remains one thing wanting which Eugene cannot supply. It is the Dolls' Dressmaker who provides the final word. Lizzie is to be Eugene's wife; only then will the reparation be complete. When, on the evening of this discovery, Lizzie enters the injured man's room, the Dolls' Dressmaker asks if he is conscious. And it is Eugene who answers the question, adding the missing word to his earlier declaration: '"He is conscious, Jenny," murmured Eugene for himself. "He knows his wife"' (742).

It was through Lizzie that Wrayburn was brought to destruction in the river, by her that he was rescued from its waters, and it is in her that he at last finds the means of true self-definition. Her voice speaking his name has the power to call him back from his wanderings, as her faith and love empower him to begin life anew, to live rather than die for her sake. She is his 'refuge' (753) and more. Through marriage to the waterman's daughter the 'T'Other Governor' finds at last 'the right course of a true man' (742), a role and an identity which fulfil his true nature. And yet it is this very marriage which sets the seal on Wrayburn's social alienation, for he can have no place in the 'good society' which sees in his love nothing more than 'a ridiculous affair' (817). Unlike Carton, Wrayburn has not found a better rest but rather a perpetual estrangement, a fate he accepts as the inevitable accompaniment of his reclaimed selfhood. If Lizzie is his 'refuge', she is also, necessarily, his only home. This is not simply a replaying of the Steerforth/Emily plot, with Eugene surviving his ordeal by water to supply the 'happy ending' earlier withheld. There is no 'ending' here, no fairy-tale banishment of Podsnap and all that he represents of repressive, inhuman and unbending social authority. Beyond their union, Lizzie and Eugene face a future of strictly limited consolations, sustained by the hope that the 'sadly wan and worn Eugene' may not be 'much disfigured by-and-bye' (811). There is no other resolution. For the Podsnap world can no more vanish than the 'Voice of Society' can be silenced. In fact, the two 'end' the novel with their perpetual uproar. It is, surely, significant that of all the participants in the final, representative 'Social Chorus', it is of Twemlow alone that Mortimer

Lightwood does not enquire ' "Now I wonder whether *you* are the Voice of Society?" ' (818). The marginality of Twemlow and the genuine moral values he represents in a world of surface, veneer and 'Podsnappery' could not be clearer. He may redefine gentlemanly status in a manner Pip himself could not have bettered: ' "I beg to say that when I use the word gentleman, I use it in the sense in which the degree may be attained by any man" ' (819–820). It is not a form that will ever pass current in 'Society'. It too, like so much else, will plainly not be 'admitted'. Wrayburn's journey ends in a determination to struggle to the last, as he must do, for the self he has reclaimed. For him, as for so many of his predecessors, the battle will always continue, this being the inescapable condition of his self-recovery. But for the two Dickens heroes to come, the conflict will at last prove fatal, as they live out, or rather die for, the implications of Eugene's spiritual progress.

CONCLUSION

The Self Destroyed:
The Dickens Hero as 'Villain'

Having begun this study with the words of Angus Wilson's classic essay, it seems appropriate to conclude with them too. For Wilson, writing once more in 'The Heroes and Heroines of Dickens', Eugene Wrayburn marks the culmination of a process of development begun with the creation of Steerforth, the end of 'all those twists and turns by which Dickens eventually transforms a somewhat stray villain into a full-sized hero'.[1] And the view forms an obvious corollary to his contention, cited in the preceding chapter, that the rehabilitated Eugene of *Our Mutual Friend*'s closing pages – '"I make no protestations," said Eugene, "who does, who means them? – I have made a resolution"' (811) – represents a 'redemption' of his wayward, and doomed, predecessor. But the process of development being traced here, the evolution of the Dickens hero and the progressive limitations of his prospects of social accommodation and integration, does not end with Wrayburn's significantly shadowed rebirth. It is not merely that the issue of Eugene's 'redemption' is itself problematic, he being more accurately vindicated in his indifferentism than redeemed from it. It is also that the fates of Wrayburn and Carton both, the one just succeeding in reclaiming his true self at the price of an enduring social estrangement, the other able to find self-fulfilment only in death, deepen still further the implications of the Dickens hero's experience. For they raise the possibility of self-destruction as the end of the search for selfhood, and it is this possibility Dickens takes up with the figures of the morally compromised and psychically alienated Bradley Headstone and John Jasper. Neither is a 'somewhat stray villain' transformed into a 'full-sized hero'. The process works, rather, the other way. They are divided souls metamorphosed into murderers and, in the case of Headstone at least, into a suicide as well. Far from culminating in 'redemption', the spiritual journey of these last Dickens heroes has no other end but moral and physical self-destruction.[2]

With Headstone and Jasper, Dickens is, in fact, giving final form to the threats which have increasingly shadowed the hero's experience, threats of a self unable at last to be reclaimed (virtually the case with Carton), or compromised too deeply (suggested with Wrayburn), or suppressed too long (a possibility half-realized with Harmon). He does so by inverting the pattern of that experience as previously established. The personal histories of the two men begin, in effect, where the story of the Dickens hero formerly ended: in a recognition of the fact of a world hostile to true selfhood, a world which can be neither defeated nor escaped. Both possess at the outset the established place and function the Dickens hero characteristically lacks, Headstone as the 'highly certificated stipendiary schoolmaster' (210), Jasper as the self-described 'poor monotonous chorister and grinder of music' (12). And this is the heart of their predicament, for the place and function distort, indeed destroy, the self they should define. The Dickens hero had previously come to accept, at his journey's end, a condition of social alienation as the inevitable accompaniment of selfhood. Headstone and Jasper begin their journey having accepted psychic estrangement as the price of a precarious social accommodation. Each is acutely conscious of the toll exacted by his social role: Jasper subduing himself and all natural 'ambition, aspiration, restlessness, dissatisfaction' (12) to the mechanical demands of his 'vocation' (12); Headstone 'watching and repressing himself daily' (291) to discharge his no less mechanical 'duties' (291). Although Jasper, with his musical performances and his 'gift of teaching' (11), is one of the few genuinely creative artists to feature in Dickens's fiction, in contrast to the comic incapables like Miss La Creevy or the impostors like Gowan, it is not this aspect of his 'vocation' which is stressed. It is rather the wearying repetitiveness of the cathedral routine that is emphasized. Jasper's music does feature as an emotional outlet Headstone is entirely denied, but only in highly sinister circumstances – when he sits 'chanting choir-music in a low and beautiful voice' (103) before his 'unaccountable' (130) excursion with Durdles, and on the afternoon of the murder, when he is again found in 'beautiful voice' (128).

Like Clennam and Harmon, like Pip, Carton and Wrayburn, both Headstone and Jasper are active participants in their own suppression. Both are indeed aware of their co-operation/co-option in negation from the outset, as their predecessors are not. Yet there is now, for them, no hope of recovery or 'redemption'. The self which ultimately breaks free of its constricting social identity proves so deformed as to be irrecoverable, finding fulfilment only in murder, and self-destruction.

It is a fate anticipated by the increasingly qualified 'resolutions' the hero's journey has found, from Clennam at large in the noisy streets to Pip left homeless and (potentially) alone, and one most clearly forecast by the virtual suicide of 'Poor Carton'. But Carton, with his 'far, far better thing', was able to recover a best, a true self in death at least if not in life. In Headstone and Jasper years of repression and subjugation have destroyed the best self that might once have existed. The true self now finds its true expression in the murderous impulses and violent sexual passions finally let loose, as Jasper finds his 'voice' on the day of his nephew's death. An analysis of Headstone's plight serves as description for both: 'It seemed to him as if all that he could suppress in himself he had suppressed, as if all that he could restrain in himself he had restrained, and the time had come – in a rush, in a moment – when the power of self-command had departed from him' (341). That self-command, so long and so painfully maintained, leaves in its place a self perverted beyond redemption.

Like Jasper, who would carve demons out of his heart as a relief from his 'daily drudging round' (11) – as the monks of the cathedral had once carved them 'out of the stalls and seats and desks' (11) – Headstone too is engaged in what is essentially a process of self-mutilation. The point is underscored by the repeated imagery of torture which accompanies his progress through the novel. And the implications of his experience seem clear. Headstone, dead among the 'ooze and scum' (802) of Plashwater Weir Mill Lock, completes the triptych formed by 'the living-dead man' (373) Harmon, restored to selfhood only through the intervention of others, and the 'sadly wan and worn' (811) Eugene, fighting it out to the last gasp for the woman who has resurrected him. Headstone represents, indeed, the darkest version of the story all three tell: the story of the self beleaguered and inevitably estranged in, and from, a society for which Veneering is the 'representative man' – 'which cannot in these times be doubted' (224) – and Lady Tippins the unsilenceable voice.

The educational automaton, who yet possesses in him 'enough of what was animal, and of what was fiery (though smouldering)' (218) to require a different fate, is confined to a machine-like 'routine of educational tricks' (546) by a world which does not 'admit' the discrepancy. Mr Podsnap no more acknowledges the possibility of spiritual starvation among the inhabitants of '"The World's Metropolis, London, Londres, London"' (132), his own young person included, than he does the fact of physical want. In a society of such surfaces Headstone's depths can find no proper channel and must, therefore, forge their own. And it will prove a 'dark and deep and stormy one, and difficult to sound' (388). There is a fatal disjunction between his imposed role – the pauper lad was, the text implies, 'told off' for teaching as he might otherwise have been 'told off for the sea' (218) – and his true self. As Eugene Wrayburn judges, the man is ' "too passionate for a good schoolmaster" ' (292), for he fails fully to dismiss his 'man's nature' (291) in forming himself to his mechanical part. Confronted with the self-possessed Eugene's cool contempt, Bradley, tormented by his own 'red and white heats of rage' (294), makes an 'errant motion of his hands as if he could have torn himself' (292). And this is what he does by acquiescing in the self-suppression demanded by his 'most respectable' (288) calling. Subduing his natural energies according to the dictates of a society that offers them no natural expression, he is tearing himself emotionally, psychologically, and morally. His final descent to murder and suicide comes as the culmination of a social accommodation that is now seen to involve nothing less than spiritual self-destruction.

And it is this same pattern of meaning which shapes the course of Headstone's murderous successor. For numerous critics of *Edwin Drood*, John Jasper is, simply, an intuitive portrait of a recognizable pathological type, a criminal schizophrenic whose self, mind and memory break into two distinct parts and hold no sort of communion. It is a view of the character most famously, and most influentially, formulated by Edmund Wilson in his essay 'Dickens: The Two Scrooges'. Quoting a frequently cited passage in the text beginning 'As in some cases of drunkenness, and in others of animal magnetism, there are two states of consciousness which never clash' (15), Wilson concludes 'John Jasper has, then, "two states of consciousness"; he is, in short, what we have come to call a dual personality.'[3] The biographical conclusions Wilson goes on to draw from this need not concern us here. But there is a corollary to his 'psychological' interpretation that is significant. For Wilson and his many followers, Jasper the schizophrenic is, in his 'normal' state, ignorant of the crime he commits and unconscious of the deadly irony with which he devotes himself to the pursuit and destruction of his nephew's murderer. Yet this emphasis on the disconnection of Jasper's opposing selves actually obscures the implications of the duality which so clearly afflicts him. For his is not, in fact, the dilemma of the unconscious schizophrenic, unaware of the conflict he embodies. Rather, Jasper is the conscious

Conclusion

instrument of his own division, wittingly suppressing in one sphere of
his existence the natural energies he expresses so unnaturally in
another. (With both Headstone and Jasper, Dickens makes it clear that
the frustration of unfulfilled sexual drives plays a large part in their
self-torment.) He is split between two personae he has himself co-
operated in creating: the 'respectable' choir master on the one hand,
the habitué of London opium dens on the other. The one identity is a
compensation for the repression the other demands. Both lead only to
further self-distortion that continues a now unbreakable cycle. In
effect, Jasper has already carved demons out of his own heart, demons
he feeds each time he 'lights his pipe, and delivers himself to the
Spectres it invokes at midnight' (38). And 'delivers', with its sense of
voluntary submission, is the key word to note.

For Wilson and the critics who follow him, Jasper's chief significance
is as a case study in psychic dislocation, Dickens having, in Wilson's
view, 'dropped away here all the burden of analyzing society' which
weighs so heavily on the other late novels, developing instead what he
calls 'the psychological interest'.[4] Yet once the 'poor monotonous
chorister' (12) immured in a routine which, in his own words, '"grinds
me away by the grain"' (11), is seen as being the co-author of his own
alienation, the 'psychological' and 'social' implications of his experience become inseparable. Jasper stands, indeed, as the culmination of
that line of self-divided protagonists, those characteristic 'heroes',
whose psychic plight increasingly forms Dickens's most profound
social indictment. Like them a participant in his own estrangement, his
co-operation, like theirs, becomes a complex response to a world that
cannot be escaped, a response at once voluntary and inevitable. Just as
Headstone could find no identity or role commensurate with his
'passionate' true self in a society of 'Podsnappery' and veneer, so
Jasper's passionate energies must stand opposed to the 'oppressive
respectability' (14) of the Cloisterham world. His is a dualism fostered
by a society whose respectability is as repressive as it is oppressive, a
deadening world inimical to living desires and energies.

Nor is Jasper the only one who suffers in the 'monotonous, silent city'
(14), dominated by a dead past in the shape of 'vestiges of monastic
graves' (14) and 'fragments of old wall, saint's chapel, chapter-house,
convent, and monastery' (14). Even Mr Crisparkle, 'Minor Canon and
good man' (6) is, as his title suggests, diminished by its constricting
influence. For he is forced to submit his goodness to the expedient
worldliness of Cloisterham's 'prudent Dean' (145), chief representative

of its respectable, and charity-less, official Christianity. While the Minor Canon would shelter the unfortunate suspect Neville in his home, 'the authority to which the Minor Canon deferred officially' (145) makes such humanity impossible: '"Mr. Crisparkle," quoth the Dean, "human justice may err, but it must act according to its lights. The days of taking sanctuary are past. This young man must not take sanctuary with us"' (145). For all his 'Muscular Christian' vitality, Crisparkle recalls the superannuated gentleman Twemlow in *Our Mutual Friend*. For he too is marginal in a world dominated 'officially' by the luke-warm, self-satisfied Dean and others of his chapter: '"It does not become us, perhaps," pursued the Dean, "to be partizans. Not partizans. We clergy keep our hearts warm and our heads cool, and we hold a judiciaious middle course"' (146). And there is something undeniably enervated about the 'quiet place in the shadow of the Cathedral' (39) which is Crisparkle's home. Its very quaintness and tranquillity derive from the sense of life and energy long past and gone which pervades all Cloisterham.

Swaggering fighting men had had their centuries of ramping and raving about Minor Canon Corner, and beaten serfs had had their centuries of drudging and dying there, and powerful monks had had their centuries of being sometimes useful and sometimes harmful there, and behold they were all gone out of Minor Canon Corner, and so much the better. Perhaps one of the highest uses of their ever having been there, was, that there might be left behind, that blessed air of tranquillity which pervaded Minor Canon Corner, and that serenely romantic state of mind – productive for the most part of pity and forbearance – which is engendered by a sorrowful story that is all told, or a pathetic play that is played out. (39–40)

As Jasper proves, this 'blessed tranquillity', in which there is more than a suggestion of sterility and stagnation, breeds something besides pity and forbearance. Nor is the 'sorrowful story' of violence, evil and suffering in Cloisterham as yet 'all told'.

Crisparkle, however, the closest thing the novel comes to a conventional, 'heroic' presence, escapes quite lightly touched by the prevailing deadness of Cloisterham. According to Forster, he was to have married Helena Landless at novel's end.[5] And if the union of the exotic foreigner with the bachelor clergyman appears somewhat unlikely, it yet marks his alliance with a representative of the living energies so conspicuously lacking in Cloisterham's moribund confines. But for Jasper the influence of the 'monotonous, silent city' and its stifling respectability proves fatal. Bradley Headstone's enforced 'suppression of so much'

(218) results in monstrously deformed impulses of self-assertion, impulses which can only find fulfilment in a violence that is finally, and inevitably, self-directed. And Jasper's self-subjugation/self-distortion follows a similar course, leading first to opium addiction and then to the utter moral disintegration of murder. In a sense, his very degeneration is a perverse mark of integrity, an embodied indictment of a society incapable of accommodating his energies and needs. There is a deliberate ambiguity to the plight of both these 'respectable' murderers that takes still further the possibility raised by Carton's and Wrayburn's careers. With them the 'dandy' rejection of social engagement emerged as a mark of potential moral superiority. With Headstone and Jasper, murder becomes the logical, even the inevitable, result of their social predicament.

But while the relation of social cause and personal effect could scarcely be clearer in the case of the schoolmaster, a residual uncertainty necessarily hangs over the choirmaster's unfinished story. Unlike Headstone, Jasper conspicuously lacks a thematically significant past – indeed he lacks any past at all – to define unequivocally the meaning of his history. Plainly, he is constricted by his life in Cloisterham in ways which have grievously affected him. The burden of his cryptic speech to his nephew in the second chapter of the novel is precisely the ' "restlessness, dissatisfaction, what shall we call it?" ' (12) which he suffers within 'the confines of its oppressive respectability' (14). Yet it is simply never revealed how Jasper came to be caught as he is, whereas the progress of Headstone's psychic maiming is clear. The social mechanism which first brought the 'grinder of music' to embrace his own suppression, as he undoubtedly does – ' "I must subdue myself to my vocation . . . It is too late to find another now" ' (12) – is left a mystery. That such self-subjugation is at the heart of his increasingly intolerable plight is clear. How it came to be so is not. Perhaps it was Jasper himself who was to have supplied the final link the existing text consistently implies, providing in his last hours not merely an account of the murder of Edwin Drood but also of the personal history of that most fearful self-tormentor his murderer. For according to Forster's well-known account, the 'originality' of *The Mystery of Edwin Drood* 'was to consist in the review of the murderer's [Jasper's] career by himself at its close, when its temptations were to be dwelt upon as if, not he the culprit, but some other man, were the tempted. The last chapters were to be written in the condemned cell, to which his wickedness, all elaborately elicited from him as if told of another, had brought him.'[6]

The clue to the still more resonant mystery of John Jasper, no less than to that of the murder of Edwin Drood, would seem to lie in one more personal history Dickens did not live to write, a narrative Jasper never supplies. Whether or not this elaborate self-analysis (another version of John Harmon's 'solo', perhaps) would have established unequivocally what now exists essentially by implication alone, this does seem the only, the necessary, conclusion to Jasper's story. Irreparably maimed by the suppression in which he has himself co-operated, he has indeed become another man. He has been made a 'villain' and the condemned cell his journey's end. Dying with the novel half-finished, Dickens never took his hero further, nor even, indeed, so far. And there is a sense in which this too seems almost inevitable. There is, perhaps, nowhere further for the Dickens hero to go.

Notwithstanding the thematic fitness of the outline Forster supplies, enthusiasts of *Edwin Drood*'s mystery have been debating John Jasper's 'true' character and motivation for well over a century. And the peculiar demands of the mystery form, together with the half-finished state of the novel, inevitably invest his figure with a significance that is, at times, highly equivocal. In contrast to this, the nature and cause of Bradley Headstone's psychic divisions are made plain from his first appearance in *Our Mutual Friend*. There is a 'want of adaptation' (217) between the 'thoroughly decent young man of six-and-twenty' (217) and the social role he constrains himself to enact. It is a disjunction which reveals itself externally in 'a kind of settled trouble in the face' (217), the index of still greater trouble within. This much is established at once. Yet it is not simply that Headstone's is a 'naturally slow or inattentive intellect' (217) forced beyond its own capacity and conscious of the strain: 'He always seemed to be uneasy lest anything should be missing from his mental warehouse, and taking stock to assure himself' (217). Nor is it that in 'forming himself for the duties' he must discharge, 'watching and repressing himself daily to discharge them well' (291), the man has long subdued all spontaneous impulses to a soul-destroying educational routine, making his mind 'a place of mechanical stowage' (217), though this too is plainly part of his dilemma. Nor is it, finally, that in embracing his 'thoroughly decent' calling Headstone has forcibly separated himself from his own past, suppressing the fact of his pauper birth as incompatible with his present 'most respectable title' (288), though he has done this too: 'Regarding that origin of his, he was proud, moody, and sullen, desiring it to be forgotten. And few people knew of it' (218).

The real heart of Headstone's predicament is that he has suffered all these things, fracturing and mutilating himself in the process, to secure an identity which fails to provide him with either a fixed status or place. He has paid the price of self-alienation and received nothing but further alienation in return, with no more positive role open to him. Philip Collins has demonstrated the extent to which Dickens was drawing upon an identifiable contemporary phenomenon with his creation of the 'highly certificated stipendiary schoolmaster' (210): that of the pauper boy educated out of his own class yet with no natural home in any other. It is a double estrangement the 'certificated teacher' was likely to suffer, exposed to 'both the jealousy of the class he had left, and the disdain of the class he aspired to enter'.[7] And the plight is significantly compounded in Headstone's case by his determination to suppress his obscure origins. From at least the time of the writing of *A Christmas Carol* (1843), the necessity of an integration of past memory and present self is a constant theme in Dickens's fiction. He returns to the subject again in the 1848 Christmas tale *The Haunted Man*, as well as in the retrospective narratives of David Copperfield and Pip, and the peculiarly intense 1868 story 'George Silverman's Explanation'. In all these otherwise quite different narratives, a time-haunted protagonist seeks a means of reconciling past and present experience and the often competing versions of the self that experience creates. And it is precisely this reconciliation which Headstone must forgo. His present 'respectable' identity depends on the suppression of his former self, and the unacceptable passions that self embodied. He is the self-made man unmade by his own success: self-help in his case identical with self-destruction. It is a bitterly ironic revision of the myth that had seduced young Pip too. Charley Hexam, another 'self-help' exemplar, stands as an object lesson in *Our Mutual Friend* of the destructive consequences of rejecting one's past and the 'softening' influence of 'the old times' (712) that lie behind. He is a monster of selfishness, characterized by the unfeeling determination never to 'look back': '"What we have to do is, to turn our faces full in our new direction, and keep straight on"' (228). And this is now the means of attaining 'perfect respectability' (712) in the society of the novel. For Headstone perfect respectability means complete self-severance, and even so his wished-for goal eludes him. He pays the ultimate price of his own 'natural' identity and receives nothing in return but deeper dislocation.

In social terms schoolmasters like Headstone were indeed displaced persons, as Collins quotes a contemporary source to prove: 'What then is his calling? Whereabouts in the sliding scale of society is his position? . . . The labourer, the mechanic, the tradesman, the professional man, the clergy, all have their place and calling in the great hive: whereabouts is the schoolmaster's, and what is it?'[8] And Headstone himself, confronted in the person of Eugene Wrayburn with an assumption of superiority as unmerited as it is unshakeable, gives voice to the anguish of the social anomaly, conscious of deserving a status he will never win: '"You reproach me with my origin," said Bradley Headstone; "you cast insinuations at my bringing-up. But I tell you this, sir, I have worked my way onward, out of both and in spite of both, and have a right to be considered a better man than you, with better reasons for being proud"' (293). It is a right 'Society' will never admit.

Headstone is, plainly, divided from, and within, himself long before meeting the woman who will prove his 'ruin' (395). And he forms in this a significant parallel to his otherwise contrasting rival Wrayburn. In both men the emotions Lizzie Hexam so innocently arouses serve to deepen an existing estrangement. But where the result is, finally, resurrection for Eugene out of virtual destruction, Headstone finds no such salvation. It is not merely that years of enforced suppression have left him no means of combating the passion and jealousy so spontaneously kindled within him. For the one-time 'pauper lad' love of the waterman's daughter means too the embrace of the poverty and obscurity he has laboured so hard to escape. In the very midst of his 'passion' he is 'contending with himself' (346) once more, resenting the weakness that has forced him to love Lizzie while yet devoting himself to securing that love's fulfilment: 'Truly, in his breast there lingered a resentful shame to find himself defeated by this passion for Charley Hexam's sister, though in the very self-same moments he was concentrating himself upon the object of bringing that passion to a successful issue' (341). And the new conflict seems to Headstone to consume the very self he has constructed at such enormous psychic cost. '"I have no resources in myself,"' he tells Lizzie, '"I have no confidence in myself, I have no government of myself when you are near me or in my thoughts. And you are always in my thoughts now. I have never been quit of you since I first saw you"' (395).

It is a speech which anticipates Wrayburn's later, no less passionate, outburst, '"You don't know what my state of mind towards you is. You don't know how you haunt me and bewilder me"' (692). For Lizzie haunts Headstone too. She is the living embodiment of all he has so long suppressed, not merely his poor origins and obscure past, but also the vital energies he has been forced to subdue and deny. With Headstone and Lizzie, Dickens inverts the social/sexual tensions which had so bound Pip to Estella. Headstone is not a poor boy aspiring to an unattainable 'lady', but a 'self-made' man caught in a socially degrading love for a woman who must be conventionally considered 'beneath' him. Lizzie represents not everything he desires but every-thing he dreads to confront once more. Where Estella had seemed to offer the self-divided Pip an escape from his 'coarse' and 'common' origins, Lizzie can only undermine still further the 'respectability' Headstone has sacrificed his true self to achieve. And here too it is a double torment in which he is caught. For the very energies Lizzie calls forth threaten every moment to consume him unless they are repressed with a force which rends him still further. Once more it is Headstone himself who gives voice to his plight in pleading with the woman who has brought him to full and bitter knowledge of 'the depths' (396) within him: ' "It is another of my miseries that I cannot speak to you or speak of you without stumbling at every syllable, unless I let the check go altogether and run mad" ' (396). Frustrated in the desires whose very ascendancy signals self-defeat, superseded by the man who represents all that he can never hope to win, Headstone will indeed 'let the check go altogether and run mad'. For that is now the only fulfilment possible for him. Lizzie brings self-knowledge to him, but it is knowledge of a self irreparably deformed. Their final exchange is prophetic as Lizzie, alarmed by the schoolmaster's violence, seeks to escape: ' "Mr. Headstone, let me go. Mr. Headstone, I must call for help!" "It is I who should call for help," he said; "you don't know yet how much I need it" ' (398).

What frightens Lizzie is 'the wild energy of the man, now quite let loose' (396), she herself having been the unwitting catalyst of the 'absolutely terrible' (396) liberation she witnesses. It is a state the more horrifying for the contrast it presents to the self-control Headstone must still exercise, 'just as usual' (400), in his daily routine. But if it is passion for Lizzie which first unleashes these frightful energies, it is jealousy and hatred of Eugene Wrayburn, his gentleman rival, which drives Headstone to their final indulgence in murder. From the first meeting of the two there is 'some secret, sure perception between them, which set them against one another in all ways' (288). Both are men whose self-image has been radically called into question by love of the same woman, a woman who represents for each a denial of the social identity which alone defines him: respectable schoolmaster, gentleman of good family. And it is the perverse bond between them, the 'secret, sure perception', which allows Wrayburn to devise the refinements of torture he inflicts upon 'the poor dogging wretch' (544) who haunts him. Expounding the 'pleasures of the chase' (543) to his friend, the careless Eugene shows a careful knowledge of his shadow's mind and heart: '"Then soberly and plainly, Mortimer, I goad the schoolmaster to madness. I make the schoolmaster so ridiculous and so aware of being made ridiculous, that I see him chafe and fret at every pore when we cross one another"' (542). (Eugene will later chafe himself at his own 'ridiculous' position with regard to Lizzie.) The torments Wrayburn nightly inflicts on his rival are 'grinding' (542) indeed, as he terms them, eating away at Headstone's self-control, breaking down all restraints until he appears, in a memorable image, 'like a haggard head suspended in the air: so completely did the force of his expression cancel his figure' (544). It is an anticipation of the self-negation which will be his ultimate fate.

For Lizzie the threat Headstone represents lies in what she perceives as his 'ungovernable rage and violence' (398). And Jenny Wren confirms her in her fear of his explosive nature, remarking of the schoolmaster's smouldering passions that '"a whole lot of gunpowder among lighted lucifer-matches in the next room might almost as well be here"' (347). In fact, as Headstone's psychic degeneration accelerates under the combined influence of frustrated desire and continued humiliation, it becomes apparent that he no longer even seeks to govern the passions which consume him. The long years of literal self-denial now find their compensation in complete self-abandonment. Just as Headstone had co-operated in his own suppression, so he now embraces his own moral and spiritual destruction, indulging the murderous impulses which transform the 'thoroughly decent young man of six-and-twenty' into a 'passion-wasted night-bird with respectable feathers, the worst night-bird of all' (555). It is the ultimate tragedy of the man, and the inevitable outcome of his systematic self-betrayal, that self-realization can now be found only in this misshapen form, the final expression of the disjunction between inner reality and outer persona. Like the various Dickens heroes who precede him, Headstone too achieves self-recognition in the course of his spiritual journey. But for him the sum of his hard-won knowledge is an admission of his own criminal potential, and an acceptance, indeed a welcoming, of the moral collapse this represents into the final solipsistic obsession of murder:

The state of the man was murderous and he knew it. More; he irritated it, with a kind of perverse pleasure akin to that which a sick man sometimes has in irritating a wound upon his body. Tied up all day with his disciplined show upon him, subdued to the performance of his routine of educational tricks, encircled by a gabbling crowd, he let loose at night like an ill-tamed wild animal. Under his daily restraint, it was his compensation, not his trouble, to give a glance towards his state at night, and to the freedom of its being indulged. (547)

Consciously feeding his 'wrath and hatred' (546) by making himself the nightly sport of Wrayburn's chase, Headstone is no less conscious of what his own tracking of Eugene will end in: 'still always going on with infinite endurance, pains, and perseverance, could his dark soul doubt whither he went?' (547). And it is precisely by embracing the role of murderer which awaits him at the end of his dark progress that he finds his true self. Adopting the disguise of 'Rogue' Riderhood's clothing to facilitate his final attack, the inner and the outer man cease for the first time to be in conflict. The paradox – discovery through disguise – lies indeed at the heart of his predicament: 'And whereas, in his own schoolmaster clothes, he usually looked as if they were the clothes of some other man, he now looked, in the clothes of some other man, or men, as if they were his own' (631). Much can be, and has been, made of Headstone and Eugene Wrayburn as symbolic doubles, inverted reflections united in a common obsession. But there is a case to be made for Charley Hexam and 'Rogue' Riderhood too as significant counterparts for aspects of the self-divided Bradley, the one an embodiment of his own past experience as a pauper lad seeking to rise in 'the scale of society' (713), the other an image of his increasingly 'passion-wasted', murderous self. Yet the inverted, and perverted, form of self-discovery Headstone achieves by means of his 'double''s disguise can lead only to the loss of self in the very release it is forced to seek. For a soul so monstrously deformed as to find its truest freedom in murder, there can be no other end. And the destruction will come from within, the inevitable culmination of a career of self-negation.

Just before the assault on Eugene, Headstone stands above Plashwater Weir Mill Lock, attended by his uncomprehending 'double' Riderhood, apparently poised between suicide and murder:

There was a very dark expression on his face; an expression the Rogue found it hard to understand. It was fierce, and full of purpose; but the purpose might have been as much against himself as against another. If he had stepped back for a spring, taken a leap, and thrown himself in, it would have been no surprising sequel to the look. Perhaps his troubled soul, set upon some violence, did hover for the moment between that violence and another. (636)

The moment is an emblematic one. For, as a necessary sequel to the violence he now contemplates, Headstone will throw himself into the lock. And he will carry Riderhood with him, the living, threatening symbol of his own degeneration. In effect, the attack upon Wrayburn constitutes a form of moral suicide. Having dipped his hands, unsuccessfully, in blood, Headstone has done more than mark himself 'a miserable tool and fool' (791). He has virtually completed the process of self-destruction begun so long ago. The fact that he finds no satisfaction in the murderous deed he has courted, but remains 'chained heavily to the idea of his hatred and his vengeance, and thinking how he might have satiated both in many better ways than the way he had done' (709), is but a further refinement of his continued self-torment. Even here there is no freedom to be found. The bond with his persecutor Eugene, now his victim, continues to the end. Blackmailed by the vengeful Riderhood as though his guilty self were now rebelling against him – ' "You did wot I'll be paid for and paid heavy for" ' (798) – abandoned by the despicable Charley Hexam, yet another surrogate self, and conscious that his desperate attempt to separate Wrayburn and Lizzie at the price of his own moral ruin has actually served to unite them at last, Headstone's is a 'blasted course' (791) indeed. Nor can there be any escape from the 'gloom of his fallen state' (713) except in death. As he returns to Plashwater Weir for the last time to confront 'the Rogue', and the implications of his own fall, the horizons of his world have contracted to this one spot, the very landscape reflecting nothing more than his own utter hopelessness. In its frozen desolation it is the outward expression of his inner blight:

In the distance before him lay the place where he had struck the worse than useless blows that mocked him with Lizzie's presence there as Eugene's wife. In the distance behind him, lay the place where the children with pointing arms had seemed to devote him to the demons in crying out his name. Within there where the light was, was the man who as to both distances could give him up to ruin. To these limits had his world shrunk. (796)

Parting from his devoted teacher and friend, Charley Hexam, now 'strictly respectable in the scale of society' (796), leaves him with a truly appalling injunction: ' "In conclusion, if you feel a sense of having injured me, and a desire to make some small reparation, I hope you will think how respectable you might have been yourself, and will contemplate your blighted existence"' (713). The contrast to the 'reparation' Eugene seeks to make (by defying 'Society' and marrying Lizzie) could not be clearer. And the words constitute the culminating irony of the 'highly certificated stipendiary schoolmaster''s career. For it is his very devotion to society's notions of strict respectability, and the self-suppression they demand, which has blighted an existence that might once have been very different. Drowning himself and Riderhood in the waters of the lock, Headstone embraces the only fate now left open to him, the only role left for him to fulfil. (He dies literally embracing an embodiment of the violence in which he sought his escape.) His journey of self-discovery ends, inevitably, in the ooze and scum of the river bottom, while the 'Voice of Society' drones on. In his 'fallen state' no other 'ending' is possible. He has no other place.

Following Headstone, as the reader does, through the increasingly inevitable stages of his downward course, there are no questions of 'who done it', or how, or why, associated with his crime. Nor is there any secret to the origins of his ultimate fate. From the introductory description of the doomed schoolmaster, with its ominous repetition of the key words 'decent' and 'mechanical', a sense of internal division and attendant emotional strain is firmly established. He is a virtual case study of socially induced self-destruction. The 'case' of John Jasper, in contrast, prime suspect in a mystery forever unsolved, is necessarily more obscure. His first appearance, unlike Headstone's, is not as an identified source of unease, but as an unnamed 'scattered consciousness' (1), fantastically piecing itself together in the novel's opening paragraph. Yet the suggestion of conflict is strong here too. Though Jasper remains unnamed to the end of the chapter, featuring successively as 'the waking man' (2), 'the watcher' (3), and 'a jaded traveller' (3), the narrative itself actually begins inside his manifestly fragmented mind. The initial displacements and uncertainties – 'An ancient English Cathedral Town? How can the ancient English Cathedral town be here!' (1) – though seemingly random, are themselves a key to his psychic dislocation. For the vision that follows reveals the scattered consciousness to be a radically divided one as well. Under the influence of the five pipes of opium he has reportedly smoked since midnight, the 'waking man' briefly fuses two worlds of experience into a single 'fantastic' landscape, superimposing an Arabian Nights fantasy of 'thrice ten thousand dancing-girls' (1) and 'countless gorgeous colours' (1) on to the 'massive grey' (1) reality of the ancient

English cathedral town. These are the opposing worlds the 'jaded traveller' moves between, worlds of sensuality and grey respectability, release and repression. They are extremes which can meet, seemingly, only in moments of conscious disintegration.

This is Jasper's predicament: he has divided himself into two halves that can never make a whole. No single 'normal' identity can unite the self he has dissevered so radically. The source of Jasper's dilemma is not some unacknowledged psychic disjunction but the deliberate disconnection of the inner and outer man. And there is, by his own account, no other alternative for him. The only 'choice' of escape he can make is the temporary release of opium, a release that brings with it only another form of subjection. Like Headstone, Jasper acquiesces in an identity and role which deny his true nature, embracing a vocation to which he must 'subdue' (12) himself in a process of self-suppression amounting to mutilation. Like the 'thoroughly decent' schoolmaster chafing beneath his 'thoroughly decent' persona, he retains enough of what is animal and passionate in him – qualities reflected in his opium dreams – to make his confined, respectable routine a daily torment. It is a slow form of suffocation he describes, ' "No whirl and uproar around me, no distracting commerce or calculation, no risk, no change of place" ' (11). And he himself co-operates in it. That is the essence of his confession to his uncomprehending nephew:

> 'The cramped monotony of my existence grinds me away by the grain. How does our service sound to you?'
> 'Beautiful! Quite celestial.'
> 'It often sounds to me quite devilish. I am so weary of it! The echoes of my own voice among the arches seem to mock me with my daily drudging round. No wretched monk who droned his life away in that gloomy place, before me, can have been more tired of it than I am. He could take for relief (and did take) to carving demons out of the stalls and seats and desks. What shall I do? Must I take to carving them out of my heart?' (11)

The 'grinder of music' (12) is, as it were, caught in his own machinery, his very voice tormenting him with reminders of his captivity. Jasper's tragedy, like Headstone's, is that he too has failed to dismiss his man's nature in forming himself to his mechanical part. It is never explicitly stated why Jasper cannot break free from this life of self-suffocation. Unlike Headstone, he would appear to be economically independent and socially secure. The implication is strong, however, that whatever the agency of his initial, and continued, immolation, it is now 'too late' (12) indeed for him to regain the wholeness he has sacrificed, to reunite his fractured self. Headstone, plainly, is caught by economic and social necessity in a terrible trap. He has been 'told off' for his profession, forced to suppress his own natural instincts in the exercise of his mechanical calling, and yet has been denied the status that might have formed the basis of a new identity. Even the love he seeks to redress these psychic wrongs offers only a further source of division. Yet, if the pressures which bind Jasper – a man seemingly both respected and at home in the society in which he moves – to his tormenting 'round' are less clearly rendered, he too is no less incapable of breaking free. Relief comes only in the form of an opium-induced secret life, a life that is itself but a further self-destruction. The point is less the hypocrisy of the choirmaster's double life, divided between cathedral and opium den, than the agony of a split that is a virtual psychic dismembering. The daily drudgery of his mechanical routine constitutes a continual self-betrayal, offering no release for the deeper energies which trouble 'even' him, cloistered 'in his niche' (12). It is a process of literal self-denial which results in ever-increasing dislocations and deformities of spirit Jasper cannot help but embrace. His passionate impulses 'take for relief' first to opium and then to murder, finding in these their only means of expression. The 'poor monotonous chorister' (12) realizes his true self only in his moments of scattered, and unconstrained, consciousness. It is the opium woman's claim, and this virtually ends the novel as it stands, that she knows her old customer ' "Better far, than all the Reverend Parsons put together know him" ' (216). And she is plainly right.

Even more than the dead-alive John Harmon, the figures of Jasper and Headstone both must raise the question of the influence of 'sensation' fiction in their creation, the mechanics of their situations being, apparently, quintessentially 'sensational'. Some dates might be of help here. *Our Mutual Friend* began appearing in 1865; *The Mystery of Edwin Drood* in 1870. Mrs Henry Wood scored her remarkable success with the 'sensational' *East Lynne* at the beginning of the decade (1860–61), to be followed by Mary Elizabeth Braddon with *Lady Audley's Secret* (1862) and *Aurora Floyd* (1863), all undeniable 'best-sellers' – time enough, undoubtedly, for the influence of the new form to be registered and even assimilated. But perhaps the most significant date for our purposes is 1868, the year of the publication of Wilkie Collins's *The Moonstone*. Collins's close association with Dickens both as writer and friend, their collaboration on theatrical productions and Christmas stories, has been extensively documented. And the presence of

'Eastern' elements in *Edwin Drood*, most notably Jasper's opium habit, has long been attributed to Dickens's desire to beat the younger novelist at his own very successful 'sensation' game. How far a spirit of conscious rivalry and/or emulation may have influenced the writing of the later novels – *The Woman in White* had been serialized, with very great success, in 1859–60 in Dickens's own weekly magazine *All the Year Round* – it is, of course, impossible to tell. Jasper's drug-taking would seem to owe something to the addict Ezra Jennings in *The Moonstone*. And it is possible too that an opium-induced reenactment of the crime might have played a part in the solution of Dickens's mystery as it had done in Collins's. Nevertheless, Angus Wilson makes a valuable point in his introduction to the Penguin edition of *The Mystery of Edwin Drood* when he notes that Dickens's contemporaries were particularly struck by its atypical cathedral setting and cast of clergymen, and that the most frequent comparison was to Trollope rather than Wilkie Collins.[9]

For this returns us to a point made in earlier discussion of John Harmon as a potential 'sensation' hero. There is nothing either new or un-Dickensian about the presence of secret guilt, murder and the whole spectrum of 'sensation' violence in the world of Dickens's novels. There is no marked change after 1860 to be attributed to the new fictional trend. Nor did Dickens require the external example of Braddon's and Wood's angelic adulteresses and childlike, golden-haired murderesses to attempt sympathetic portraits of figures conventionally reserved for unmitigated moral condemnation and a reassuring dismissal to justice in 'chapter the last'. Bill Sikes and Jonas Chuzzlewit both testify to Dickens's early interest in exploring the internal experience of his 'villains', creating murderers who become, in fact, more rather than less human as a result of their crime. Moving within the mind of Sikes during his lonely flight from London, or Jonas as he returns to confront his own guilty self, the narrative forges an imaginative identification which effectively subverts the conventional divisions between 'good' and 'bad' characters. Though the 'sensational' aspect of their violence may be fully exploited, it is the psychological effect of the murder upon the murderer, as much as its melodramatic potential, which interests Dickens even in these early studies.

Headstone and Jasper, then, continue a line of development rather than inaugurate a pronounced shift in mode. Their importance lies not in the atmosphere of violence encompassing them – that dates from the London of *Oliver Twist* at least, if not of the inset tales of *Pickwick* – but in the fact that this is now seen to be the fate of the Dickens hero. He lives in a world of murder and guilt, and cannot escape its taint. Indeed, he is brought finally to embrace violence as his truest self-expression. Whatever 'sensation' influences Dickens may or may not have absorbed, he has assimilated them to thematic purposes very different from those shaping the novels of Braddon, Wood, or even the much more gifted Collins. If he retains, as they do, a large dimension of melodrama in both plot and character, it loses much of its reassuring, simplifying, insulating effect. The typical 'sensation' novel's reliance on mystery and disclosure, on 'plot' as the source of both form and meaning, necessarily leaves the prospect of narrative resolution not merely unchallenged, but reinforced, and this is precisely what Dickens calls into question. Recent studies of the 'sensation' genre have very usefully called attention to its implicit 'social' content, most notably in its preoccupation with deviant femininity as embodied in a whole range of transgressive 'heroines'. But if there is a 'social secret' informing the 'sensation' novel it is that middle-class respectability can *mask* murder, violence and guilt, not that it breeds them. At novel's end the secret is told, the murder uncovered, the lurking evil purged and the sanctity of the respectable home restored. But the secret that lies at the heart of the Dickens hero's experience proves increasingly resistant to this kind of narrative containment. It is a secret of inevitable, and perpetual, estrangement which undermines the very prospect of closure, leaving, as in *Edwin Drood*, a problem that cannot be resolved at the centre of a story that never ends. Bradley Headstone's *act* of violence is not, finally, the focus of his story. It comes in the last hundred pages of the novel and occupies a brief three paragraphs in the doing. The interest is rather in the spiritual journey the self-divided sufferer undertakes which leads him inexorably to the crime which has become his fate. The social and psychic mechanisms driving the respectable schoolmaster to murder and suicide, and, even more, the inevitable interrelation of the two, are Dickens's ultimate concern. The 'sensation' superstructure of thwarted passion, long pursuit, disguise and sudden attack only achieves its full meaning as the external correlative of a spiritual plight that has long been taking shape in all its desolation. These are the marks of a double alienation that has destroyed the Dickens hero at last. And we might remember here Forster's remark that the 'originality' of *Edwin Drood* was to have consisted in Jasper's own account of the journey he has undertaken, a journey that leads him inexorably to the condemned cell and death. The 'sensation' elements of murder, violence and mystery constitute no 'originality' in the development of Dickens's art. It is the use to which they were consciously to be put that would distinguish the novel.

To return, then, to the issue of Jasper and his 'sensational' drug-taking. His recourse to opium is more than an attempt to import 'exotic' elements for their melodramatic appeal, or to borrow a leaf, quite literally, from Wilkie Collins's book. It may be one or both indeed, but it is also an external expression of the complex interplay of compulsion and co-operation informing the 'respectable' choirmaster's moral ruin. For he is an addict, a fact revealed by the old woman who supplies him with his drug – '"I didn't suppose you could have kept away, alive, so long, from the poor old soul with the real receipt for mixing it"' (205) – with an addict's helpless dependence on what was once a voluntary indulgence. And the dependence is itself both a function and a symbol of his inability to find any other means of self-fulfilment in the life-denying world he inhabits. Whatever else he may be, Jasper is not *simply* evil, a drug-taking hypocrite with a penchant for murder to compare with Collins's embezzling, womanizing 'philan-thropist' Godfrey Ablewhite, the revelation of whose double life provides the exciting denouement of *The Moonstone*. Although the actual process of addiction predates the action of the novel, Jasper's own words clearly indicate that he has been driven to opium as an escape from the divisions which rend him. It is a release, providing an outlet for passionate energies for which no other allowance is made in the cloistered existence of Cloisterham's 'worthy and respected Choir Master' (101). '"I thought you had so exactly found your niche, Jack,"' Edwin Drood comments in dismay after his uncle's startling confession of discontent. '"I know you thought so"' is the answer. '"They all think so"' (11). It is precisely because he has found his 'niche', and is walled up alive in it, that he must turn to opium for release.

Yet the very 'release' itself further deforms impulses which will at last find their only satisfaction in murder. Under the influence of the drug, the self-divided man can enact the crime he will ultimately commit. Not, as has frequently been suggested, to bring himself to the point of execution his 'normal' consciousness forbids, but rather as a deliberate, and necessary, surrogate for the thing itself. Like Headstone 'worrying' his murderous impulses with a compulsive pleasure in the act, it is the compensation the 'worthy and respected Choir Master' requires for the life of suppression he is daily forced to lead. '"Yes, I came on purpose,"' he tells the opium woman. '"When I could not bear my life, I came to get the relief, and I got it"' (208). And his words recall his more guarded confession to young Drood in the novel's second chapter: '"I have been taking opium for a pain – an agony – that sometimes overcomes me. The effects of the medicine steal over me like a blight or a cloud, and pass"' (10). Jasper's illness is, in fact, past the cure of any medicine but this. That he can find relief in nothing else is itself an indication of the extent to which the self has been maimed by the 'agony' of its long repression. The psychic 'blight' which will destroy him has settled on him well before the addiction which now emerges less as its cause than its inevitable result.

Although the point is never made explicit in the novel as it stands, Jasper's own words do suggest that a major source of the 'torment' (170) for which he sought his opium 'relief' was his frustrated passion for Rosa Bud. His frenzied declaration of love to her would seem to indicate as much, though she does not comprehend the allusion: '"In the distasteful work of the day, in the wakeful misery of the night, girded by sordid realities, or wandering through Paradises and Hells of visions into which I rushed, carrying your image in my arms, I loved you madly"' (170–171). The chronology is, perhaps, somewhat obscure. But whether it was Rosa's image which first sent him rushing to embrace the 'relief' which blights him, or whether it was a later accompaniment to a journey already undertaken – the basic disjunction between self and persona would seem to precede this additional torment – it is clear that for him, as for Headstone, there can be no redemption through love. There is no social barrier dividing Jasper and Rosa as there is between Headstone and Lizzie. And yet he was, prior to Edwin's death, no less cut off from her, first by virtue of her engagement to another man, secondly by his own near relation to that man to whom he himself stands as guardian. Crisparkle's judgment of Neville Landless's comparatively innocent love for Rosa is unequivocal: such a thing is 'outrageously misplaced' (83). There is no 'natural' outlet for Jasper's sexual energies, any more than for Headstone's. His 'mad' (171) passion, exploding after Edwin's death in a 'fierce extreme of admiration' (171), compounds rather than resolves the divisions within him. Love itself, if it can be called so, has become deformed and monstrous. The mere fact of Jasper's passion constitutes a betrayal of faith to the nephew whose wife Rosa was to have been, as he himself confesses to her: '"Let me have hope and favour, and I am a forsworn man for your sake"' (173). What Rosa does not yet know, though she instinctively fears, is that it was precisely the mixture of thwarted desire and jealousy Jasper's love arouses which has transformed the respectable choirmaster into a murderer. As with the schoolmaster, the very emotion proves irreparably tainted, finding expression only in a 'frightful vehemence' (173), a 'violence of look and delivery' (171), which speak of years of suppression and denial and the psychic wounds they have inflicted. Jasper is horrible in the fierceness of his passion and yet more so in the unnatural 'composure' (171) with which he masks it. To Rosa the opposition of inner and outer man, now plainly apparent, is 'hideous' (171). What she is witnessing is the monstrosity of the self-divided man, constrained to subdue his real nature to the point of deformity. Jasper ends his declaration much as Headstone did his, with a return to the suppression which is his 'normal' life: ' "Rosa, I am self-repressed again" ' (171). Mr Grewgious's portrait of the true lover 'living at once a doubled life and a halved life' (95) has a significance he clearly does not envision. And there is for Jasper no unity to be found in his terrible passion, still less in the desperate means by which he seeks to gratify it.

Jasper turns to murder to relieve the intolerable pressures which divide him, pressures caused by energies too long suppressed as well as passions unsatisfied. He moves from the surrogate to the thing itself in an inevitable progression. As he later confesses to the opium woman, it was always necessary for him to enact his murderous 'journey' of imagination under the influence of the drug, before he could obtain the other 'relief' of opium-induced fantasy: ' "Yes! I always made the journey first, before the changes of colours and the great landscapes and glittering processions began. They couldn't begin till it was off my mind. I had no room till then for anything else" ' (208). Absorbed in the one idea of surrendering to impulses so long denied, there is both 'pleasure' (207) and a necessary release in the acting out of this ultimate gesture of self-assertion. Yet when the murder is finally committed, it fails to provide the imagined satisfaction. The reality appears as one more vision: ' "It has been too short and easy. I must have a better vision than this; this is the poorest of all" ' (208). Jasper clearly misses something in the deed itself – ' "No struggle, no consciousness of peril, no entreaty" ' (208) – possibly a compensatory affirmation of self that should have been provided by the victim's response, and his own sense of power over the life he takes. As with Headstone, the anticipated relief proves but a further source of self-torment. He too appears to remain chained heavily to the idea of his crime. As the wretched schoolmaster finds himself condemned to be 'always doing the deed and doing it better' (709) in his tortured imagination, so Jasper seems drawn back to the opium woman, driven to 'have a better vision' than the one he has become a murderer to realize. Like Headstone, Jasper discovers his true self by embracing the monstrous role and the discovery is the culmination of his long process of self-destruction. Once again, the paradox is the essence of the predicament.

Making his preparations for murder, the choirmaster achieves a harmony he has never known before, and the word is used advisedly. For his newly acquired, and patently sinister, unity receives expression in an astonishing 'melodious power': 'He has never sung difficult music with such skill and harmony, as in this day's Anthem. His nervous temperament is occasionally prone to take difficult music a little too quickly; to-day his time is perfect' (128). Like the schoolmaster dressed in his murderer's 'disguise' and prepared to strike the blow, Jasper has reconciled self and role. The inner and the outer man are finally in accord as he is poised to effect his own moral ruin with his nephew's death. This is his tragedy: identity can be achieved only through disintegration. After the murder Jasper records an oath in his journal that is plainly more significant than even he knows, vowing 'That I will fasten the crime of the murder of my dear dead boy, upon the murderer. And that I devote myself to his destruction' (146). Adherents of the Jasper-as-schizophrenic theory see in this proof of his ignorance of the guilt he has incurred. But the device seems more an obvious ruse, a conscious hypocrisy on his part, with Jasper exploiting his very self-estrangement to provide his own alibi. The entry in the journal is written specifically for exhibition to Mr Crisparkle, whose unsuspecting goodness Jasper has already skilfully manipulated. Headstone's attempts to implicate Riderhood in his crime only hasten his catastrophe. He is defeated by his very lack of skill in the murderous games 'the Rogue' has long practised, and he remains in this a helpless victim. Jasper, in contrast, early proves capable of using the very social forces which so oppress him, making Sapsea, the Dean, even Crisparkle, unknowing participants in his murderous plans.

Yet there is a very real irony here too. For Jasper has already devoted himself to his own destruction by embracing the role of murderer, as he could not help but do. In much the same way he had earlier been compelled to 'deliver' himself to his opium 'Spectres' (38). Finding his true identity in murder, Jasper discovers a self that is 'a horrible wonder apart' (175), a spirit so fearfully deformed as to be 'in moral accordance or interchange with nothing around him' (203). It is the ultimate expression of his enduring predicament. Like Bradley Headstone, he has found selfhood to be identical with a spiritual alienation more profound even than the social isolation which has previously attended the Dickens hero's search. His journey has but one end: the condemned cell. The self, so long condemned to suppression, is now fit for no other home. Charles Forsyte, in his *The Decoding of Edwin Drood*, has proposed that Jasper's career, like Headstone's, would in fact have culminated in suicide, the condemned man forestalling the hangman by his own act.[10] It is one of the more reasonable 'solutions' the mystery has spawned. For the suggestion has an undoubted symbolic consonance, however speculative its basis, Jasper having been for so long the accomplice of his own ruin. Driven to moral and psychic disintegration already, he certainly seems destined for death, and not simply as the necessary 'justice' for his 'villainous' crime (as the 'sensation' novel would demand). The worlds of the ancient English cathedral town and the opium landscapes alike offer him nothing else. His death is the inevitable terminus of the journey he could not but undertake, as it is of the long miles of road which had opened to the view of the Dickens hero with the closing paragraphs of *David Copperfield*. The shadows which so faintly, yet so undeniably, troubled David's final happy accommodation – shadows cast by Ham's grave, Emily's enduring penance, and Mrs Steerforth's and Rosa Dartle's blighted lives – opened to the hero the prospect of a much darker voyage than any David undertook, and a much more uncertain goal. And these too find their logical end here. For the Dickens hero, over the course of the progress David initiates, closure has become steadily more elusive, 'resolution' increasingly less possible. It seems only fitting that his final journey should, as it were, stop short in *The Mystery of Edwin Drood* in the permanent suspension of an unsolved mystery, and a narrative that will never 'end'.

Notes

Introduction

[1] A. Wilson, 'The Heroes and Heroines of Dickens', in J. Gross and G. Pearson (eds.), *Dickens and the Twentieth Century*, p. 3.

[2] M. Oliphant, 'Charles Dickens', *Blackwood's Magazine* 78 (1855), pp. 451–2.

[3] Forster, *Life*, pp. 715–16.

[4] Ibid., p. 618.

[5] W. M. Thackeray, *The History of Pendennis*, D. Hawes (ed.) (Harmondsworth: Penguin Books, 1972), p. 34.

[6] W. M. Thackeray, *The English Humourists of the Eighteenth Century: The Works of W. M. Thackeray* vol. 23 (Smith, Elder and Co., 1879), pp. 297–8.

[7] E. Kahler, *The Inward Turn of Narrative*, pp. 65–6.

[8] F. Moretti, *The Way of the World: The Bildungsroman in European Culture*, p. 26.

Chapter 1 – Young Men Out of Nature: The Early Heroes

[1] G. K. Chesterton, *Criticisms and Appreciations of the Works of Charles Dickens*, p. 32.

[2] Forster, *Life* p. 722.

[3] I have not been able to locate any contemporary reviews of *Nicholas Nickleby* objecting to Nicholas as being insufficiently 'heroic'. But, given Dickens's known practice of answering criticism in his subsequent prefaces (as in his defence of Krook's spontaneous combustion in the preface to *Bleak House*), it is entirely possible that his additional 'remark' was intended to rebut a specific objection.

[4] Forster, *Life*, p. 473.

[5] Ibid., p. 473.

[6] Ibid., p. 473.

[7] Ibid., p. 473.

[8] G. Orwell, 'Charles Dickens', in *The Decline of the English Murder and Other Essays*, p. 110.

[9] Forster, *Life*, p. 146.

[10] Ibid., p. 146.

[11] Ibid., p. 479.

[12] Ibid., p. 473.

[13] Ibid., p. 473.

[14] Ibid., p. 473.

[15] Ibid., pp. 308–9.

[16] Ibid., pp. 305–6.

[17] Ibid., p. 471.

[18] Ibid., p. 477.

[19] Ibid., p. 477.

[20] G. Pearson, 'The Old Curiosity Shop', in Gross and Pearson (eds.), Dickens and the Twentieth Century, p. 90.

Chapter 2 – David Copperfield and the Emergence of the Homeless Hero

[1] Thackeray, The History of Pendennis, p. 785. The allusion is to a device used by the anti-slavery movement showing a picture of a slave being whipped, and bearing the inscription 'Am I not a Man and a Brother?'

[2] E. Gaskell, The Life of Charlotte Brontë, A Shelston (ed.) (Harmondsworth: Penguin Books, 1975), p. 308. This was not a new design for Brontë. In her Introduction to The Professor, written in 1846 but not published until 1857, another first-person narrative, she declared her intention of creating a 'real living' hero: 'I said to myself that my hero should work his way through life as I had seen real living men work theirs – that he should never get a shilling he had not earned – that no sudden turns should lift him in a moment to wealth and high station; that whatever small competency he might gain, should be won by the sweat of his brow ... that he should not even marry a beautiful girl or a lady of rank. As Adam's son he should share Adam's doom, and drain throughout life a mixed and moderate cup of enjoyment.'

Like Dickens with his ostensibly 'natural' Nicholas Nickleby, however, Brontë's prefatory remarks did not prevent her from rewarding her 'real living' hero with a highly conventional happy ending at novel's close.

[3] Q. D. Leavis, Introduction to Jane Eyre (Harmondsworth: Penguin Books, 1975), p. 28. Leavis expands her discussion in the appendix to her chapter on David Copperfield in Dickens the Novelist, 'Oliver Twist, Jane Eyre and David Copperfield'.

[4] Forster, Life, p. 525.

[5] B. Westburg, The Confessional Fictions of Charles Dickens, pp. 39–40.

[6] Leavis, Dickens the Novelist, p. 47.

[7] P. Collins, Charles Dickens: David Copperfield, p. 29.

[8] Forster, Life, p. 553.

[9] A. Welsh, The City of Dickens, Chapter 11 'Two Angels of Death', passim.

[10] R. Gilmour, 'Memory in David Copperfield', Dickensian 71 (1975), p. 37.

Chapter 3 – The Dickens Hero and the Social Cause: Bleak House and Hard Times

[1] Orwell, 'Charles Dickens', p. 87.

[2] Forster, Life, p. 547.

[3] It might perhaps be argued that two other later heroines, Amy Dorrit and Estella, equally qualify by virtue of their semi-orphan status and deprived childhoods as Dickens heroes. Unlike Esther, however, they do not suffer the psychic division which is the hallmark of the hero, nor is there, in either case, a process of reintegration, successful or not, to be charted.

[4] R. Garis, The Dickens Theatre, p. 136.

Notes

[5] See M. Slater, *Dickens and Women*, Chapter 14 'The Womanly Ideal', especially pp. 306–15.

Chapter 4 – Arthur Clennam, John Harmon and the Problem of Will

[1] S. Marcus, *Dickens: From Pickwick to Dombey*, p. 47.
[2] Ibid., p. 47.
[3] L. Trilling, '*Little Dorrit*', in *The Opposing Self*, pp. 57ff.
[4] G. Lukács, *The Theory of the Novel*, p. 136.
[5] H. M. Daleski, *Dickens and the Art of Analogy*, p. 232.
[6] S. Gill, Introduction to *Our Mutual Friend* (Harmondsworth: Penguin Books, 1971), p. 22.
[7] Quoted in W. Hughes, *The Maniac in the Cellar: Sensation Novels of the 1860s*, pp. 121–2.
[8] Gill, Introduction, p. 22.

Chapter 5 – Will and Gentility: *Great Expectations* and the Problem of the Gentleman

[1] R. Gilmour, *The Idea of the Gentleman in the Victorian Novel*, p. 2.
[2] Ibid., p. 137.
[3] Ibid., p. 125.
[4] Ibid., p. 123.
[5] Ibid., p. 126.
[6] Ibid., p. 143.
[7] J. Moynahan, 'The Hero's Guilt: The Case of *Great Expectations*', *Essays in Criticism* 10 (1960), p. 70.
[8] J. Hillis Miller, *Charles Dickens: The World of His Novels*, pp. 268–9.

Chapter 6 – The 'Dandy' Vindicated: Sydney Carton, Eugene Wrayburn and the Reclaimed Self

[1] E. Moers, *The Dandy: From Brummell to Beerbohm*, pp. 12–13.
[2] Ibid., p. 13.
[3] Ibid., p. 35.
[4] J. Gross, '*A Tale of Two Cities*', in Gross and Pearson (eds.), *Dickens and the Twentieth Century*, pp. 189–90.
[5] A. Wilson, 'The Heroes and Heroines of Dickens', in J. Gross and G. Pearson (eds.), *Dickens and the Twentieth Century* p. 8.

Conclusion – The Self Destroyed: The Dickens Hero as 'Villain'

[1] Wilson, 'The Heroes and Heroines of Dickens', p. 8.
[2] It is not my intention to add anything to the literature on the 'true' solution to the mystery in *The Mystery of Edwin Drood*. For the purposes of this chapter I follow the outline given by Forster of Dickens's intentions for the novel and assume: that Edwin Drood was murdered; that the murder was committed by Jasper; and that he was to be caught in the manner Forster details (*Life*, p. 808).

Notes

3 E. Wilson, 'Dickens: The Two Scrooges', in *The Wound and the Bow*, p. 92.

4 Ibid., p. 84.

5 Forster, *Life*, p. 808.

6 Ibid., p. 808.

7 P. Collins, *Dickens and Education*, p. 168.

8 Ibid., p. 160.

9 A. Wilson, Introduction to *The Mystery of Edwin Drood* (Harmondsworth: Penguin Books, 1974), p. 14.

10 C. Forsyte, *The Decoding of Edwin Drood*, p. 99.

✺
Bibliographic Essay

Introduction

Mario Praz's *The Hero in Eclipse in Victorian Fiction* is obviously highly relevant to this introductory discussion of the changing dimensions of the nineteenth-century literary hero. Alexander Welsh's *The Hero of the Waverley Novels* is equally useful for an assessment of Scott's role in the process. Other works of particular relevance to the discussion in this chapter are Gerard Barker's *Grandison's Heirs: The Paragon's Progress in the late Eighteenth-Century Novel* and Peter Thorslev's *The Byronic Hero: Types and Prototypes*. On the theme of the search for selfhood in Victorian literature, in addition to Steven Cohan's *Violation and Repair in the English Novel*, Philip Weinstein's *The Semantics of Desire: Changing Models of Identity from Dickens to Joyce* is also suggestive, as is Dirk den Hartog's *Dickens and Romantic Psychology*. Its subtitle, *The Self in Time in Nineteenth-Century Literature*, indicates the different approach it takes to the problem of self-discovery in Dickens's novels, focusing primarily on the influence of Wordsworthian ideas of psychological continuity through memory.

Chapter 1

The recent revival of interest in Dickens's early fiction has resulted in a proliferation of criticism. The following is simply a selection of the studies most relevant to the problem of the 'hero', not an overview of the existing literature.

Michael Slater's introduction to the Penguin edition of *Nicholas Nickleby* offers a very useful discussion of the ambiguous function of theatrical (and particularly melodramatic) convention in the novel. Jerome Meckier's 'The Faint Image of Eden: The Many Worlds of *Nicholas Nickleby*', *Dickens Studies Annual* 1 (1970), pp. 129–46, is suggestive on the presence of 'tragic' elements within *Nickleby*'s comic structure and their influence in undermining, or at least troubling, the ideal world the narrative seeks to establish at its close. Garrett Stewart's account of Dick Swiveller as an exemplar of the principle of imaginative grace in his *Dickens and the Trials of the Imagination* has influenced in obvious ways this chapter's discussion of the potential thematic function of this comic 'hero'. On *Martin Chuzzlewit*, Barbara Hardy's two essays, in Gross and Pearson's *Dickens and the Twentieth Century* and her own *The Moral Art of Charles Dickens*, provide an extensive assessment of the novel's weaknesses and failures, particularly as exemplified by young Martin and his 'conversion'. Sylvere Monod's more recent, and more sympathetic, reconsideration, simply titled *Martin Chuzzlewit*, is also of interest on this point. Finally, Elliot Engel's *The Victorian Novel Before Victoria: British Fiction During the Reign of William IV, 1830–1837* offers a usefully brief overview of the sort of novels, and 'heroes', Dickens was reacting to in his own early work.

Chapter 2

Robin Gilmour's admirable essay 'Memory in *David Copperfield*', cited in the chapter notes, offers an excellent account of the novel's peculiar cadences of loss and regret. John Lucas's *The Melancholy Man: A Study of Dickens's Novels* is also suggestive on the related issue of the novel's temporal vision. For an interesting assessment of *Copperfield*'s twin concerns of memory and literary heroism, and their relation to other contemporary fiction, Carl Dawson's *Victorian Noon: English Literature in 1850* is worth consideration, particularly the chapters 'Men of Letters as Hacks and Heroes' and 'the Lamps of Memory: Wordsworth and Dickens'. George Orwell's classic essay 'Charles Dickens', first published in 1940 and reprinted in the Penguin collection *Decline of the English Murder and Other Essays*, is still particularly illuminating on *David Copperfield* and the implications of young David's 'social' plight. On the convention and role of the orphan figure, two studies are of special interest here: Harry Stone's *Dickens and the Invisible World: Fairy Tales, Fantasy and Novel-Making* and, more generally, John Reed's *Victorian Conventions*. (Stone is also suggestive on the role of Uriah Heep as David's inverted 'double'.) Of the innumerable journal articles *David Copperfield* has spawned, two are of interest for the alternative readings they provide of themes explored in this chapter. Neil Grill's 'Home and Homeless in *David Copperfield*', *Dickens Studies Newsletter* 11 (1980), pp. 108–11, briefly considers the image of home as a stable refuge in a world of change, impermanence and flux. J. O. Jordan's 'The Social Sub-text of *David Copperfield*', *Dickens Studies Annual* 14 (1984), pp. 61–92, relates David's doubts as to the identity of his narrative 'hero' to a confusion of heroism and gentility, analysing his history in terms of a class anxiety that remains essentially unresolved.

Chapter 3

Alexander Welsh, in *From Copyright to Copperfield: The Identity of Dickens*, offers a detailed study of the novel's 'personal' character and its implication for the development of Dickens's 'social' concerns. The issue of Esther's role in *Bleak House* has been canvassed extensively. William Axton's 'The Trouble with

Esther', *Modern Language Quarterly* 26 (1965), pp. 545–57, and Alex Zwerdling's 'Esther Summerson Rehabilitated', *PMLA* 88 (1973), pp. 429–39, assess her function as a divided, self-repressed personality in terms which have influenced the discussion in this chapter. Axton's essay 'Esther Summerson's Nicknames: A Study in Relevance', *Dickensian* 62 (1966), pp. 158–63, provides an interesting supplement to his argument, tracing the association of the various identities imposed upon her to a variety of witches, old women and widows of popular song, nursery rhyme and folklore. In contrast, Robert Donovan and A. E. Dyson, in *The Shaping Vision: Imagination in the English Novel from Defoe to Dickens* and *The Inimitable Dickens* respectively, offer a very different assessment of Esther, finding in her narrative a normative voice that provides an ordered alternative to the disorder of Chancery and the third-person narration. On the issue of Tom Gradgrind's ambiguous moral status, Taylor Stoehr's *Dickens: The Dreamer's Stance* is interesting for its attempt to account for Dickens's 'inexplicable' hostility to Tom, seeing in it a palpable failure of imaginative control rather than the deliberate innovation analysed in this chapter.

Chapter 4

The issue of the 'endings' of Dickens's later novels has received considerable attention from a variety of critical perspectives, commentators generally finding in them either the index of a changing social vision or the mark of a continuing imaginative failure. J. Hillis Miller's brief account, in his *Charles Dickens: The World of His Novels*, of the disappearance of an alternative world of untroubled stasis by the end of *Our Mutual Friend* has particularly influenced the discussion in this chapter. Although arriving at very different conclusions concerning their implications, John Kucich in *Excess and Restraint in the Novels of Charles Dickens* offers an interesting assessment of the necessary form the novels' endings must take. Deirdre David's *Fictions of Resolution in Three Victorian Novels* is also suggestive on the increasing difficulties of transcendence in *Our Mutual Friend* and the narrative intervention this prompts. On the convention of wills and inheritance in Victorian fiction generally, John Reed's *Victorian Conventions* is, once again, illuminating. For an account of Arthur Clennam's spiritual progress which sees it as concluding in an unintentional, and unassimilated, irresolution, see Richard Barickman's 'The Spiritual Journey of Amy Dorrit and Arthur Clennam: 'A Way in which there is No Ecstasy''', *Dickens Studies Annual* 7 (1978), pp. 163–89. On the 'problem' of the Harmon plot in general, and his 'solo' in particular, Stephen Gill's Introduction to the Penguin edition of the novel, cited in the chapter notes, is completely unsympathetic but thorough. A more balanced assessment of its technical failure of realization but underlying psychological and symbolic validity is offered by P. J. M. Scott in his *Reality and Comic Confidence in Charles*

Dickens. Steve Connor's *Charles Dickens*, in the Basil Blackwell Rereading Liteature series, is also interesting, if ultimately unconvincing, in its attempt to present Harmon's 'solo' as part of a pattern of competing perceptual modes offered by a narrative conscious of the disintegrative potential of language.

Chapter 5

In addition to Robin Gilmour's *The Idea of the Gentleman in the Victorian Novel*, cited extensively in the chapter notes, G. R. Stange's essay 'Expectations Well Lost: Dickens's Fable for His Times', collected in George Ford and Lauriat Lane's *The Dickens Critics*, is illuminating on the social/historical implications of the novel. Jerome Buckley in his *Season of Youth: The Bildungsroman from Dickens to Golding* offers an analysis of *Great Expectations* as a variant on the traditional apprenticeship novel. On the issue of Orlick's role in Pip's history, Harry Stone's *Dickens and the Invisible World* provides an account of his dual function as a manifestation of primal evil as well as an objectification of Pip's own repressed hostilities that is rather less determinedly subversive of the novel's narrative structure than Moynahan's similar interpretation. The cancelled ending of the novel has been reprinted in Forster's *Life* and as an appendix to the Penguin edition of the novel. Discussion of the 'true' ending can be found in, among many others, M. Millhauser's '*Great Expectations*: The Three Endings', *Dickens Studies Annual* 2 (1972), pp. 267–77; A. L. French's 'Old Pip: The Ending of *Great Expectations*', *Essays in Criticism* 29 (1979), pp. 357–60; and Edgar Rosenberg's 'Last Words on *Great Expectations*: A Textual Brief of the Six Endings', *Dickens Studies Annual* 9 (1981), pp. 87–116. Taylor Stoehr, in *Dickens: The Dreamer's Stance*, offers a reading of all extant endings as a failure of conviction on Dickens's part that allows Pip to sidestep the deepest implications of his predicament. It is an analysis that effectively disregards the highly qualified nature of the 'resolution' Pip actually achieves.

Chapter 6

For accounts of the Victorian response to the idea and figure of the 'dandy', Part Four of Moers's *The Dandy: From Brummel to Beerbohm*, 'The Victorian Reaction', can be usefully supplemented by Chapter 10 of Walter Houghton's *The Victorian Frame of Mind 1830–1870*, entitled 'Earnestness', particularly the section 'Moral Earnestness and the Social Crisis'. Geoffrey Thurley in *The Dickens Myth: Its Genesis and Structure*, offers a brief but interesting consideration of Steerforth, not as a prototypal Dickens 'dandy', but rather as a 'bourgeoisified' Byronic hero, Dickens's response to the Romantic cult of the self-destructive hero. On the satirical function of Dickens's 'dandy' figures, Sylvia Manning's *Dickens as Satirist* is suggestive. Interesting assessments of Charles Darnay's central role in the thematic economy of *A Tale of Two Cities* can be found in Edwin Eigner's essay 'Charles Darnay and Revolutionary Identity', *Dickens Studies Annual* 12 (1983), pp. 147–59, and several pieces collected by Charles Beckwith in *Twentieth Century Interpretations of A Tale of Two Cities*, particularly G. R. Stange's 'Dickens and the Fiery Past: *A Tale of Two Cities* Reconsidered'. Andrew Sanders offers representative analyses of the 'redemptive' character of Carton's history, and its social implications, in both his *The Victorian Historical Novel 1840–1880* and *Charles Dickens: Resurrectionist*. The titles of the works themselves explain the slight differences in emphasis. John Gross's essay, cited in the chapter notes, provides a brief but very suggestive assessment of Carton's sacrifice from the opposite perspective, as a gesture of despair. It is a point developed more extensively in all its implications in the chapter discussion. Graham Smith in *Dickens, Money and Society* is illuminating on the equally despairing character of Wrayburn's union with Lizzie Hexam, and his view too has been influential in formulating this chapter.

Conclusion

The Mystery of Edwin Drood has spawned an enormous amount of literature, much of it, at least until quite recently, devoted to the solution of its detective puzzle. There are, however, a number of studies relevant to the discussion of the meaning of its mystery. A. E. Dyson's account of the novel in *The Inimitable Dickens* is particularly suggestive on the nature, and implications, of Jasper's psychic divisions, seeing in them a conscious strategy rather than an unconscious plight. Lawrence Frank's 'The Intelligibility of Madness in *Our Mutual Friend* and *The Mystery of Edwin Drood*', *Dickens Studies Annual* 5 (1976), pp. 150–95, is also interesting for its analysis of Jasper as a social rebel whose crime testifies to a perverse form of moral integrity. For a very different view, which essentially discounts the social implications of the choirmaster's divisions, see Frank Kaplan's *Dickens and Mesmerim: The Hidden Springs of Fiction*. Rather less critical energy has been expended on the figure of Headstone, but P. J. M. Scott's *Reality and Comic Confidence in Charles Dickens* is illuminating on the importance of the self-divided schoolmaster to *Our Mutual Friend*'s exploration of the individual's inescapable social predicament. On the 'sensation' novel's potential social content, Jenny Bourne Taylor's *In the Secret Theatre of Home: Wilkie Collins, Sensation Narrative, and Nineteenth-Century Psychology* is very suggestive, though her focus is primarily the implications of the theories of mind and mental process underlying Collin's 'sensation' plots. For a fascinating account of two real-life 'sensation' crimes and the response in both journalism and fiction, see Richard Altick's *Deadly Encounters: Two Victorian Sensations*. It is particularly illuminating on the historical context of the 'sensation' vogue and the significance attached to the phenomenon by contemporary observers.

Bibliography

NOTE: Unless otherwise specified, the place of publication in all instances is London.

Dickens

Adrian, Arthur. *Dickens and the Parent–Child Relationship*. Ohio: Ohio University Press, 1984.

Axton, William. 'The Trouble with Esther', *Modern Language Quarterly* 26 (1965) pp. 545–57.

———— 'Esther Summerson's Nicknames: A Study in Relevance', *Dickensian* 62 (1966) pp. 158–63.

———— *Circle of Fire: Dickens' Vision and the Popular Victorian Theatre*. Lexington: University of Kentucky Press, 1966.

Barickman, Richard *et al. Corrupt Relations: Dickens, Thackeray, Trollope, Collins and the Victorian Social System*. New York: Columbia University Press, 1982.

Barickman, Richard. 'The Spiritual Journey of Amy Dorrit and Arthur Clennam: "A Way in which there is No Ecstasy"', *Dickens Studies Annual* 7 (1978) pp. 163–89.

Beckwith, Charles (ed.). *Twentieth Century Interpretations of A Tale of Two Cities*. New Jersey: Prentice Hall, 1972.

Brown, James. *Dickens: Novelist in the Market Place*. Macmillan, 1982.

Butt, John and Tillotson, Kathleen. *Dickens at Work*, Methuen, 1957.

Carey, John. *The Violent Effigy: A Study of Dickens' Imagination*. Faber and Faber, 1973.

Caserio, Robert. *Plot, Story, and the Novel: From Dickens and Poe to the Modern Period*. Princeton: Princeton University Press, 1979.

Chase, Karen. *Eros and Psyche: The Representation of Personality in Charlotte Brontë, Charles Dickens and George Eliot*. New York: Methuen, 1984.

Chesterton, Gilbert Keith. *Criticisms and Appreciations of the Works of Charles Dickens*. J. M. Dent, 1933.

Cockshut, A. O. J. *The Imagination of Charles Dickens*. Collins, 1961.

Collins, Philip (ed). *Dickens: The Critical Heritage*. New York: Barnes and Noble, 1971.

Collins, Philip. *Dickens and Education*. Macmillan, 1963.

————— *Dickens and Crime*. Macmillan, 1965.

————— *Charles Dickens: David Copperfield*. Edward Arnold, 1977.

Connor, Steve. *Charles Dickens*. Oxford: Basil Blackwell, 1985.

Dabney, Ross. *Love and Property in the Novels of Dickens*. Chatto and Windus, 1967.

Daldry, Graham. *Charles Dickens and the Form of the Novel*. Croom Helm, 1987.

Daleski, Herman. *Dickens and the Art of Analogy*, Faber and Faber, 1970.

David, Deirdre. *Fictions of Resolution in Three Victorian Novels: North and South, Our Mutual Friend and Daniel Deronda*. Macmillan, 1981.

Davis, Earle. *The Flint and the Flame: The Artistry of Charles Dickens*. Columbia: University of Missouri Press, 1963.

den Hartog, Dirk. *Dickens and Romantic Psychology: The Self in Time in Nineteenth-Century Literature*. Macmillan, 1987.

Donovan, Robert. *The Shaping Vision: Imagination in the English Novel from Defoe to Dickens*. Ithaca: Cornell University Press, 1966.

Dyson, A. E. *The Inimitable Dickens*. Macmillan, 1970.

————— *Dickens: Bleak House, A Casebook*. Macmillan, 1983.

Eigner, Edwin. *The Metaphysical Novel in England and America: Dickens, Bulwer, Melville and Hawthorne*. Berkeley: University of California Press, 1978.

————— 'Charles Darnay and Revolutionary Identity', *Dickens Studies Annual* 12 (1983) pp. 147–59.

Engel, Monroe. *The Maturity of Dickens*. Cambridge, Mass.: Harvard University Press, 1967.

Fielding, K. J. *Charles Dickens: A Critical Introduction*. Longmans, Green, 1958.

Ford, George. *Dickens and his Readers: Aspects of Novel Criticism Since 1836*. New York: W. W. Norton, 1965.

Ford, George and Lane, Lauriat (eds.). *The Dickens Critics*. New York: Cornell University Press, 1961.

Forsyte, Charles. *The Decoding of Edwin Drood*. Victor Gollancz, 1980.

Frank, Lawrence. 'The Intelligibility of Madness in *Our Mutual Friend* and *The Mystery of Edwin Drood*', *Dickens Studies Annual* 5 (1976) pp. 150–95.

————— *Charles Dickens and the Romantic Self*. Lincoln: University of Nebraska Press, 1984.

French, A. L. 'Old Pip: The Ending of *Great Expectations*', *Essays in Criticism* 29 (1979) pp. 357–60.

Garis, Robert. *The Dickens Theatre*. Oxford: Clarendon Press, 1965.

Giddings, Robert (ed.). *The Changing World of Charles Dickens*. Vision Press, 1983.

Golding, Robert. *Idiolects in Dickens*. Macmillan, 1985.

Grill, Neil. 'Home and Homeless in *David Copperfield*', *Dickens Studies Newsletter* 11 (1980) pp. 108–11.

Gross, John and Pearson, Gabriel (eds.). *Dickens and the Twentieth Century.* Routledge and Kegan Paul, 1962.

Hardy, Barbara. *The Moral Art of Charles Dickens.* Athlone Press, 1970.

Hornback, Bert. *Noah's Arkitecture: A Study of Dickens' Mythology.* Ohio: Ohio University Press, 1972.

Horton, Susan. *The Reader in the Dickens World: Style and Response.* Macmillan, 1981.

House, Humphry. *All in Due Time.* New York: Books for Libraries Press, 1972.

————— *The Dickens World* (2nd edn). Oxford: Oxford University Press, 1950.

Johnson, Edgar. *Charles Dickens: His Tragedy and Triumph* (2 vols.). Gollancz, 1953.

Jordan, J. O. 'The Social Sub-text of *David Copperfield*', *Dickens Studies Annual* 14 (1984) pp. 61–92.

Kaplan, Frank. *Dickens and Mesmerism: The Hidden Springs of Fiction.* Princeton: Princeton University Press, 1975.

Kincaid, James, *Dickens and the Rhetoric of Laughter.* Oxford: Clarendon Press, 1971.

Kucich, John. *Repression in Victorian Fiction: Charlotte Brontë, George Eliot and Charles Dickens.* Berkeley: University of California Press, 1987.

————— *Excess and Restraint in the Novels of Charles Dickens.* Athens, Georgia: University of Georgia Press, 1981.

Leavis, F. R. and Q. D. *Dickens the Novelist.* Chatto and Windus, 1970.

Lettis, Richard and Morris, William (eds.). *Assessing Great Expectations.* San Francisco: Chandler Publishing, 1960.

Lucas, John. *The Melancholy Man: A Study of Dickens's Novels.* Sussex: Harvester Press, 1980.

McMaster, Janet. *Dickens the Designer.* New Jersey: Barnes and Noble, 1987.

Manning, Sylvia. *Dickens as Satirist.* New Haven: Yale University Press, 1971.

Marcus, Steven. *Dickens: From Pickwick to Dombey.* Chatto and Windus, 1965.

Meckier, Jerome. 'The Faint Image of Eden: The Many Worlds of *Nicholas Nickleby*', *Dickens Studies Annual* 1 (1970) pp. 129–46.

Miller, J. Hillis. *Charles Dickens: The World of His Novels.* Cambridge, Mass.: Harvard University Press, 1959.

Millhauser, M. '*Great Expectations*: The Three Endings', *Dickens Studies Annual 2* (1972) pp. 267–77.

Monod, Sylvere. *Dickens the Novelist.* Norman: University of Oklahoma Press, 1968.

————— *Martin Chuzzlewit.* George Allen and Unwin, 1985.

Moynahan, J. 'The Hero's Guilt: The Case of *Great Expectations*', *Essays in Criticism* 10 (1960) pp. 60–79.

Newman, S. J. *Dickens at Play.* Macmillan, 1981.

Nisbet, Ada and Nevius, Blake (eds.). *Dickens Centennial Essays.* Berkeley: University of California Press, 1971.

Bibliography

Oliphant, M. 'Charles Dickens', *Blackwood's Magazine* 78 (1855) pp. 451–4.

Orwell, George. 'Charles Dickens', in *Decline of the English Murder and Other Essays*. Harmondsworth: Penguin Books, 1979.

Partlow, Robert (ed.). *Dickens the Craftsman: Strategies of Presentation.* Carbondale: Southern Illinois University Press, 1970.

Raina, Badri. *Dickens and the Dialectic of Growth.* Madison: University of Wisconsin Press, 1986.

Romano, John. *Dickens and Reality.* New York: Columbia University Press, 1978.

Rosenberg, Edgar. 'Last Words on *Great Expectations*: A Textual Brief of the Six Endings', *Dickens Studies Annual* 9 (1981) pp. 87–116.

Sadoff, Diane. *Monsters of Affection: Dickens, Eliot and Brontë on Fatherhood.* Baltimore: Johns Hopkins University Press, 1982.

Sanders, Andrew. *Charles Dickens: Resurrectionist.* Macmillan, 1982.

Schlicke, Paul. *Dickens and Popular Entertainment.* George Allen and Unwin, 1985.

Schwarzbach, F. S. *Dickens and the City.* Athlone Press, 1979.

Scott, P. J. M. *Reality and Comic Confidence in Charles Dickens.* Macmillan, 1970.

Slater, Michael (ed.). *Dickens 1970.* Chapman and Hall, 1970.

Slater, Michael. *Dickens and Women.* J. M. Dent, 1983.

Smith, Graham. *Dickens, Money and Society.* Berkeley: University of California Press, 1974.

Stange, G. R. 'Expectations Well Lost: Dickens's Fable for His Times', in Ford and Lane (eds.), *The Dickens Critics*, 1961.

———— 'Dickens and the Fiery Past: *A Tale of Two Cities* Reconsidered', in Beckwith (ed.), *Twentieth Century Interpretations*, 1972.

Stewart, Garrett. *Dickens and the Trials of the Imagination.* Cambridge, Mass.: Harvard University Press, 1974.

Stoehr, Taylor. *Dickens: The Dreamer's Stance.* Ithaca: Cornell University Press, 1975.

Stone, Harry. *Dickens and the Invisible World: Fairy Tales, Fantasy and Novel-Making.* Bloomington: Indiana University Press, 1979.

Storey, Graham. *Charles Dickens: Bleak House.* Cambridge: Cambridge University Press, 1987.

Sucksmith, Harvey. *The Narrative Art of Charles Dickens: The Rhetoric of Sympathy and Irony in His Novels.* Oxford: Clarendon Press, 1970.

Thurley, Geoffrey. *The Dickens Myth: Its Genesis and Structure.* Routledge and Kegan Paul, 1976.

Tomlinson, E. W. F. (ed.). *Charles Dickens 1812–1870: A Centenary Volume.* Weidenfeld and Nicolson, 1969.

Trilling, Lionel. '*Little Dorrit*', in *The Opposing Self.* Secker and Warburg, 1955.

Watkins, Gwen. *Dickens in Search of Himself: Recurrent Themes and Characters in the Work of Charles Dickens.* Macmillan, 1987.

Welsh, Alexander. *The City of Dickens*. Oxford: Clarendon Press, 1971.
———— *From Copyright to Copperfield: The Identity of Dickens*. Cambridge, Mass.: Harvard University Press, 1987.
Westburg, Barry. *The Confessional Fictions of Charles Dickens*. Dekalb: Northern Illinois University Press, 1977.
Wilson, Angus. *The World of Charles Dickens*. Panther Books, 1983 (Secker and Warburg, 1970).
Wilson, Edmund. 'Dickens: The Two Scrooges', in *The Wound and the Bow*. New York: Oxford University Press, 1965.
Zwerdling, Alex. 'Esther Summerson Rehabilitated', *PMLA* 88 (1973) pp. 545–57.

General

Adburgham, Alison. *Silver Fork Society: Fashionable Life and Literature from 1814 to 1840*. Constable, 1983.
Alter, Robert. *The Rogue's Progress: Studies in the Picaresque Novel*. Cambridge, Mass.: Harvard University Press, 1964.
———— *Partial Magic: The Novel as Self-Conscious Genre*. Berkeley: University of California Press, 1978.
Altick, Richard. *Deadly Encounters: Two Victorian Sensations*. Philadelphia: University of Pennsylvania Press, 1986.
Ball, Patricia. *The Central Self: A Study in Romantic and Victorian Imagination*. Athlone Press, 1968.
Barker, Gerard. *Grandison's Heirs: The Paragon's Progress in the Late Eighteenth-Century Novel*. Newark: University of Delaware Press, 1985.
Beebe, Martin. *Ivory Towers and Sacred Founts: The Artist as Hero in Fiction from Goethe to Joyce*. New York: New York University Press, 1964.
Bell, Michael. *The Sentiment of Reality: Truth of Feeling in the European Novel*. George Allen and Unwin, 1983.
Bjornson, Richard. *The Picaresque Hero in European Fiction*. Madison: University of Wisconsin Press, 1977.
Blackburn, Alexander. *The Myth of the Picaro: Continuity and Transformation of the Picaresque Novel 1554–1954*. Chapel Hill: University of North Carolina Press, 1979.
Bloomfield, M. W. (ed.). *The Interpretation of Narrative: Theory and Practice*. Cambridge, Mass.: Harvard University Press, 1970.
Briggs, Asa. *Victorian Cities* (rev. edn). Harmondsworth: Penguin Books, 1968.
Brooks, Chris. *Signs for the Times: Symbolic Realism in the Mid-Victorian World*. George Allen and Unwin, 1984.
Brooks, Peter. *Reading for the Plot: Design and Intention in Narrative*. Oxford: Clarendon Press, 1984.

Bibliography

Buckley, Jerome (ed.). *The World of Victorian Fiction*. Cambridge, Mass.: Harvard University Press, 1975.

———— *Season of Youth: The Bildungsroman from Dickens to Golding*. Cambridge, Mass.: Harvard University Press, 1974.

Butt, John (ed.). *The Victorians and Social Protest*. Devon: David and Charles, 1973.

Cazamian, Louis. *The Social Novel in England 1830–1850*. M. Fido (trans.). Routledge and Kegan Paul, 1973.

Chapman, Raymond. *The Sense of the Past in Victorian Literature*. Croom Helm, 1986.

Clayton, Jay. *Romantic Vision and the Novel*. Cambridge: Cambridge University Press, 1987.

Cohan, Steven. *Violation and Repair in the English Novel: The Paradigm of Experience from Richardson to Woolf*. Detroit: Wayne State University Press, 1986.

Cox, Stephen. *'The Stranger Within Thee': Concepts of the Self in Late-Eighteenth-Century Literature*. Pittsburgh: University of Pittsburgh Press, 1980.

Danon, Ruth. *Work in the English Novel: The Myth of Vocation*. Croom Helm, 1985.

Dawson, Carl. *Victorian Noon: English Literature in 1850*. Baltimore: Johns Hopkins University Press, 1979.

Engel, Elliot. *The Victorian Novel Before Victoria: British Fiction During the Reign of William IV 1830–1837*. Macmillan, 1984.

Fleishman, Avrom. *The English Historical Novel: Walter Scott to Virginia Woolf*. Baltimore: Johns Hopkins University Press, 1971.

Garber, Frederick. *The Autonomy of the Self from Richardson to Houysmans*. Princeton: Princeton University Press, 1982.

Garrett, Peter. *The Victorian Multiplot Novel: Studies in Dialogical Form*. New Haven: Yale University Press, 1980.

Gilmour, Robin. *The Idea of the Gentleman in the Victorian Novel*. George Allen and Unwin, 1981.

Goodin, George (ed.). *The English Novel in the Nineteenth Century: Essays on the Literary Mediation of Human Values*. Urbana: University of Illinois Press, 1972.

Gose, Elliott. *Imagination Indulged: The Irrational in the Nineteenth-Century Novel*. Montreal: McGill–Queen's University Press, 1972..

Gregor, Ian (ed.). *Reading the Victorian Novel: Detail into Form*. Vision Press, 1980.

Halperin, John. *Egoism and Self-Discovery in the Victorian Novel: Studies in the Ordeal of Knowledge in the Nineteenth Century*. New York: Burt Franklin, 1974.

Hardy, Barbara. *Forms of Feeling in Victorian Fiction*. Peter Owen, 1985.

Harvey, William. *Character and the Novel*. Ithaca: Cornell University Press, 1965.

Hochman, Baruch. *The Test of Character: From the Victorian Novel to the Modern.* New Jersey: Associated Universities Press, 1983.

Houghton, Walter. *The Victorian Frame of Mind 1830–1870.* New Haven: Yale University Press, 1957.

Hughes, Winifred. *The Maniac in the Cellar: Sensation Novels of the 1860s.* Princeton: Princeton University Press, 1980.

Irwin, Michael. *Picturing: Description and Illusion in the Nineteenth-Century Novel.* George Allen and Unwin, 1979.

Johnson, Wendell. *Sons and Fathers: The Generation Link in Literature 1780–1980.* New York: Peter Lang, 1985.

Kahler, Erich. *The Inward Turn of Narrative.* R. and C. Winston (trans.). Princeton: Princeton University Press, 1973.

Kawin, Bruce. *The Mind of the Novel: Reflexive Fiction and the Ineffable.* Princeton: Princeton University Press, 1982.

Kincaid, James and Kuhn, Albert. *Victorian Literature and Society.* Ohio: Ohio State University Press, 1984.

Langbaum, Robert. *The Mysteries of Identity: A Theme in Modern Literature.* New York: Oxford University Press, 1977.

Levine, George. *The Realistic Imagination: English Fiction from Frankenstein to Lady Chatterley.* Chicago: University of Chicago Press, 1981.

Lukács, Georg. *The Theory of the Novel.* A. Bostock (trans.). Merlin Press, 1971.

Lyons, John. *The Invention of the Self: The Hinge of Consciousness in the Eighteenth Century.* Carbondale: Southern Illinois University Press, 1978.

McMaster, Janet and R. D. *The Novel from Sterne to James: Essays on the Relation of Literature to Life.* Macmillan, 1981.

Marshall, William. *The World of the Victorian Novel.* New York: A. S. Barnes and Co., 1967.

Miller, D. A. *Narrative and Its Discontents: Problems of Closure in the Traditional Novel.* Princeton: Princeton University Press, 1981.

Miller, J. Hillis. *The Form of Victorian Fiction.* Ohio: Arete Press, 1968.

Miller, Karl. *Doubles: Studies in Literary History.* Oxford: Oxford University Press, 1985.

Miyoshi, Masao. *The Divided Self: A Perspective on the Literature of the Victorians.* New York: New York University Press, 1969.

Moers, Ellen. *The Dandy: From Brummell to Beerbohm.* Secker and Warburg, 1960.

Morretti, Franco. *The Way of the World: The Bildungsroman in European Culture.* Verso, 1987.

Parker, Alexander. *Literature and the Delinquent: The Picaresque Novel in Spain and Europe 1599–1753.* Edinburgh: Edinburgh University Press, 1967.

Peckham, Morse. *Beyond the Tragic Vision: The Quest for Identity in the Nineteenth Century.* Cambridge: Cambridge University Press, 1981 (1962).

Praz, Mario. *The Hero in Eclipse in Victorian Fiction.* A. Davidson (trans.). Oxford University Press, 1969.

Price, Martin. *Forms of Life: Character and Moral Imagination in the Novel.* New Haven: Yale University Press, 1983.

Rathburn, Robert and Steinmann, M. (eds.). *From Jane Austen to Joseph Conrad.* Minneapolis: University of Minneapolis Press, 1958.

Ray, Gordon. *The Letters and Private Papers of William Makepeace Thackeray* (4 vols.). Cambridge, Mass.: Harvard University Press, 1946.

Reed, John. *Victorian Conventions.* Ohio: Ohio University Press, 1975.

Reed, Walter. *Meditations on the Hero: A Study of the Romantic Hero in Nineteenth-Century Fiction.* New Haven: Yale University Press, 1974.

————— *An Exemplary History of the Novel: The Quixotic Versus the Picaresque.* Chicago: University of Chicago Press, 1981.

Sanders, Andrew. *The Victorian Historical Novel 1840–1880.* Macmillan, 1978.

Schorer, Mark (ed.). *Society and Self in the Novel.* New York: Columbia University Press, 1956.

Shaffner, R. P. *The Apprenticeship Novel: A Study of the 'Bildungsroman' as a Regulative Type in Western Literature.* New York: Peter Lang, 1984.

Spacks, Patricia. *Imagining a Self: Autobiography and the Novel in Eighteenth-Century England.* Cambridge, Mass.: Harvard University Press, 1976.

Stang, Richard. *The Theory of the Novel in England 1850–1870.* New York: Columbia University Press, 1966.

Stone, Donald. *The Romantic Impulse in Victorian Fiction.* Cambridge, Mass.: Harvard University Press, 1980.

Taylor, Jenny Bourne. *In the Secret Theatre of Home: Wilkie Collins, Sensation Narrative, and Nineteenth-Century Psychology.* Routledge, 1988.

Thorslev, Peter. *The Byronic Hero: Types and Prototypes.* Minneapolis: University of Minnesota Press, 1962.

Tillotson, Kathleen. *Novels of the Eighteen-Forties.* Oxford: Clarendon Press, 1956.

Torrance, Robert. *The Comic Hero.* Cambridge, Mass.: Harvard University Press, 1978.

Watt, Ian (ed.). *The Victorian Novel: Modern Essays in Criticism.* Oxford: Oxford University Press, 1971.

Watt, Ian. *The Rise of the Novel: Studies in Defoe, Richardson and Fielding.* Chatto and Windus, 1974 (1957).

Weinstein, Arnold. *Fictions of the Self 1550–1800.* Princeton: Princeton University Press, 1981.

Weinstein, Philip. *The Semantics of Desire: Changing Models of Identity from Dickens to Joyce.* Princeton: Princeton University Press, 1984.

Welsh, Alexander. *The Hero of the Waverley Novels.* New Haven: Yale University Press, 1963.

Bibliography

Williams, D. A. *The Monster in the Mirror: Studies in Nineteenth Century Realism.* Oxford: Oxford University Press, 1978.

Index

Index

revision of, 140–43, 148, 167
Darnay, Charles, 144, 145–6, 147,
148
David Copperfield, 5, 24, 30, 42, 43–6,
47, 49, 54, 62, 66, 67, 68–70, 71,
74, 75, 81, 97, 121, 140, 184
David, Deirdre, 191
Dawson, Carl, 190
den Hartog, Dirk, 189
Disraeli, Benjamin, 140; *The Young
Duke*, 11
Dombey and Son, 5, 15, 16, 32, 33, 34,
41, 44, 68, 69, 72
Donovan, Robert, 191
D'Orsay, Alfred, 140
Dyson, A. E., 191, 193

Eigner, Edwin, 193
Eliot, George, 2, 3; *Middlemarch*, 47
Engel, Elliot, 190

Fielding, Henry, 10, 11, 18; *Tom
Jones*, 2, 4; Jones, Tom 11, 12, 13,
43; Andrews, Joseph, 12
Ford, George, 192
Forster, John, 3, 5, 10, 13, 16, 22,
34, 41, 72, 166, 168, 179, 192; *Life
of Charles Dickens* quoted, 3, 15,
16, 17, 31, 32, 33, 38, 44–5, 52,
69, 167
Forsyte, Charles, 184
Frank, Lawrence, 193

Garis, Robert 72, 84, 85
Gaskell, Elizabeth, 2; *Life of
Charlotte Brontë* quoted, 43
Gay, Walter, 5, 15, 16, 17, 18, 22,
24, 31–4, 35, 36, 37–8, 40, 41, 44,
47, 72, 73, 81
gentility, the hero and, 37, 59;
'false', 118–20, 130, 132; 'true',
120–21, 123, 135, 137, 160

'George Silverman's Explanation',
169
Gill, Stephen, 116, 191
Gilmour, Robin, 66, 118, 119, 123,
190, 192
Gowan, Henry, 101–2, 140–43, 144,
148, 155
Gradgrind, Tom, 6, 67, 73–5, 85–9,
90, 92, 93, 94, 97, 98, 99
Great Expectations, 46, 47, 117, 118,
119, 123, 126, 127, 128, 132, 136,
137
Grill, Neil, 190
Gross, John, 143, 190, 193

Hard Times, 6, 36, 67, 68, 69, 70, 73,
75, 86, 87, 89, 90, 140
Hardy, Barbara, 189–90
Harmon, John, 47, 91–6, 99, 104,
107–16, 117, 118, 120, 121, 122,
125, 128, 131, 143, 144, 147, 148,
149, 153, 158, 162, 163, 177, 178
Harthouse, James, 73, 74, 87, 140–
43, 144, 153
Haunted Man, The, 169
Headstone, Bradley, 90, 92, 108,
145, 149, 155, 161–5, 166, 167,
168–75, 176, 177, 178–9, 180, 181,
182–3, 184
Heep, Uriah, 57–8, 60, 61–2, 74,
128
'hero', the, 1–5, 9; Dickens's opinion
of, 3; Dickens's parody of, 19–22,
29–31, 36; Byronic hero, 19, 20,
31, 141; Dickens's parody of, 29;
paragon hero, 3, 4, 5, 14
heroism, Dickens and, 3–5, 13, 14,
15, 16, 19–22, 29–31, 36;
'natural', 5, 11–15, 18, 19–20, 21,
24, 25, 30, 32, 35–6, 41–2, 44, 60,
86; 'moral', 30–31, 47, 62, 85
home and homelessness, 5, 6, 7, 44,
46–7, 49, 51–2, 54, 57, 91, 121–2

204

Index

Houghton, Walter, 192

Jasper, John, 90, 92, 145, 146, 149, 150, 161–8, 175–84, 187
Jordan, J. O., 190

Kahler, Erich, 5
Kaplan, Frank, 193
Kucich, John, 191

Lane, Lauriat, 192
Leavis, Q. D., 43, 45
Le Sage, Alain René, 11; *Gil Blas*, 43
Little Dorrit, 46, 75, 93, 95, 96, 97, 98, 101, 102, 104, 107, 108, 111, 118, 137, 140
Lucas, John, 190
Lukács, Georg, 96

Manning, Sylvia, 192
Marcus, Steven, 91, 92
Marryat, Frederick, 10
Martin Chuzzlewit, 15, 16, 27, 31, 32–3, 34, 36, 41, 44, 60, 62, 68, 69, 112, 139, 140
Meckier, Jerome, 189
Miller, J. Hillis, 132, 191
Millhauser, M., 192
Moers, Ellen, 139, 140, 192
Monod, Sylvere, 190
Moynahan, Julian, 127–8, 129, 192
Mystery of Edwin Drood, The, 67, 164, 167, 168, 177, 178, 179, 184, 187

narrative closure, the hero and, 7–8, 14, 24, 34, 40, 64–6, 70, 80–1, 91–2, 107–8, 137–8, 159–60, 163, 179, 184
Nicholas Nickleby, 9, 10, 11, 13, 15, 16, 19, 22, 32, 34, 36, 37, 40, 139, 140, 185, 186
Nickleby, Nicholas, 5, 6, 7, 9–15,

16, 17, 18–24, 25, 26, 28, 29, 31, 32, 33, 34, 35, 36, 37, 40, 41, 42, 44, 45, 46, 60, 81, 82, 91, 106

Old Curiosity Shop, The, 15, 16, 17, 34, 35, 36, 37, 38, 39, 41–2, 68
Oliphant, Margaret, 1
Oliver Twist, 9, 10, 178
Orlick, Dolge, 120, 127–8
orphanhood, the hero and, 44, 47, 90, 92, 99
Orwell, George, 17, 52, 69, 190
Our Mutual Friend, 3, 73, 93, 94, 95, 96, 104, 107, 108, 111, 112, 115, 116, 118, 140, 153, 154, 155, 161, 166, 168, 169, 177

Pearson, Gabriel, 40, 41, 190
Pickwick Papers, The, 9, 68, 112, 178
Pickwick, Samuel, 9, 10, 82, 91
Pinch, Tom, 15, 25, 26, 30–31, 60, 62, 85
Pip, 1, 40, 41, 46, 52, 91, 99, 112, 117–38, 143, 144, 148, 149, 150, 153, 157, 160, 162, 163, 169, 171
Pocket, Herbert, 131, 134, 135
Praz, Mario, 189

Radcliffe, Ann, 13
Richardson, Samuel, 2; Grandison, Sir Charles, 2
Reed, John, 190
Rosenberg, Edgar, 192

Sanders, Andrew, 193
Scott, P. J. M., 191–2, 193
Scott, Walter, 3, 10, 36, 146; Waverley, Edward, 147
self-help, 45, 46, 55, 116; Dickens's inversion of, 117, 135, 169, 171
sensation novels, 111; Dickens and, 111–12, 177–80, 184
Sketches By Boz, 17